Case Studies
in
NEUROSCIENCE
Critical Care
Nursing

Aspen Series of Case Studies in Critical Care Nursing
John M. Clochesy, MS, RN, CS, FCCM, Series Editor
Instructor, Acute and Critical Care Nursing
Frances Payne Bolton School of Nursing
Case Western Reserve University
Cleveland, Ohio

Case Studies in Cardiovascular Critical Care Nursing
Mickie D. Welsh and John M. Clochesy, Editors

Critical Care of the Burn Patient:
A Case Study Approach
Evelyn Gonzales McLaughlin, Editor

Case Studies
in
NEUROSCIENCE
Critical Care
Nursing

Edited by

Susan M. Johnson, RN, MN, CCRN

Nurse Manager
Neurosurgery and Trauma
Intensive Care Units
UCLA Medical Center
and
Assistant Clinical Professor
UCLA School of Nursing
Los Angeles, California

Aspen Series of Case Studies in Critical Care Nursing
John M. Clochesy, Series Editor

AN ASPEN PUBLICATION®
Aspen Publishers, Inc.
Gaithersburg, Maryland
1991

Library of Congress Cataloging-in-Publication Data

Case studies in neuroscience critical care nursing / edited by Susan M. Johnson.
    p. cm. — (Aspen series of case studies in critical care nursing)
                                   Includes bibliographical references.
                                                      Includes index.
                                        ISBN: 0-8342-0218-2
1. Neurological nursing—Case studies. 2. Neurological intensive care—Case
studies. I. Johnson, Susan M., R.N. II. Series. [DNLM: 1. Central Nervous
                     System Diseases—nursing—case studies.
              2. Critical Care—case studies.   WY 160 C337]
                                      RC350.5.C37   1991
                                      610.73'68—dc20
                                           DNLM/DLC
                                   for Library of Congress
                                            90-14561
                                                CIP

The authors have made every effort to ensure the accuracy of the information
herein, particularly with regard to drug selection and dose. However, appropriate
information sources should be consulted, especially for new or unfamiliar drugs or
procedures. It is the responsibility of every practitioner to evaluate the appro-
priateness of a particular opinion in the context of actual clinical situations and with
due consideration to new developments. Authors, editors, and the publisher cannot
be held responsible for any typographical or other errors found in this book.

Editorial Services: Lisa Hajjar

Library of Congress Catalog Card Number: 90-14561
ISBN: 0-8342-0218-2

Printed in the United States of America

1 2 3 4 5

Dedicated to my mother, Grace McCormick,
for her infinite wisdom, courage, and loving support.
To my children, Jesse Talbot and Deija Lei,
for all the tears and laughs of motherhood.

Table of Contents

Contributors

Jacques Dion, MD

Assistant Professor
Endovascular Services
Department of Radiology
UCLA Medical Center
Los Angeles, California

Laura L. Drobnich, RN, MN, CCRN

Assistant Head Nurse
Neurosurgical Intensive Care Unit
The Ohio State University Hospitals
Columbus, Ohio

Lorena A. Gaskill, RN, MN, CEN

Clinical Nurse Specialist
Emergency Services
Riverside Medical Center
Minneapolis, Minnesota

Elizabeth A. Henneman, RN, MS, CCRN

Clinical Nurse Specialist
Medical Intensive Care Unit
UCLA Medical Center
and
Assistant Clinical Professor
UCLA School of Nursing
Los Angeles, California

Carol F. Holt, RN, MN

Clinical Nurse Specialist
UCLA Medical Center
Los Angeles, California

Susan M. Johnson, RN, MN, CCRN

Nurse Manager
Neurosurgery and Trauma Intensive Care Units
UCLA Medical Center
and
Assistant Clinical Professor
UCLA School of Nursing
Los Angeles, California

Evangeline Martin-Thomson, RN, BSN, MBA, CNRN

Neurosurgical Liaison Nurse
Department of Neurosurgery
Los Angeles County University of Southern
    California
Los Angeles, California

Maureen A. Mielcarek, RN, MN, CCRN

Nurse Manager
Medical Surgical Areas
Veterans' Administration Hospital
Sepulveda, California

Susan M. More, RN, MN

Clinical Nurse Specialist
Division of Neurosurgery
UCLA Medical Center
Los Angeles, California

Kathleen Thomas, RN, MN

Clinical Nurse Specialist
Division of Neurosurgery
UCLA Medical Center
Los Angeles, California

Foreword

With the proclamation of the 1990's as the Decade of the Brain, there is increased awareness by both the public and health care professionals of neurologic diseases and their impact on members of our society. This increased awareness should become the impetus to improve the multi-faceted practice of the neuroscience nurse, that of caregiver, educator and researcher.

Case Studies in Neuroscience Critical Care Nursing includes a case study presentation of each neuroscience disease, as well as nursing managment and a specific nursing care plan for each disease process. This prepares the nurse for his or her role as caregiver. With increased knowledge of pertinent nursing care, the nurse will be able to meet the patient's nursing care needs with confidence. The pathology related to the disease process, and the common medical management outlined in the chapter are good references to educate the nurse in the specifics of each disease process presented. With an expanded knowledge base, the nurse can be the educator of the patient and the family. The general knowledge of each disease, along with the specific treatment plans prescribed by the physician, will answer the patient's questions, decrease fears of the unknown, and return a sense of equilibrium obtained from this new knowledge.

After increasing our knowledge base, we can then begin inquiries into improving the standard of care. Nursing research can promote change and improvement in the nursing care we deliver, but knowledge is an essential prerequisite.

Neuroscience nursing is an intellectually challenging specialty, and we in the field are charged to keep our knowledge current. This book can help us meet the challenge.

Jeanne K. Clancey, RN, MSN, CNRN
Clinical Coordinator
West Penn Neurosurgery, PC
Pittsburgh, Pennsylvania

Preface

As the body of knowledge and scope of practice related to neurosurgery and neurology has expanded, so too has neuroscience nursing, which has finally earned a place within the specialties of critical care nursing. Throughout the United States sophisticated neurosurgery intensive care units are being designed to meet these complex patient needs. With this development, the need for information related to critical care neuroscience nursing will increase. *Case Studies in Neuroscience Critical Care Nursing* was written to help meet the educational needs of the nursing and other health care team members caring for these patients.

The book is organized around specific case studies which illustrate the concepts applicable to neuroscience nursing. Each case study represents an actual patient that the chapter author either had direct care responsibilities for or served as a consultant with the physicians or nursing staff caring for the patient. Although the details of each case study are individualized, the cases themselves are representative of patients with the same diagnoses. The book is not meant to contain an all-inclusive list of cases that may be admitted to a neuroscience critical care unit. Instead, it highlights some of the more common diagnoses.

Each chapter begins with the case study presentation followed by a review of the anatomy and physiology as it relates to the disease process. The clinical manifestations are presented and illustrated by the case study. Discussions of state of the art diagnostic tests and procedures, as well as the medical and surgical treatment, are included. Nursing interventions and a nursing care plan are found at the end of each chapter. To avoid repetition, some of the nursing care plans have prioritized the nursing diagnoses, thereby listing only the most relevant for that particular case. Although the psychological needs of these patients and their families are tremendously important to their recovery, the focus in this book is on physiological needs of the patient during the critical care phase of hospitalization.

Although procedures and practice may vary, the material found in this book represents the standard of practice found in the literature and in each author's own clinical experience. In the spirit of academic growth, the authors encourage and invite criticism of error or inaccuracy.

I wish to express my genuine gratitude to the contributors of this book. Their knowledge of neuroscience nursing and their compassion for their patients is a tribute to our profession.

Acknowledgments

I wish to thank the staff of the 2E/7W Neurosurgery and Trauma Intensive Care Units at the UCLA Medical Center. It is a privilege to work with such outstanding neuroscience nurses. They are a continuous source of creativity, endurance, and inspiration. Thanks also to the nursing staff of the 6E/9E General Surgery/Transplant Intensive Care Units for their expert practice and interest in learning about neurosurgical nursing. Thanks to Barbara Anderson for her friendship and her ability to keep humanism alive and well in the ICU. Thanks to Margie Vallejo for helping to keep the other half of my professional responsibilities in meticulous order. I wish to thank Laurel Torczon for all the hours of consultation she provides continuously. Special thanks to Kathy Thomas, Susan More, Alice Hester Leipzig, and Maureen Keckeisen for all their encouragement and support. Thanks to Drs. John Frazee and Dave Adelson for their review of sections of this book. Thanks also to Lisa Hajjar of Aspen Publishers for her editorial assistance and encouragement throughout the entire process.

Chapter 1

Head Injury

Susan M. Johnson

INTRODUCTION

Injury to the brain is one of the most devastating experiences known to man. According to most recent statistics, every 15 seconds someone in the United States sustains a head injury; every five minutes, one of those people dies and another becomes permanently disabled.[1] There are over two million head injuries every year, and 75,000 to 100,000 of these victims die.[1] Head injury is tragic because the majority of the patients involved are young and healthy and the injury is unexpected. With the advent of improved and expanded emergency medical systems, patient outcomes have improved. Increasing numbers of patients survive with less severe neurological deficits than in the past. There are two major goals in managing these patients: (1) preventing secondary injury to the brain (ie, cerebral edema, ischemia) and (2) providing an environment that optimizes recovery for the compromised brain. This chapter addresses the main concepts of head injury, including pathophysiology, clinical manifestations, diagnostics, surgical management, and nursing interventions. A nursing care plan with current North America Nursing Diagnosis Association (NANDA)-approved diagnoses is also included.

* * * * *

CASE STUDY

A 43-year-old female (A.J.) was involved in a motor vehicle accident. She was in the driver's seat and drove off a freeway overpass going approximately 60 mph; the car fell 40 feet onto another freeway level. Paramedics responded to the scene within 10 to 15 minutes and resuscitated the patient in the field. A.J.'s vital signs were unstable: HR 60 with premature ventricular contractions (PVCs), BP 72/30, RR 8 shallow and irregular, Glasgow coma score 4. She was unresponsive to verbal or painful stimuli. Her right pupil was 4 to 5 mm in diameter and reacting sluggishly, and the left was 2 mm with brisk response to light. Her corneal cough and gag reflexes were intact.

In addition to neurological damage, her other injuries were: a near-complete amputation of the right lower extremity with a possible fracture of the distal tibia and fibula above the right ankle, an open fracture of the tibia and fibula of the left leg with arterial bleeding, an open fracture of the right wrist, nonpalpable radial and ulnar pulses, multiple lacerations, and abrasions.

She was orally intubated without difficulty, two 18-gauge intravenous lines were started and normal saline was infused wide open, and a backboard and cervical collar were applied for spinal stability. Her injured extremities were stabilized and she was transported to the emergency room of a nearby university medical center.

When admitted to the emergency room her status was unchanged. She was immediately typed and cross-matched for six units of packed cells, complete laboratory studies were obtained, extensive x-rays were taken, and a head computed tomography (CT) scan was done. The head CT scan was negative for intracranial bleeding. Efforts to stabilize her vital signs continued and she was placed on a ventilator with settings of Fio$_2$ 80%, assist control (AC) 20, tidal volume (TV) 750, PEEP 5. She was scheduled for emergency surgery and underwent an exploratory laparotomy that resulted in no significant findings. Her right hand was explored with a fasciotomy, the right radius fracture repaired, the right radial artery explored, open reduction and internal fixation of the left tibia and fibula performed along with repair of the tibial nerve, primary reanastomosis of the left posterior tibial artery done, and the right leg amputated above the knee.

She was transferred to the neurotrauma intensive care unit (ICU) after surgery. Within four hours her neuro status began to deteriorate. Her right pupil was now 6 to 7 mm in diameter and non-responsive, she was still flaccid, and she did not respond to verbal or painful stimuli. A second CT scan was performed emergently and a right subdural hematoma, a right intraventricular hemorrhage, and a right posterior fossa contusion were discovered. She was taken back to surgery by the neurosurgical team who noted during surgery that she had a right occipital contusion. The procedure performed included a right frontotemporalparietal craniotomy, evacuation of the right convexity subdural hematoma, evacuation of the right temporal hematoma, a right temporal lobectomy, a right suboccipital craniotomy, evacuation of the right posterior fossa subdural hematoma, and a right occipital craniectomy. A left frontal Camino intracranial pressure (ICP) catheter was inserted and she was transferred back to the neurotrauma ICU.

During her entire month and a half in the ICU, the focus of her treatment was to stabilize her neurological status, specifically her ICP/CPP (cerebral perfusion pressure), and to wean her off the ventilator. Details of her neurological management will be reviewed at appropriate intervals throughout the chapter, and the patient's outcome will be discussed in the conclusion section.

* * * * *

PATHOPHYSIOLOGY

The major causes of head trauma are motor vehicle accidents with injury either to passengers or pedestrians, falls, violent acts, and sports-related activities. There are many methods to use when classifying head trauma. The Core Curriculum for Neuroscience Nursing has specified six classifications of head injury

1. pathological mechanisms
2. mechanisms of injury
3. types of injury
4. severity of brain damage
5. cognitive levels
6. outcome[2]

For the purposes of this chapter and its focus on critical care nursing, the second and third classifications will be reviewed.

Mechanisms of Injury

Direct impact injuries can occur by acceleration, which means that a rapidly moving object (ie, a baseball bat) hits the head and injury usually occurs directly under the point of impact. Deceleration occurs when the head hits a stationary object (ie, a car windshield, the street, or a wall).

Rotational injury occurs when the brain rotates within the cranial vault due to a lateral blow. Indirect injuries occur when there is trauma to the body (other than the head) and the brain is affected. An example is falling and landing on the buttocks.

Blunt injuries are closed, non-penetrating injuries, which are also called closed head injuries. These injuries are similar to direct impact injuries. There is no break in the integrity of the protective structures (ie, bony skull).

Penetrating injuries, which are also called open head injuries, are a result of actual penetration of the brain tissue. These injuries can be caused by missile objects that can fragment and either remain in the head or exit. Sharp instruments, such as knives or scissors, can cause this type of injury as well. The patient is always at a greater risk for infection any time the protective layer of the brain, the dura, has been interrupted. Depending on the object's size and velocity these injuries can cause considerable damage. It is of utmost importance that nurses understand that neither term—closed or open head injury—gives any indication of the extent of severity of cerebral injury.[3(p337)]

Compression injuries are frequently present with other types of injuries. The brain is crushed due to the skull being compressed between two objects.

Types of Injury

The types of injury reviewed in this section include scalp injuries, skull fractures, primary brain and brain-stem damage, intracranial hemorrhage, secondary brain and brain-stem damage, cranial nerve injuries, and vascular injuries.

Scalp Injuries

Scalp injuries can involve lacerations, avulsion, burns, and abrasions. Lacerations can take almost any form. Avulsion usually occurs in the loose areolar tissue between the galea and pericranium. Most scalp avulsions occur when a portion of hair is pulled at a tangential angle.[4] Due to the rich blood supply present in the scalp, these injuries may at times appear spectacular, but it should be kept firmly in mind that they may not be a lethal injury, and nursing care must not be misdirected.[4]

Fracture Injuries

Fractures of the skull may be classified as linear, depressed, comminuted, compound, or basilar. The type of fracture depends on many factors, such as point of impact on the cranium, velocity, and force of the impact. Linear fractures constitute 80% of skull fractures; they are simple breaks or cracks in the bone but no actual separation of the bone, similar to a drinking glass that holds water but has several cracks on its surface. Linear fractures start at the point of impact and travel out, somewhat like a starburst design.

Depressed fractures are defined as a break in the continuity of the skull so that bone fragments are depressed to the thickness of the skull. These fractures may be either open or closed, although open depressed fractures are more common. Usually twisted or turned bony fragments and dural tearing are present.

Comminuted fractures produce small fragments of bone. At the point of impact, the skull is forced inward and the immediate surrounding area is forced outward; thus the linar fracture occurs. But if the force is great enough, the skull will be interrupted and the bone will fragment.

Any fracture that results in a communication between the scalp and the brain or dura is considered a compound fracture. This injury is considered contaminated because foreign objects, dirt, and bony fragments can be forced into the brain tissue. Compound fractures can also result in a protrusion of brain tissue outside the fracture site.

Among the most serious fractures are basilar fractures. The usual locations are the petrous portion of the temporal bone, the orbital surface of the frontal bone, and the basiocciput.[5] These fractures commonly involve the paranasal sinuses; when this occurs there is invariably a tear in the dura. Basilar fractures are difficult to visualize on x-ray and are sometimes diagnosed by clinical presence of rhinorrhea and or otorrhea. The presence of periorbital ecchymosis (raccoon's eyes) and rhinorrhea (cerebrospinal fluid and/or bloody drainage from the nose) is an indication of anterior fossa fracture. Ecchymosis of the mastoid bone (Battle's sign) and otorrhea (cerebrospinal fluid and/or bloody drainage from the ear) are an indication of temporal petrous bone fracture.

Brain Tissue Injury

Injury to the brain tissue itself can either be focal or diffuse. Focal injuries result from localized damage and account for approximately 50% of all hospital admissions for head injury.[6] Examples of focal injuries are contusions, lacerations, and epidural, subdural, and intracerebral hemorrhages (Figure 1-1).

Contusions are wedge-shaped bruised areas that extend into the underlying white matter beneath the site of impact. They are due to the disruption of small blood vessels; they are also called coup injuries. Contrecoup contusions are due to the inertial effects of the brain rapidly moving about in the cranial vault. There is stress on the vascular area opposite the site of impact and therefore injury.

Epidural hemorrhages are the result of bleeding between the skull and the dura, and 40% to 50% of the time the middle meningeal artery is most commonly involved. The remaining injuries occur from either venous hemorrhage from the fracture site or laceration of the dural venous sinuses. These hemorrhages are typically located in the temporal or frontal regions, and are frequently associated with skull fractures. The hematoma that is created is oval shaped and causes pressure on the underlying brain, which can lead to increased ICP, shifting of midline structure (ventricles), herniation and eventually death if left untreated. The blood within an epidural hematoma is clotted, unlike that of the subdural hematoma in which the blood is often a mixture of liquid and clotted blood.

Subdural hematomas are a collection of blood between the dura mater and the arachnoid layer of the meninges, usually resulting from rupture of the small bridging veins between the cortex and dura or other small branches of surface arteries. These are more common than epidural hematomas, and usually result in a more serious head injury; the mortality rate is 60% to 70%.[7]

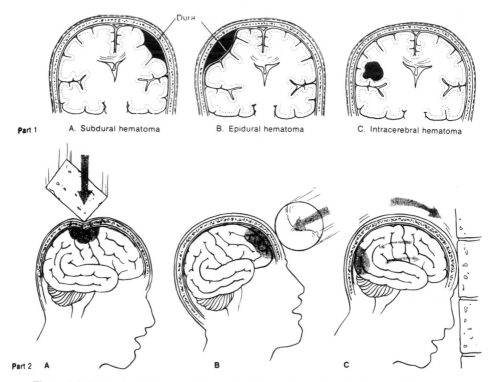

Dura

Part 1   A. Subdural hematoma   B. Epidural hematoma   C. Intracerebral hematoma

Part 2   A   B   C

Figure 1-1 Epidural, subdural, and intracerebral hemorrhages (from Luckman and Sorenson). **Part 1:** Different types of hematoma. **Part 2:** Some mechanisms of head injury. Head injury results from penetration or impact. **A,** A direct injury (blow to skull) may fracture the skull. Contusion and laceration of the brain may result from fractures. Depressed portions of the skull may compress or penetrate brain tissue. **B,** In the absence of skull fracture, a blow to the skull may cause the brain to move enough to tear some of the veins going from the cortical surface to the dura. Subsequently, subdural hematoma may develop. Note areas of cerebral contusion (*shaded*). **C,** Rebound of the cranial contents may result in an area of injury opposite the point of impact. Such an injury is called a "contrecoup injury." In addition to the three injuries depicted, secondary phenomena may result from the injury and cause additional brain dysfunction or damage. For example, ischemia, especially cerebral edema, may occur, elevating intracranial pressure. *Source:* Reprinted from *Medical-Surgical Nursing: A Psychophysiologic Approach* (p 662) by J Luckman and KC Sorensen with permission of WB Saunders, © 1980.

Intracerebral hemorrhage is a bleed into the parenchyma of the brain associated with severe contusions, lacerations, and subdural hematomas. They most frequently occur in the frontal and temporal lobes and they are commonly seen as two or more distinct areas of hemorrhage.

Subarachnoid hemorrhage is a common result of head injury and can be seen in combination with other injuries. The collection of blood in the subarachnoid space can impede normal circulation of CSF and reabsorption to the degree that increased ICP can occur and lead to secondary injury and brain herniation. A serious and rather common complication of subarachnoid hemorrhage is vasospasm. This narrowing of the cerebral arteries is thought to be a reaction to blood byproducts at the cellular level. Severe impedance to circulation can result in irreversible ischemia and infarction.

A.J., the patient in the case study presented above, sustained a posterior fossa subdural, a right temporal subdural, and a right occipital contusion.

Diffuse injuries are associated with widespread brain damage, and often there is no visible injury to the brain. Two examples of diffuse injuries are concussions and diffuse axonal injury (DAI). The Latin meaning of the word concussion is "to shake violently." There is no permanent structural damage in the concussed brain.

The mechanism of injury in diffuse axonal injury is acceleration, usually occurring in motor vehicle accidents when the individual suffers violent impact to the windshield or dashboard of the vehicle. Microscopic findings consist of widespread shearing of the white matter throughout both hemispheres, and in severe cases the cerebellum and brain stem are affected. Focal injuries can occur with DAI as well. Basically all the connections are disconnected and, depending on the severity of injury, the patient can remain in a comatose state for a long time.

Secondary Brain Injury

One of the major goals of critical care nursing is to prevent secondary injury to the brain. Prevention of primary injuries involves social and political issues such as public education; enforcement of existing laws related to seat belts, driving under the influence of drugs and alcohol; and legislation directed toward gun control and mandatory motorcycle helmet requirements. These issues, of course, are out of the realm of the practice of the critical care nurse. Therefore the focus of the nurse and the area in which he or she will have the greatest impact on the patient is prevention of secondary damage to the brain.

Secondary injury, triggered by the initial insult to the brain, compounds the destructive effect on already compromised brain tissue. There is a reaction to cellular injury, usually due to a decrease in oxygen. The four main categories of secondary injury to the brain discussed in this section are

1. cerebral metabolism
2. intracranial hemodynamics
3. intracranial pressure
4. brain water balance

Cerebral Metabolism and Intracranial Hemodynamics

Although the human brain weighs only 2% of the total body weight, it uses approximately 20% of cardiac output. These statistics give one a sense of the dimension and importance of cerebral blood flow (CBF). The brain has literally no capacity to store oxygen or glucose, its main energy sources. Adequate CBF is difficult to determine because of the many factors that influence oxygen uptake (ie, metabolic needs, severity of injury). However normal CBF is felt to be at flow levels of about 50 cc/100 grams/minute. When CBF decreases below this level, the brain may become ischemic.[8(p188)] Cerebral hypoxia results from metabolic uncoupling, which is an imbalance between the demands of the cerebral tissue and the blood flowing through the tissue (supply). One example is increased oxygen and glucose demand, such as during seizures, coupled with insufficient supply. When this occurs, normal aerobic glycolysis can no longer be supported and the brain shifts to anaerobic metabolism. Lactate is generated in addition to limited production of high energy adenosine triphosphate (ATP). Increased levels of lactate, hypoxia, hypercapnia, and acidosis contribute to vasodilatation and vasomotor paralysis, a state of reduced cerebrovascular tone.

In the case presentation, A.J.'s field vital signs showed pronounced hypotension and inadequate respiratory effort. Both of these factors may contribute to global cerebral ischemia. In the normal brain, the CBF is maintained at a relatively constant rate by a process known as autoregulation, which is the ability of the cerebral resistance vessels (arteries) to change their diameter in response to the systemic blood pressure in order to maintain a normal CBF.

There are three mechanisms that influence autoregulation: myogenic, metabolic, and neurogenic factors.[9] Myogenic control involves the cerebral vessel tone fluctuation in response to arterial blood pressure. Metabolic control relates to increased blood flow in positive correlation with increased metabolic needs (ie, seizures, CO_2, oxygen, and pH). Autoregulation is impaired when the mean arterial pressure (MAP) is less than 50 torr. This was the situation in A.J.'s case; therefore, her ability to autoregulate may have been impaired and her CBF may have been compromised. Outside the limits of autoregulation the CBF becomes passively dependent on changes in perfusion pressure. Small decreases in blood pressure then result in ischemia.[10]

A.J.'s inadequate respiratory effort at the scene resulted in hypoventilation, CO_2 retention, and hypoxia, according to her arterial blood gases. Carbon dioxide (CO_2) is a potent vasoactive substance because it easily crosses the blood-brain barrier and can change extravascular pH instantaneously. CBF can change 4% per mm Hg change in CO_2.[8(p189)] Increased levels of CO_2 cause vasodilatation (maximum dilatation occurring at P_{CO_2} of 60 mm Hg) and decreased levels cause vasoconstriction (maximum constricting occurring at Pco_2 of 20 mm Hg).[8(189)] It is thought that pH rather than CO_2 is the mediator facilitating this change in vessel diameter. Hypoxia, Pao_2 at 50 mm Hg, will also result in vasodilatation.

One could speculate that some degree of vasodilatation exceeding the cerebral metabolic needs may have occurred in this case study, and possibly cerebral hyperemia, or luxury perfusion, which is an increase in cerebral blood volume vasogenic cerebral edema and leads to further increases in ICP.

Another concept that is important in understanding intracranial hemo-dynamics in head injury is cerebral perfusion pressure. CPP is defined as the blood pressure gradient across the brain and is calculated as the difference between the incoming mean arterial blood pressure and the opposing intra-cranial pressure on the arteries (CPP = MAP − ICP). The average range of CPP is 80 to 100 mm Hg. CPP must be at least 60 mm Hg to provide minimally adequate blood supply to the brain.[3(p249)] It is not sufficient to monitor the ICP alone; because ICP does not give an accurate assessment of the cerebral circulation, CPP should be calculated as well. A.J. did not have an adequate CPP. She was admitted with a MAP of 43 mm Hg and her first ICP reading after her Camino ICP monitor was inserted was 18 mm Hg. Therefore, her CPP was 25 mm Hg, a level that could lead to severe lasting neurological deficits.

Increased Intracranial Pressure

The skull is a rigid vault that contains incompressible contents. These include the brain and interstitial fluid (80%), CSF (10%), and blood (10%). The Monroe-Kellie doctrine states that with increased levels of volume (ie, CBF) in the cranial vault, the brain will compensate so that pressure (ICP) will not increase. These compensatory measures consist of intracellular de-hydration, increased CSF reabsorption, and translocation of CSF to the spi-nal subarachnoid space. Once the brain has reached compensatory capacity, even a small amount of volume will result in increased pressure (Figure 1-2). Any space-occupying lesion (ie, subdural hematoma or cerebral edema) can result in increased ICP. This was one of the many pathological processes occurring in A.J. that resulted in her increased ICP.

The concept of brain compliance is important in the research and manage-ment of these patients. Alterations in the elastance or compliance of the brain is a characteristic that is difficult to measure, although it is invaluable in terms of an accurate overall assessment of the state of the brain. It cannot be assumed that a normal ICP implies normal compliance. Compliance is de-fined as the ratio of the change in volume to the resulting change in pressure. A method of evaluating compliance is the volume pressure response (VPR). This can be determined by injection or withdrawal of 1 mL CSF (or normal

DYNAMIC PATHOLOGY

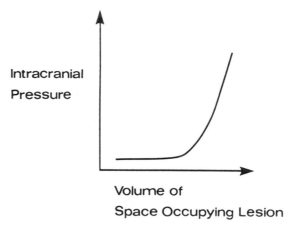

Figure 1-2 Changes in intracranial pressure as an intracranial lesion progressively increases in size. Initial phase of compensation is followed by an exponentially increasing pressure.

saline in the case of instillation), and noting the response in ICP. An increase in ICP of 5 mm Hg or more is considered an abnormal response and indicates a decrease in compliance.[8(p191)]

The pressure volume index (PVI) is a more accurate measurement of overall compliance because it takes into account the patient's changing ICP. It is calculated by the following equation: $PVI = \delta V/\log 10 \times (Pp/Po)$, where δV is the amount injected, Po is the baseline ICP, Pp is the ICP reached after injection.[8(p191)] In the average healthy brain (normal ICP and normal compliance), the PVI is 25 cc, which means that 25 cc are required to increase the ICP 10 mm Hg. If compensatory efforts are exceeded, volume added to the brain will increase pressure. Although neither VPR nor PVI is frequently calculated in practice, and was not obtained in this case study, research in computerized ICP waveform analysis as it relates to brain compliance may, in the near future, make continuous, accurate compliance monitoring easier to obtain. In this case study, one can speculate that A.J. had some degree of decreased compliance.

In cases of severe compression, herniation may occur. Herniation is defined as the protrusion of an organ or substance outside of its normal compartment.[11(p287)] The three herniation syndromes are: cingulate or across the falx, uncal or lateral, and central or intratentorial (Figure 1-3). Herniation may be classified as supratentorial or infratentorial. Dysfunction above the tentorium threatens the quality of life while dysfunction below the tentorium threatens life itself.[11(p288)]

Brain Water Balance

The water content of the brain is approximately 80% in normal gray matter and 70% in the white matter. Most of the water in the brain is intracellular and derived from the blood supply. Cerebral edema is an abnormal accumulation of fluid in the intracellular or extracellular spaces within the brain; it can be focal or diffuse. There are two types of cerebral edema, cytotoxic and vasogenic. Cytotoxic edema results from failure of the ion pumps within the cell that is due to disruption of cellular membrane integrity, as in the case of cerebral ischemia. In brain trauma, a situation is created in which there is insufficient ATP and therefore normal cellular functions are inhibited. So-

MANAGEMENT OF HEAD INJURIES

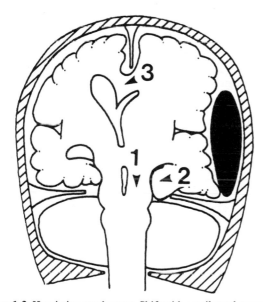

Figure 1-3 Herniation syndromes. Shift with a unilateral supratentorial hematoma:
 1. Downward displacement of brain stem
 2. Herniation of uncus of temporal lobe into tentorial hiatus
 3. Herniation of cingulate gyrus below falx cerebri
Note also shift of the ventricles, compression of the ventricle on the same side as the clot, and dilatation on the opposite side. *Source:* Reprinted from *The Diagnosis of Stupor and Coma* (p 64) by F Plum and J Posner with permission of the FA Davis Company, © 1981.

dium goes into the cell and potassium goes out, which causes an influx of water as well, and the cells become edematous.

Vasogenic edema is more commonly associated with brain tumors, abscess, and head injury. Normally the endothelial cells of the cerebral blood vessels prevent movement of large molecules from the vascular space to the extracellular space. This phenomenon is known as the blood-brain barrier. In vasogenic edema there is an increase in hydrostatic pressure within the cerebral vessels and increased permeability across the capillary membrane. This result may be due to a disruption of the blood-brain barrier. Plasma proteins are able to move across the blood-brain barrier, and fluid begins to leak across the vascular bed into the interstitial spaces. The arterial pressure is the driving force behind vasogenic edema so that, in some cases, if the MAP is decreased, vasogenic edema can be slowed.

Vasogenic edema is the more common of the two types of cerebral edema. Both types of edema have a negative impact on the brain in that they contribute to increased volume and therefore increased ICP. Once the pathological condition resolves, the fluid moves into the ventricular system and is reabsorbed.

Cranial Nerve Injury

Cranial nerve injuries can be a result of direct trauma or altered blood flow. Although any combination of injuries can result in cranial nerve dysfunction, Table 1-1, derived from the core curriculum of the American Association of Neuroscience Nurses (AANN), provides a brief guideline.[2]

Vascular Injuries

In any form of insult to the brain, there can be minor injuries to the capillary bed that result in contusions. The injuries that result in the various forms of intracranial hemorrhages (ie, subdural, epidural, or intracerebral bleeds) have previously been discussed. The remaining vascular injuries consist of traumatic aneurysm and carotid-cavernous fistula.

Traumatic aneurysms are most commonly caused by blunt injuries to the head. They involve the arteries on the surface of the brain and are usually found directly beneath the point of impact. They result from vessel compression against bony structures or rigid dural edges. With the increased use of CT and decreased use of angiography for diagnosis of head injury, traumatic aneurysms are sometimes missed. These aneurysms are rarely recognized until their presence is heralded by delayed subarachnoid hemorrhage or delayed neurologic deterioration. Subarachnoid hemorrhage secondary to the ruptured traumatic aneurysm usually occurs between 15 to 20 days after injury.[12] The possibility of traumatic aneurysm in any head-injured patient

Table 1-1 Cranial Nerve Involvement in Head Injury

Cranial Nerve	Location or Type of Injury
I and II	Anterior fossa or generalized shearing injuries
II	Frontal lobe
III, IV, and VI	Sphenoid sinus or cavernous sinus
V	Superior orbital fissure or basal fractures
VII and VIII	Parietal-temporal regions of petrous ridge (middle fossa)
IX, X, and XI	Foramen magnum
XII	Rare
II and III	Orbital plate fractures
I	Cribriform plate fracture

should never be ruled out until further assessment and cautious monitoring of the patient's neurological status.

A carotid-cavernous sinus fistula is an abnormal communication between the carotid artery and the cavernous sinus. It can occur spontaneously but a posttraumatic fistula is three times more common in males than females.[12] Blunt trauma is the most common cause but it may be seen in penetrating trauma as well. It is frequently associated with basilar skull fractures. The fistula is formed when there is arterial and venous injury that results in a direct communication between the carotid artery and the venous sinus. This communication in turn results in a redirection of blood flow and increased pressures within the venous system. In most cases, posttraumatic fistulas are high-flow and high-pressure shunts and the cavernous sinus fills rapidly; therefore, the exact point of injury is difficult to detect.[13] Although carotid-cavernous fistulas do not pose a significant threat to the patient, any head-trauma patient with symptoms of exophthalmos, chemosis, and bruit should be evaluated for this condition. If the fistula is severe enough to cause visual disturbances or an unacceptable appearance, treatment should be undertaken by either craniotomy or balloon angioplasty.

CLINICAL MANIFESTATIONS

The clinical manifestations of the head-injured patient can take many different forms, depending upon the location and severity of injury and the presence of secondary injury, such as cerebral edema, ischemia, and herniation. The information included in this section will focus on the findings from the neurologic assessment. The most valuable tool the neuroscience critical care nurse can use is his or her assessment skills. The nurse who has fine-tuned these critical skills can save a patient's life. It is the subtle changes that, if recognized early, can lead to immediate intervention and ultimately make a difference in the outcome for the patient.

Table 1-2 has been designed to include all types of head injury, but it is wise to remember that patients do not always follow the textbook and may vary considerably.

In the case study, A.J. demonstrated signs of a severe head injury. Her Glasgow coma score (GCS) was extremely low and she was unconscious. Information gathered at the initial field assessment indicated that she had changes in vital signs (irregular respirations). These changes indicate possible injury to the brain stem (specifically, the medulla) because the respiratory center is located in that region, although her brain stem reflexes (cough and gag) were intact. Pupil or eye movement changes indicate possible damage to cranial nerves III, IV, VI on the ipsilateral side of the injury; this damage can be the result of compression by uncal herniation. Obviously a diagnosis cannot be made without a CT, but the nurse can make a nursing diagnosis and get a general sense of the location and possible extent of the injury from the neurologic assessment.

Once again, it is important not to be caught off guard by relying solely on the results of technology rather than the clinical presentation of the patient. A.J.'s initial CT was negative for intracranial bleeding. Several hours later the second CT was performed and it showed a right subdural hematoma, right intraventricular hemorrhage, and right posterior fossa contusion, all of which could explain the dilated pupil on her right side in addition to the poor GCS and decreased level of consciousness.

DIAGNOSTIC PROCEDURES

Although a detailed account of how the injury occurred may be difficult if not impossible to obtain, the nurse must attempt to gather this information from family members or others who may have witnessed the event. Information related to vital signs, level of consciousness, neurologic status, and the presence of seizure activity in the field is helpful to compare to the patient's current condition. Past medical history that is relevant to the situation should be documented because an underlying disease process, such as hypertension, coagulopathy, or chronic obstructive pulmonary disease could have a pre-ventable negative impact on the patient's hospital course.

Complete serial neurologic assessments are probably the most important

Table 1-2 Clinical Manifestations

Type of Injury	Signs and Symptoms
Skull fractures	
Anterior fossa (Paranasal sinuses)	Conjunctival hemorrhage Ecchymosis of periorbital areas (raccoon's eyes) Rhinorrhea
Middle fossa	Ecchymosis of mastoid process of the temporal bone (Battle's sign) Hemotympanum Facial palsy Deafness Otorrhea
Dural tears	Otorrhea Rhinorrhea Postnasal drip Hemotympanum
Concussion	Transient neurodysfunction Unconsciousness (immediate and lasts seconds, minutes, or hours) Loss of reflexes Change in vital signs Retrograde and posttraumatic amnesia Irritability Drowsiness Headache Visual disturbances Vertigo Gait disturbances Contusion
Postconcussional syndrome	Headache Vertigo Nervousness Irritability Emotional instability Fatigue Insomnia Poor concentration Poor memory Difficulty with abstraction Difficulty with judgment Decreased judgment Decreased inhibitions Decreased libido Avoidance of crowds Weeks to years after head injury

continues

Table 1-2 *continued*

Diffuse axonal injury	Immediate prolonged unconsciousness Deep coma Decerebration Increased ICP, BP, and temperature
Primary brain stem	CN injury III-XII Petechial hemorrhage
Midbrain	Deep coma Pupils fixed at midpoint Ophthalmoplegia Decerebration
Pons	Coma Small nonreactive pupils Ophthalmoplegia Decerebration
Intracranial hemorrhages Epidural	Momentary unconsciousness then lucid period followed by decreased level of consciousness Headache Seizures Vomiting Hemiparesis (usually contralateral) Dilated ipsilateral pupil Irregular respirations (deep and labored) Decreased heart rate Increased systolic BP and temperature Changes in vital signs (late finding)
Subdural Acute	Headache Drowsiness Agitation Confusion Ipsilateral pupil dilated Hemiparesis (contralateral)
Subacute	Associated with less severe underlying conditions Signs and symptoms similar to those of acute
Chronic	May be months before symptoms appear Headaches Confusion Drowsiness Seizure Papilledema Ipsilateral pupil dilated and sluggish Hemiparesis (late finding)

Table 1-2 *continued*

Subarachnoid	Nuchal rigidity Headache Decreased level of consciousness Hemiparesis (contralateral) Ipsilateral dilated pupils
Intracerebral hematoma	Decreased level of consciousness that may lead to unconsciousness; this occurs from onset of bleeding Headache Hemiplegia on contralateral side Dilated pupil on ipsilateral side

part the nurse can play in the diagnostic process. The GCS is helpful in that it allows all levels of the medical staff to communicate in a concise form, but it should not be substituted for a detailed and thorough assessment. Vital signs, level of consciousness, pupil function, and motor and sensory function should all be included, as well as brain-stem reflexes and cranial nerves.

The level of consciousness is the most critical part of the neurologic exam and can be determined by the degree of stimulus required to have the patient respond in an appropriate manner. There are various terms used to describe levels of coma: alert, lethargic, stuporous, semicomatose, and comatose. Pupillary observation is an integral part of the neurologic assessment. Pupil size, shape, position and reactivity to light should be evaluated frequently. There are classical patterns of pupil abnormality that can assist in localizing the cerebral lesion (Figure 1-4).

If ocular movements cannot be assessed due to the patient's inability to respond, then the oculocephalic response (doll's eyes) can be tested. The head is gently elevated approximately 30 degrees and turned briskly side to side. The normal response is for the eyes to attempt to maintain their position in space and therefore move opposite to the direction in which the head was moved. This response is known as doll's eyes and the brain stem is considered to be intact. If this test is not possible due to possible cervical spine involvement or if the results are questionable, then the oculomotor pathways can be assessed by a stronger physiologic response test, the oculovestibular or cold caloric test. Prior to performing this test, the nurse must ensure the integrity of the tympanic membrane. The head is again elevated approximately 30 degrees and the ear is irrigated with 10 to 20 cc of ice-cold water. A response should occur within 20 to 60 seconds and can last several minutes. The normal response is a tonic deviation of both eyes to the ipsilateral

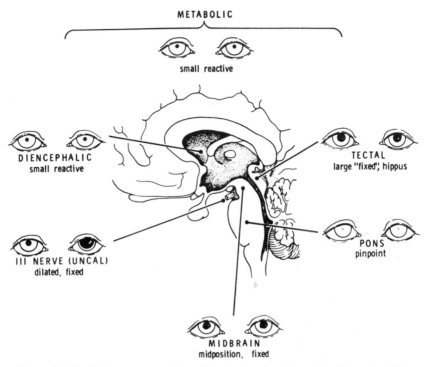

Figure 1-4 Pupils in comatose patients. *Source.* Reprinted from *The Diagnosis of Stupor and Coma* (p 46) by F Plum and J Posner with permission of the FA Davis Company, © 1981.

side. Repeated irrigations should be performed if there is no response or a questionable one.

Motor function and the presence of abnormal posturing (decorticate or decerebrate) should be assessed as well. This will enable the gross evaluation of the motor strip and spinal cord integrity.

The corneal and gag reflexes are evaluated by two simple tests performed in a matter of minutes; yet the tests contribute significant information related to the integrity of cranial nerves V, VII, IX and X.

Either a body-system approach or head-to-toe assessment is critical to the accurate diagnosis of the patient. Many times the patient does not have an isolated head injury and the nurse, as in the case study, may be faced with other life-threatening injuries. Confirmation of the absence of cervical spine injury is imperative to prevent cord injury.

The gold standard for diagnosis in head trauma is computed tomography. Since its introduction in 1972, this procedure has become the rule for diagnosis in many neurological disease processes but especially in head trauma. This completely noninvasive procedure enables the neurosurgeon and/or radiologist to assess changes in tissue density, displacement of structures and abnormalities in size, shape, or location of cerebral anatomy. The computerized visualization relates to tissue density can provide information related to the contents of various structures or lesions (ie, blood). In some rare situations, it may be desirable to perform a CT with contrast to enhance visualization. If this is the case, an iodinated radiopaque substance will be injected into the patient's venous access. The advantages of the CT are numerous: it is noninvasive, a complete scan can be accomplished within 30 minutes, serial scans can be used to measure patient progress, and radiation exposure is relatively low.

Although it is still recognized as a useful tool, especially in cases of suspected skull fracture, the skull film has been replaced by the CT for the symptomatic patient. The information obtained from the CT is far more conclusive and therefore more valuable in emergent situations, such as severe head trauma.

The magnetic resonance imaging study has yet to become practical for head-injured patients because the equipment requires that no metallic objects be attached to the patient and that the patient be perfectly still, both of which may be literally impossible for the trauma patient.

Baseline and continuous monitoring of the electrical activity of the brain is becoming more valuable as newly developed computerized methods of electroencephalogram (EEG) analysis (brain mapping and computerized spectral array) simplify interpretation and offer the clinician immediate information related to abnormal electrical activity. Asymmetrical changes or diffuse slowing of the electrical activity in the brain can be detected at an early stage of ischemia or injury, well before the patient may demonstrate clinical signs of neurological deterioration.

Lumbar puncture is contraindicated for the diagnosis or treatment of head-injured patients. In the presence of increased intracranial pressure, the patient is at risk for herniation if a lumbar puncture is performed. If the cerebral spinal fluid must be accessed, then a ventriculostomy should be performed.

Angiography is not indicated for head-trauma patients unless there is a reason to suspect traumatic aneurysms or arteriovenous fistulae, such as the cavernous sinus fistula discussed in Chapter 4.

Laboratory assessment of the head-injured patient can provide useful information related to arterial blood gas determination, hematocrit, coagulation studies, electrolytes, and alcohol or drug screening.

MEDICAL AND NURSING MANAGEMENT

The two goals stated in the introduction of this chapter were preventing secondary injury and providing an environment that optimizes recovery for the compromised brain. The nurse's main responsibility is to prevent secondary injury and limit the extent of neurological injury to that of the primary insult.

Initial stabilization and management of the patient are of utmost importance for head-trauma patients because every second counts and any delays in airway management or failure to respond rapidly to hypotension can make a critical difference. During a head-to-toe assessment of the patient, the critical care nurse must anticipate accomplishing several procedures soon after the patient is admitted to the ICU and he or she should be ready with the appropriate equipment.

The following information is applicable to the postoperative head-injury patient or the patient whose injury does not indicate surgery; the intent is to provide complete information in terms of nursing care, including major points related to the medical regimen. The focus of the information presented is on intensive care. The following section provides a nursing care plan using NANDA-approved nursing diagnoses. This section provides detailed information of nursing interventions as well.

Pulmonary. The airway should be evaluated and the patient intubated if he or she is unresponsive or has inadequate arterial blood gases (ABG). The patient must be evaluated for the possibility of a cervical spine injury, and the neck must be kept in a neutral position until this is ruled out by either x-ray or CT scan. The use of mild hyperventilation (CO_2 25-30) is indicated unless the ABG results dictate otherwise. Further hyperventilation may lead to severe cerebral vasoconstriction and ischemia. Continuous monitoring of mixed venous oxygen saturation (SVO_2) will provide valuable information related to oxygen delivery and consumption. The SVO_2 measurement is often the first warning related to subtle changes in the patient's pulmonary status.

The lungs should be auscultated frequently and pulse oximetry as well as end-tidal CO_2 monitoring should be used to provide continuous evaluation of the oxygenation and ventilation status of the patient. If possible, positive end-expiratory pressure (PEEP) should be avoided because it increases intrathoracic pressure and decreases venous return, both of which may lead to further increases in the ICP. Careful pulmonary toileting is necessary to prevent respiratory complications, such as aspiration, atelectasis, or pneumonia.

Cardiovascular. Determining heart rate, rhythm, and blood pressure is vital to establishing appropriate interventions. Cardiac dysrhythmias are common in the head-injured patient, and it is the responsibility of every physician and nurse caring for these patients to be certified in the Advanced Cardiac Life Support (ACLS) course offered by the American Heart Association. When the dysrhythmia is identified, the appropriate algorithm should be followed.

In cases of multiple trauma, the patient may be hypotensive due to hemorrhage, and immediate resuscitation with isotonic volume (normal saline) expansion is necessary. The neurologic examination of a hypotensive patient can contrast greatly with an examination of the same patient after blood pressure has been stabilized due to changes in the CPP. Of course, the cause of the hemorrhage must be identified and corrected immediately. Vasopressor drugs should also be considered in the event of an unsatisfactory response to fluid resuscitation.

Neurologic. The diagnosis of increased ICP should be made at the time of the neurological examination. The decision to monitor the ICP with a fiberoptic subdural catheter or ventriculostomy will depend upon the physician's preference but also whether or not there is a suspected need to drain the CSF in order to control ICP. This procedure can be performed in the emergency room, ICU, or the operating room, but strict sterile technique must be employed in preparing equipment and inserting the monitoring device. Regional cerebral blood flow monitoring can also be done in the ICU. This relatively new thermal diffusion technique provides additional information relative to the cerebral hemodynamics of the injured area.

Mannitol can be given intravenously (20% Mannitol, 1 gm/kg over 15 minutes) if the patient's neurological status deteriorates, cerebral edema is present, or ICP increases. Although it is considered protocol in many institutions, the use of glucocorticosteroids remains controversial, and there are many articles in the literature citing both the benefits and the lack of effect.[14(p175)]

Seizures in this patient population can lead to secondary injury by increasing metabolic needs that cannot be met in the injured brain. Therefore, every head-trauma patient should be on a seizure precaution protocol. The protocol may differ among institutions but all patients should be on anticonvulsant drug therapy, which is instituted with a loading dose of phenytoin of 18 mg/kg infused at approximately 50 mg per minute. Lorazepam IV in 2 mg doses can be used as needed for control of ongoing seizures. Although pentobarbital coma is not induced frequently, in situations of refractory increased ICP, it is useful in decreasing the cerebral metabolic rate and thereby blood flow and ICP. The side effects are significant and include hypotension, cardiac dysrhythmias and pulmonary complications. Drug titration is achieved by continuous monitoring of the EEG to maintain burst suppression. Although the practicality of continuous computerized EEG monitoring in the ICU is still being resolved, it may become a useful tool in identifying ischemia at an early stage as well as monitoring burst suppression.

In patients that are particularly difficult to ventilate, combative, or continuously posturing, a neuromuscular blocking agent such as pancuronium or vecuronium may be useful. Of course, in awake or alert patients this protocol would not be appropriate, but if it is selected, the patient would require placement on a ventilator and sedation as well.

Gastrointestinal. The head-injured patient is always at risk for aspiration, so the insertion of a nasogastric (NG) tube would be part of standard care. These patients are also at risk for gastric ulcer. The pH of the NG tube drainage should be checked every six hours and the patient treated with antacids to maintain the pH at greater than 5.0. Prophylactic histamine blockers, such as cimetidine or tagamet, should be part of the standard care as well.

The demanding nutritional needs of the head-injured patient are clearly documented in the literature. Once bowel sounds have returned and there are no internal injuries contraindicating NG feedings, the feedings should be started. Starting at half strength and checking residuals are part of this regimen. There are many commercial preparations available and although consultation with a nutritionist is not necessary, it can be helpful, especially in the face of multiple wounds, infection, or a hypermetabolic state.

Fluids and electrolytes. Emergency fluid resuscitation was previously discussed, but once again the importance of adequate venous access cannot be overemphasized. Intravascular volume expansion can assist in correcting hypotension as well as controlling vasospasm. Fluids that minimize free water loading, such as normal saline, should be given.[14(p166)] The use of a Swan-Ganz catheter and pulmonary artery wedge pressure can aid in titration of this therapy as well as preventing fluid overload and pulmonary edema. Lab values such as complete blood count, serum and urine electrolytes and osmolarity should be monitored every six hours initially, then at least once every 24 hours.

In any neurological injury there is a risk of hormonal changes that may lead to the development of diabetes insipidus or the syndrome of inappropriate antidiuretic hormone. Table 1-3 clearly differentiates between these two complications and describes appropriate interventions.

Other injuries. It is not within the scope of this chapter to address all the aspects of trauma nursing but a few broad concepts need mention. Certainly intraabdominal and thoracic injuries must be ruled out as part of the initial

Table 1-3 Symptoms and Treatment for Diabetes Insipidus and SIADH*

	Symptoms	*Treatment*
Diabetes insipidus	Electrolyte imbalances Increased urine output Decreased urine osmolarity Increased serum osmolarity	DDAVP (desmopressin acetate) Replace fluids and electrolytes
SIADH	Increased urine output Increased urine Na Decreased serum Na (<120 mEq/L) Nausea/vomiting Hyperirritability Disorientation	Restrict free fluids NaCl supplements

*Syndrome of inappropriate secretion of antidiuretic hormone.

assessment. Sepsis can be a fatal complication; therefore, all patients with open wounds, compound fractures, and open head injury are treated with broad-spectrum antibiotics.

Hyperthermia can lead to increased ICP, increased metabolism, and increased oxygen and caloric demand. Every attempt to control the patient's temperature by cooling blankets or antipyretics should be instituted.

Orthopedic surgery can be performed as soon as the patient is stable enough to tolerate anesthesia and the operative procedure. Life-threatening internal injuries, such as a severely lacerated aorta, may even take precedence over neurosurgical procedures.

Surgical procedure. The need for surgery will depend upon the type and extent of injury seen on CT. The most common mass lesion that demands surgery is a subdural hematoma. Prompt and decisive intervention is essential because increased mortality is directly correlated with increased time intervals from injury to operation. Whether a craniotomy or burr hole procedure is performed, the information mentioned previously would apply.

NURSING CARE PLAN

The actual nursing care plan used in this case study is presented here. The nursing diagnoses were made after a complete assessment of the patient. The interventions are individualized for this particular patient, but they can be modified for different patients. Some of the nursing interventions are in accordance with specific nursing department policies and may not be applicable to all patient situations. The format can be refigured to conform to any nursing process design and type of nursing documentation. The problem list for a patient like this can be endless; therefore, the three diagnoses directly related to the patient's neurologic injury were prioritized and are presented below. All procedures should be explained to the patient and family members and documented with the patient response in the nursing notes.

1. Nursing Diagnosis: Alteration in Cerebral Tissue Perfusion Related to Head Injury and Cerebral Edema

Expected Patient Outcome

The cerebral tissue perfusion will be within normal limits as evidenced by:

1. normal or stabilized neuro exam
2. normal or stabilized CPP

Nursing Interventions

1. Perform neuro assessment every one to two hours.
2. Monitor ICP and CPP, drain CSF if ICP greater than 15 mm Hg, not to exceed 30 cc/hr.
3. Keep head of bed elevated 30 degrees and neck in neutral alignment to promote venous drainage.
4. Avoid trach ties or endotracheal tube (ET) tape that is constrictive; do not allow ET tube tape to go around patient's neck.
5. Avoid any unnecessary procedure that would create a Valsalva maneuver (straining at bowel movement, vigorous suctioning).
6. Maintain adequate oxygenation (saturation > 95%) and mild hyperventilation (Pco_2 25-30) to promote mild cerebral vasoconstriction.
7. Administer osmotic diuretics as ordered by physician.
8. Maintain MAP above 50 mm Hg to provide adequate CPP.
9. Administer sedation and neuromuscular blockers as needed.

2. Nursing Diagnosis: Alteration in Gas Exchange As Related to Mechanical Ventilation and Pneumonia

Expected Patient Outcome

The patient will experience normal gas exchange as evidenced by arterial blood gases within normal limits, lungs clear, and chest x-ray within normal limits.

Nursing Interventions

1. Perform pulmonary assessment every one to two hours.
2. Perform ventilation adjustments to maintain oxygen saturation $> 95\%$ and CO_2 25-30.
3. Use suction as needed per auscultation. Hyperventilate and oxygenate prior to suctioning; do not take patient off ventilator.
4. Do chest physiotherapy as needed and according to patient tolerance. (Caution—monitor ICP carefully).
5. Provide kinetic bed therapy to prevent secretion collection, atelectasis and further pulmonary complications.
6. Maintain sterile technique when suctioning or performing tracheostomy care.
7. Administer antibiotics as ordered.

3. Nursing Diagnosis: Alteration in Fluid and Electrolytes Related to SIADH

Expected Patient Outcome

Patient will maintain normal fluid balance and electrolytes as evidenced by:

1. balanced intake and output
2. normal electrolyte values of serum and urine

Nursing Interventions

1. Monitor hourly intake and output, with possibility of needing to limit fluids.
2. Take weight daily.
3. Monitor urine specific gravity and lab tests as ordered.
4. Administer medications as ordered.

CONCLUSION

This case study illustrates the etiology, pathophysiology, medical and nursing care of the head-trauma patient. Examples of primary and secondary injury to the brain were reviewed. The goal in neuroscience critical care nursing is to provide an environment where the compromised brain can recover from injury without the threat of potentially lethal secondary injuries.

The patient in this case study sustained bilateral craniotomies and an above-the-knee amputation of her right leg. After several weeks in a comatose state on a ventilator with pulmonary complications and sepsis, this patient survived and was discharged to a rehabilitation center. She is presently able to function at her pre-injury state. Her mental functions, with the exception of memory and mild difficulty with word finding, are completely normal.

This case study demonstrates how critical the role of the neuroscience critical care nurse can be in terms of creating a positive patient outcome. We are fortunate to participate and contribute to the expanding body of knowledge needed to care for these most challenging patients. The challenge posed to every nurse in the critical care arena is to explore ways to delicately blend the art of caring with the complexities of neuroscience nursing so that we can deliver care in a more humanistic way.

NOTES

1. *Interagency Head Injury Task Force Report.* Washington, DC: US Dept of Health and Human Services, Public Health Services, National Institute of Neurological Disorders and Stroke; February 1989.

2. Cammermeyer M, Appledorn C, eds. *Core Curriculum for Neuroscience Nursing.* Park Ridge, Ill: American Association of Neuroscience Nurses; 1990;1:1.

3. Hickey J. *The Clinical Practice of Neurological and Neurosurgical Nursing.* Philadelphia: JB Lippincott Co; 1986.

4. Barwick WJ. Scalp injuries. In: Wilkins R, Rengachary S, eds. *Neurosurgery.* New York: McGraw-Hill Book Co; 1985;2:1615.

5. McLaurin R, McLennan J. Diagnosis and treatment of head injury in children. In: Youmans J, ed. *Neurological Surgery.* Philadelphia: W.B. Saunders Co; 1982:2084.

6. Gennarelli T, Thibault L. Cranial trauma. In: Wilkins R, Rengachary S, eds. *Neurosurgery.* New York: McGraw-Hill Book Co; 1985;2:1531.

7. McCormick W. Pathology of closed head injury. In: Wilkins R, Rengachary S, eds. *Neurosurgery.* New York: McGraw-Hill Book Co; 1985;2:1548.

8. Ward J, Moulton R, Muizelaar P, Marmarou A. Cerebral homeostasis and protection. In: Wirth F, Ratcheson R, eds. *Neurosurgical Critical Care.* Baltimore, Md: Williams & Wilkins Co; 1987;1.

9. Reed G, Devous M. Southwestern Internal Medicine Conference: cerebral blood flow, autoregulation, and hypertension. *Am J Med Sci.* 1985;289:38.

10. Rockoff M, Kennedy S. Physiology and clinical aspects of raised intracranial pressure. In: Ropper A, Kennedy S, eds. *Neurological and Neurosurgical Intensive Care.* Gaithersburg, Md: Aspen Publishers, Inc; 1988:13.

11. Mauldin R, Coleman L. Intracerebral herniation. *J Neurosci Nurs.* 1983;15(5).

12. Martin E, Hummelgard A. Traumatic aneurysms. *J Neurosci Nurs.* 1986;18(2):90.

13. Martin E, Hummelgard A. Detachable balloon occlusion of carotid-cavernous sinus fistula. *J Neurosci Nurs.* 1987;19(3):134.

14. Swann K. Management of severe head injury. In: Ropper A, Kennedy S, eds. *Neurological and Neurosurgical Intensive Care.* Gaithersburg, Md: Aspen Publishers, Inc; 1988.

Chapter 2

Cerebral Vasospasm following Subarachnoid Hemorrhage

Laura L. Drobnich

INTRODUCTION

Subarachnoid hemorrhage (SAH) from a ruptured cerebral aneurysm is a potentially lethal yet manageable disease. More than 25,000 people in the United States suffer from a SAH each year.[1] About 50% of these patients die or become permanently disabled after the initial hemorrhage. Twenty percent of these patients die before reaching the hospital. Approximately 30% of those hospitalized die during the next several days or months as a result of either the initial hemorrhage or its complications.[1]

The morbidity and mortality associated with SAH remains high despite many advances in the treatment of intracranial aneurysms. Rebleeding was once thought to be the major cause, but now more recent studies demonstrate that cerebral infarction secondary to vasospasm is the leading cause of disability and death following SAH.[2,3]

This chapter explores how the nurse can face the challenges of caring for patients who have suffered from SAH. The chapter will review the pathophysiologic changes of cerebral vasospasm as they relate to symptomatology, as well as perioperative management for the treatment of cerebral vasospasm. A case study will be presented to illustrate unique aspects of this treatment. Nursing diagnoses specific to care of the SAH patient are included.

* * * * *

CASE STUDY

D.S., a 56-year-old male, complained of sudden onset of severe headache after lifting heavy machinery at work. The headache was immediately followed by two episodes of vomiting and a decrease in his level of consciousness. The emergency squad was called, and the patient was transported to a medical center.

On arrival at the emergency room, D.S. was comatose, responding only with intermittent bilateral decerebrate posturing to noxious stimuli. His pupils were equal and reactive to light at 3 mm diameter; nuchal rigidity was present. On the Hunt and Hess scale of classifying aneurysms, the patient was a Grade IV (Table 2-1).[4] His vital signs on admission were: blood pressure (BP) 180/110, pulse 120 (electrocardiogram was sinus rhythm), temperature 101° F, and respirations 30 to 40 per minute with periods of apnea. The patient was electively intubated and mechanically ventilated. The physician suspected increased intracranial pressure and the patient was hyperventilated. The ventilator settings were as follows: tidal volume 900 mL, assist control of 16, oxygen of 35%. The arterial blood gases were: pH 7.50, Po_2 135, Pco_2 29, HCO_3 18, and O_2 99%. D.S. exhibited no seizure activity.

After interviewing his wife, the nurse discovered that D.S. had a prior history of hypertension and was noncompliant in taking his antihypertensive medication. Two days prior to his hospitalization, he complained of a generalized headache that he attributed to his hypertension.

The diagnosis of subarachnoid hemorrhage was initially made based on the patient's signs, symptoms and neurologic exam. The patient underwent an emergent computerized tomography (CT) scan that revealed blood in the left sylvian fissure and intraventricular blood in the left lateral ventricle. A four-vessel angiogram was performed following the CT scan. A left middle cerebral artery aneurysm was discovered along with the presence of significant vasospasm confirming the diagnosis of SAH.

* * * * *

DEFINITION OF CEREBRAL VASOSPASM

What is a cerebral vasospasm and why does it occur following a SAH? An understanding of these mechanisms is vital for the treatment of cerebral vasospasm.

Cerebral vasospasm is defined as the constriction or narrowing of an artery of the circle of Willis or its major vessels as demonstrated by angiography. The vasospasm may be diffuse, segmented, or focal. Diffuse spasm occurs when there is a generalized narrowing of the cerebral arteries. A segmented or focal spasm occurs when there is selective narrowing of the artery, with the majority of the artery maintaining its normal diameter.[5] Cerebral vasospasm can occur as a result of severe head trauma, spinal cord injury, meningitis, and arteriovenous malformation and following surgery of the hypothalamic-pituitary axis.[6]

Arterial vasospasm was initially believed to be a biphasic event.[7] The first phase occurs after the rupture of the aneurysm when a platelet plug forms to control the bleeding. The second phase, which occurs 4 to 14 days after aneurysm rupture, is due to the spasm of arteries adjacent to the site of the aneurysm.[8] This is considered true vasospasm and produces a serious threat to the patient's survival and neurologic recovery. True vasospasm may persist for days to weeks.

Cerebral vasospasm may be classified as angiographic or clinical vasospasm. Angiographic vasospasm is a narrowing of the major cerebral arteries and their branches as demonstrated by angiography. Clinical vasospasm is a syndrome of the ischemic consequences of cerebral artery narrowing, producing neurologic deficits.[9]

Seventy percent of patients develop arterial narrowing following SAH, although only 20% to 35% exhibit any neurologic deficit.[3] This is an important point to remember when caring for SAH patients. The patient may not exhibit any neurologic deficits but have angiographic evidence of vasospasm. Neurologic deficits do not always accompany vasospasm because the brain is supplied with about twice the amount of blood flow required for normal functioning. Other factors involved with providing sufficient blood flow include the collateral circulation of the brain, blood viscosity, perfusion pressure, and the brain's metabolic demands.[10] Therefore, neurologic deficits do not become apparent until the arterial constriction reduces cerebral blood flow to a critical level.

Clinical or angiographic vasospasm occurs three to four days following the initial hemorrhage and peaks in incidence by day seven to ten.[9] Vasospasm usually resolves 15 to 21 days after hemorrhage.

Rebleeding is also a dangerous complication following subarachnoid hemorrhage. Rerupture of the aneurysm can occur on the day of the initial hemorrhage and up to weeks following the hemorrhage.

THE ETIOLOGY OF CEREBRAL VASOSPASM

The cause of chronic cerebral vasospasm following subarachnoid hemorrhage remains unknown. Age, sex, hypertension, arteriosclerosis, diabetes, and the size or location of aneurysm do not correlate with development or severity.[11,12]

Various hypotheses have been proposed. The two major hypotheses regarding the pathogenesis of vasospasm include the following:

1. contraction of the cerebral arterial smooth muscle after exposure to vasoactive substances found in the cerebrospinal fluid released from the subarachnoid clot
2. impairment of the vasodilatory activity of the cerebral artery

Other hypotheses proposed include

1. proliferative vasculopathy
2. an immunoreactive process
3. an inflammatory process
4. mechanical phenomena, which can occur alone or in conjunction with the other pathogenic processes[9,10,13]

Vasospasm develops in arteries surrounded by thick blood clots, and it has been thought that some factor found in the blood clot may be responsible for the subsequent development of vasospasm. Research to identify and validate the specific spasmogenic substances continues. No specific substance has consistently produced and sustained vasospasm in the laboratory; therefore, it is unlikely that any single spasmogenic substance is a causative factor. Potential spasmogens include serotonin, prostaglandins, catecholamines (norepinephrine and epinephrine), angiotensin, lysed erythrocytes, thrombin, plasmin, fibrin degradation products, hydroperoxides, potassium, histamines, and others.[3,9,13-15]

Vasospasm may be caused by the failure of the arterial smooth muscle to contract and relax due to improper regulation of calcium and cyclic adenosine monophosphate (cAMP).[14] Proper regulation of calcium and cAMP may be altered by a spasmogenic substance released from the subarachnoid clot. The spasmogenic substance acts on a receptor site and alters the characteristic of the vascular smooth muscle membrane. The cell membrane may be unable to maintain the appropriate calcium gradient. Normal contraction and relaxation of the arterial smooth muscle thus becomes impaired.

It is also believed that irritation from spasmogenic substances may cause morphologic changes in the vessel walls and loss of portions of the endothelial lining followed by necrosis and hyperplasia of the cerebral vessels. Arterial narrowing can occur. The arterial narrowing increases the resistance in the vessel, and blood flow is further decreased. It is uncertain whether these morphologic changes cause vasospasm, although the lumenal narrowing could be a factor in its development.

ASSESSMENT OF THE PATIENT WITH CEREBRAL VASOSPASM

Neurologic Assessment

The neurologic assessment performed by the nurse is the single most important component in the care of the subarachnoid hemorrhage patient.

This constant bedside assessment is often the only means of identifying the new onset of subtle changes.

The clinical manifestations of vasospasm vary from patient to patient depending on the artery or arteries involved in aneurysm rupture or vasospasm. Vasospasm may involve vessels nearby or distant to the site of the SAH. It is usually more severe on the side of the brain ipsilateral to the aneurysm.[9]

An altered level of consciousness may be the initial finding following SAH. Assessment should include the type and amount of stimulation required to arouse the patient and the patient's level of orientation (person, place, time, reason for hospitalization). The patient's speech and ability to understand what is being said should also be assessed. Diffuse vasospasm results in widespread or nonlocalized symptoms, such as decreased level of consciousness. Regional or focal alterations in blood flow affect specific neurologic functions, such as speech or ability to follow commands with a motor response. The cranial nerve (CN) exam also aids in the determination of global or focal dysfunction. Since many of the cranial nerves exit from the midbrain, compression of these nerves may indicate midbrain pathology. Focal ischemia or compression of the oculomotor nerve (CN III) from an aneurysm can produce ptosis, diplopia, and dilation of the pupil, which may be the cardinal sign for impending rupture. Other cranial nerves need to be assessed: extraocular eye movements (CN III, IV, VI), corneal response (CN V, VII) as well as the swallow/gag reflex (CN IX, X) in the comatose patient. A thorough neurologic exam can be performed in the awake patient.

Motor function assessment includes testing the strength of the hand grasp and bilateral extremities. Pronator drift is a subtle sign of weakness. Decreased motor strength may progress to hemiparesis or hemiplegia, depending on the degree of altered blood flow as well as the region impaired.

Clinical meningitis may later lead to meningeal thickening and scarring and damage the cerebrospinal fluid absorption process. Neurologic assessment becomes important in the early detection of hydrocephalus. The patient may require intracranial pressure monitoring with ventricular drainage. A ventricular shunt may also be required if the hydrocephalus does not resolve. The severe headache, nausea, nuchal rigidity and elevated temperature seen in patients with SAH are due to the meningeal irritation of blood in the subarachnoid space.

Part of the neurologic assessment includes classifying the patients according to grade. The classification of Hunt and Hess (Table 2-1) is one of the most accepted grading systems used by neurosurgeons.[4] Clinical grading is based on the severity of neurologic deficit and the intensity of the meningeal inflammatory reaction. At this time, it provides the best clinical criteria for the estimate of surgical risk. Patients with poorer grades have been noted to

Table 2-1 Hunt and Hess Classification of Patients with Intracranial Aneurysm According to Surgical Risk

Grade	Symptoms
0	Unruptured aneurysm
I	Asymptomatic or minimal headache and slight nuchal rigidity
IA	No acute meningeal or brain reaction, but with fixed neurologic deficit
II	Moderate to severe headaches, nuchal rigidity, no neurologic deficit other than cranial nerve palsy
III	Drowsiness, confusion, or mild focal deficit
IV	Stupor, moderate to severe hemiparesis, possibly early decerebrate rigidity, and vegetative disturbances
V	Deep coma, decerebrate rigidity, moribund appearance

Source: Reprinted from "Surgical Risk as Related to Time of Intervention in the Repair of Intracranial Aneurysms" by W. Hunt and R. Hess with permission of the Journal of Neurosurgery (1968; 28:14–20), © 1968.

have an increased incidence of developing vasospasm, are poorer surgical risks, and have less favorable outcomes.

Cardiovascular Assessment

Blood pressure control is important, as is the brain's ability to maintain its autoregulation. Cerebral blood flow in the normal brain is constant despite a wide range of mean arterial blood pressures. The autoregulatory mechanism of the brain automatically regulates the diameter of the resistance vessels (arterioles) to maintain constant blood flow when cerebral perfusion pressure changes. Cerebral perfusion pressure (CPP) is defined as the blood pressure gradient across the brain. This is calculated as the difference between the mean arterial blood pressure and the intracranial pressure (CPP = MAP − ICP). Perfusion of the brain depends on a favorable relationship between the arterial blood pressure and intracranial pressure. Adequate CPP is 60 to 80 mm Hg.[15(p249)]

In ischemic brain regions, autoregulation may be lost and cerebral blood flow parallels the mean of arterial blood pressure at hypotensive or hypertensive levels. Hypotension may lead to further ischemia due to decreased blood flow, while hypertension carries the risk of hemorrhage. In patients who develop vasospasm after SAH, hypertension increases the risk of aneurysm rerupture. Other problems associated with the loss of autoregulation may result when the brain is injured by an ischemic insult. Increases in systemic blood pressure may not be accompanied by an increase in cerebral blood flow due to the phenomenon of false autoregulation. There is the danger of increased brain edema and intracranial pressure; when there is increased systemic blood pressure and cerebral vasomotor paralysis, vasogenic edema may result. If cerebral microvascular damage has occurred from decreased blood flow, a significant increase in systemic pressure can produce a hemorrhagic infarct.[16]

The hyperactivity of the sympathetic nervous system that occurs after SAH produces an increase in the level of blood and urine catecholamines. Elevated circulating catecholamines may be responsible for hypertension and tachycardia. With sympathetic hyperactivity, there are also electrocardiogram (EKG) changes associated with SAH. These include T-wave distortions, U-waves, prolonged QT segments, and arrhythmias. Careful EKG monitoring is warranted, since further cardiovascular compromise could alter CPP.

Patients who suffer a SAH are hypovolemic after the hemorrhage.[17] It appears that hypovolemia contributes to the development of vasospasm and cerebral ischemia. Possible causes for hypovolemia include bed rest, supine diuresis, pooling of blood in the peripheral vascular beds, and a negative nitrogen balance. The use of a Swan-Ganz catheter can provide information about the patient's intravascular volume.

The patient's electrolytes must be monitored. Hyponatremia following SAH can occur as a result of physiologic changes from hyperactivity of the sympathetic nervous system or due to increased natriuresis. Urine electrolytes should be obtained to differentiate between salt wasting and water retention. The level of potassium, urea nitrogen, and creatinine can provide information about fluid balance and intravascular volume.

The patient's hemoglobin and hematocrit should also be monitored. Blood viscosity alterations seen in hemodilution can improve blood flow to the ischemic brain. Hemodilution with various colloid agents (low molecular weight dextran and albumin) enhances the rheologic characteristics of the blood. The viscosity of blood influences cerebral vascular resistance. When the blood viscosity is reduced, there is an increase in cerebral blood flow; blood flows with less intrinsic resistance. The optimum hematocrit in ischemic situations has not been established, but most neurosurgeons maintain the hematocrit at approximately 30% to 35%. Levels below 30% impair the oxygen-carrying capacity of the blood.

Pulmonary Assessment

Respiratory patterns may change in patients with altered cerebral blood flow or brain pathology. The rate and depth of respirations need to be assessed. Lungs should be auscultated for adventitious breath sounds.

Arterial blood gases should be monitored for carbon dioxide ($Paco_2$) and oxygen levels (Pao_2). Carbon dioxide is the most potent vasodilator affecting the cerebral vessels. Hypercarbia (increased Pco_2) increases cerebral blood flow. Hypercapnia or low levels of arterial Pco_2 produces marked vasoconstriction that reduces cerebral blood flow. The $Paco_2$ should be maintained at 35 to 45 mm Hg to maintain adequate cerebral blood flow. In cases of increased intracranial pressure, the $Paco_2$ should be maintained at 25 to 30 mm Hg.[15(p281)]

Oxygen does not have as profound an effect on cerebral circulation as carbon dioxide. Low levels of oxygen (hypoxia) produce cerebral vasodilation and an increase in cerebral blood flow. Hypoxia may cause an increase in cerebral blood flow from stimulation of the carotid body receptors. Cerebral blood vessels do not respond to changes in arterial oxygen until the Pao_2 is 50 mm Hg or lower. The level of oxygen should be maintained at a Pao_2 of 70 mm Hg or equal to or greater than 95% oxygen saturation.

DIAGNOSTIC TESTING

Once a history and physical exam are performed, all patients should have a computerized tomography scan. Studies have shown that a high correlation exists between the development of severe vasospasm and the presence of thick clots in the subarachnoid cisterns and fissures as seen on CT.[18] A CT scan can identify the presence of a hematoma, cerebral edema, or hydrocephalus; such pathology often occurs following SAH.

Other diagnostic tests used to identify vasospasm include the transcranial doppler ultrasound, continuous EEG monitoring, and regional cerebral blood flow monitoring. The transcranial doppler ultrasound is useful in identifying vasospasm involving the internal carotid, middle cerebral, anterior communicating, and posterior communicating arteries. The doppler measures the blood flow in the arteries affected by vasospasm. When the artery spasms, there is an increase in the velocity of blood flow in an attempt to deliver adequate blood.[19] EEG monitoring detects areas of relative ischemia. Regional cerebral blood flow measures blood flow to general regions of the brain, and is not artery specific.

A CT scan performed on D.S.'s admission to the hospital showed hemorrhage in the left sylvian fissure with blood in the left lateral ventricle (Figure 2-1). A four-vessel angiogram performed the day after D.S.'s hemorrhage revealed a left middle cerebral artery aneurysm (Figure 2-2).

MEDICAL TREATMENT

When cerebral vasospasm occurs, cerebral blood flow may be compromised as a result of impaired autoregulation in the affected region. Adequate

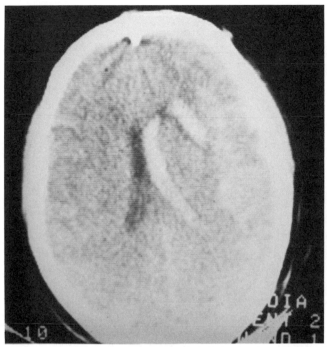

Figure 2-1 Computerized tomography scan on admission showing hemorrhage with blood in the lateral ventricle. *Source:* Reprinted from "Observations on the Perioperative Management of Aneurysmal Subarachnoid Hemorrhage" by S. Finn, S. Stephenson, C. Miller, L. Drobnich, and W. Hunt with permission of the *Journal of Neurosurgery* (1986;65:48–62), © 1986.

cerebral blood flow is related to the interaction of systemic blood pressure, intracranial pressure, cardiac function, and intravascular volume.[16,17,20]

Protocols developed for perioperative management of aneurysmal SAH are based on laboratory and clinical observations. Medical management and the guidelines to be described depend on frequent neurologic assessments and hemodynamic monitoring before and after therapies are initiated. Manipulation of cardiovascular parameters, correction of serum electrolytes, and pain control are factors that improve cerebral blood flow and the patient's neurologic status.

Importance of the Hourly Neurologic Assessment

Meticulous monitoring of the neurologic status is vital. The assessment performed by the neuroscience nurse is the single most important method of

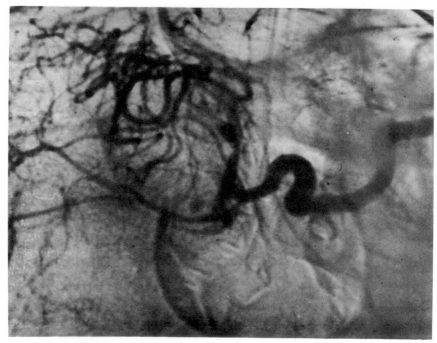

Figure 2-2 Angiogram on post-hemorrhage day 1 showing a left middle cerebral artery aneurysm. *Source:* Reprinted from "Observations on the Perioperative Management of Aneurysmal Subarachnoid Hemorrhage" by S. Finn, S. Stephenson, C. Miller, L. Drobnich, and W. Hunt with permission of the *Journal of Neurosurgery* (1986;65:48–62), © 1986.

evaluating neurologic status. The nurse must be attuned to subtle changes that may be the first signs of vasospasm.

The hourly exam should include a complete and identical assessment of areas sensitive to altered cerebral blood flow. The patient's level of consciousness should be assessed, including the type and amount of stimulation needed to arouse the patient, the patient's response to orientation questions (person, place, and time), and the patient's speech. The pupillary response, extraocular eye movements, and other pertinent cranial nerve functions should be tested. The motor response should be assessed in all extremities for strength and symmetry. A complete review of all the cranial nerves, motor function, and sensory response every hour is not always possible in the intensive care setting, but they should be assessed on every shift and more frequently if a neurologic deficit occurs. The neuroscience nurse should also be aware of the arteries that may be involved with vasospasm and tailor the neurologic assessment to focal symptoms of vasospasm that depend on the location of the aneurysm.

Laboratory Values

The arterial blood gases are monitored every 6 to 24 hours or as needed, especially when ventilator settings are changed. Arterial blood gases measure the oxygen and carbon dioxide levels, and pH. Oxygen levels should be maintained at 100 to 120 mm Hg or at an oxygen saturation greater than 95%. Patients should be intubated and mechanically hyperventilated if neurologic deterioration occurs. The carbon dioxide and pH values are important to monitor when hyperventilating the patient. The carbon dioxide ($Paco_2$) level should be maintained at 30 mm Hg. Hyperventilation will decrease cerebral edema. Vasoconstriction and reduced cerebral blood can occur when $Paco_2$ levels are less than 25 mm Hg.

The patient's other lab values provide information regarding treatment protocols and should be closely monitored. Serum electrolytes, serum osmolarity, glucose levels, and hematocrit and hemoglobin values should be obtained every 4 to 24 hours. The BUN (blood urea nitrogen), creatine, prothrombin time over partial thromboplastin time (PT/PTT), platelet values, and anticonvulsant levels are obtained every 24 hours or as needed.

Electrolyte disturbances can occur in SAH patients. Potassium levels should be maintained at 3.5 mEq/L to 5.0 mEq/L. Hyponatremia, defined as a serum sodium level less than 135 mEq/L, can be caused by increased natriuresis, water retention (SIADH), or diabetes insipidus (DI). Serum sodium levels should be maintained at 130 mEq/L to 145 mEq/L. Urine electrolytes are obtained at the same time serum electrolytes are drawn to differentiate the cause of electrolyte imbalance. Electrolytes must be promptly corrected. Abnormal levels can cause neurologic changes and fluid shifts.

Hemodynamic Monitoring and Cardiovascular Parameters

All patients admitted to the intensive care unit require close observation. An arterial line, central venous pressure line (CVP) and/or a Swan-Ganz catheter are placed to allow for continuous hemodynamic monitoring and immediate vascular access for medical treatment. The baseline blood pressure (BP) measured by cuff and arterial line, the pulmonary artery diastolic pressure (PADP), the pulmonary artery wedge pressure (PWP), and the cardiac index (CI) provide the necessary information required for the manipulation of treatment protocols. Intracranial pressure (ICP) monitoring is used in cases of severe neurologic deterioration or edema with shift or when hydrocephalus is seen on the CT scan. An intraventricular catheter and drainage system permits maintenance of a normal ICP (0 to 15 mm Hg).

The BP, PADP, CVP, and ICP should be recorded hourly. Abnormal hemodynamic values need to be evaluated and medical interventions may be necessary. The CI, as determined by thermodilution, and the PWP should be noted every four to six hours or as needed. The PWP and PADP may correlate closely in some patients.

Blood Pressure

The arterial line allows for continuous monitoring of the blood pressure. In patients with unclipped aneurysms, the BP is maintained at as low a level as the neurologic exam permits. In reducing the BP parameter, the neurosurgeon often uses the patient's level of consciousness as an indicator.[21] These parameters are adjusted for the individual patient. The systemic BP may be maintained at less than 150 mm Hg and greater than 100 mm Hg as long as the patient remains asymptomatic. Blood pressure values greater than 150 mm Hg induce the risk of rebleeding in patients with an unclipped aneurysm. Once the aneurysm is clipped, the blood pressure may be maintained at a greater value because the risk of rebleeding is decreased.

The control of BP in the unclipped aneurysm is vital. The use of narcotics (meperidine or morphine sulfate) has many benefits. The ICU patient may be experiencing anxiety or pain and discomfort. All SAH patients experience severe headaches that can cause restlessness and agitation. Narcotics, by reducing pain, promote hemodynamic stability. Narcotics are known to block the sympathetic response to pain and stress, decreasing the amount of catecholamines.[22] Narcotics also reduce pulse and respiratory rate and act as a vasodilator, thus reducing BP.[23]

Naloxone hydrochloride should be readily available to reverse the effects of the narcotic in cases of neurologic changes. A neurologic change, particularly a change in the patient's level of consciousness, may be due to narcotic administration or changes in arterial blood flow from the vasospasm.

Other medications used to control BP include calcium channel blockers, nitrates, and sodium nitroprusside (Nipride). Nifedipine provides prompt reduction in BP and can be administered orally or sublingually. Nitroglycerin is administered sublingually or topically. Nipride is given as an intravenous drip and is easily and rapidly titrated to control BP. Thiocyanate levels must be monitored when Nipride is used for several days to prevent drug toxicity. Often other antihypertensive medications are used in conjunction with sodium nitroprusside, so that the drug may be titrated and discontinued as soon as possible. Clonidine hydrochloride and hydralazine (Apresoline) are not used frequently because these drugs can cause a fall in BP that cannot be promptly reversed. Diuretics are not usually used in patients with SAH because they can cause electrolyte disturbances as well as lower intravascular volume. If hypotension occurs, antihypertensive medications are reduced, and volume expanders and vasopressor agents are administered.

Central Venous Pressure

The CVP is a measurement of the pressure of blood entering the right atrium or vena cava. It provides information about intravascular volume and the efficiency of the right side of the heart. The CVP does not accurately assess intravascular volume or approximate the PWP. This is evident in patients who are elderly or have underlying heart or lung disease.[24] The CVP can be useful as a gauge of intravascular volume.

Cardiovascular Parameters

The Swan-Ganz catheter, which measures cardiovascular function, is valuable when using intravascular volume expansion. Adequate cardiovascular monitoring requires measuring the PWP and the CI. Pulmonary artery wedge pressure reflects the left ventricular end-diastolic pressure and indirectly measures intravascular volume. In patients with no significant pulmonary vascular disease, the pulmonary artery diastolic pressure (PADP) approximates the pulmonary artery wedge pressure (PWP). A normal PWP (assuming an adequate cardiac index) is 5 to 12 mm Hg in the normal heart. When the PADP correlates closely with the PWP, the PADP values can be used.

The cardiac index is a measure of the cardiac output per square meter of body surface area. Cardiac output changes markedly with body size. The CI is a value by which the cardiac output of different-size persons can be compared with each other. The normal average CI for adults is approximately 3.0 ± 0.05 L/min/m^2.

In determining optimal volume status for a particular patient, the cardiac index is compared to the PWP. A Frank-Starling curve of the heart demonstrates the relationship between the left ventricular filling pressure (PWP) and the stroke volume, or CI (Figure 2-3). The Starling curve varies from patient to patient. One would expect that as the PWP increases with volume expansion, the CI also increases. In the normal heart, small increases in PWP are associated with significant increases in cardiac performance. In the case of myocardial dysfunction, however, the curve is much flatter and the

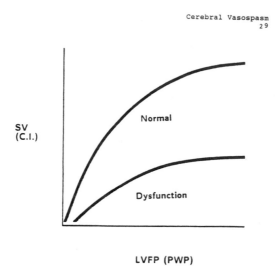

Cerebral Vasospasm
29

Figure 2-3 The Frank-Starling curve demonstrating the relationship between left ventricular filling pressure (PWP) and stroke volume (CI). *Source:* Reprinted from *The Pulmonary Artery Catheter: Methodology and Clinical Applications,* (p 111) by CL Sprung (Ed), Aspen Publishers, Inc., © 1983.

---

increase in CI is less for a similar PWP. Individuals with myocardial dysfunction thus require a high PWP in order to maintain an adequate CI. As the nurse gives fluids to increase intravascular volume, a point may eventually be reached when the CI begins to decrease despite an elevation of PWP. Once this occurs, complications of fluid overload, such as pulmonary hypoxia, congestive heart failure, pulmonary edema, and myocardial infarction, can result.

Correlation of PWP and Neurological Deficit

By recording the PWP (or PADP), BP, and neurologic assessment every hour, neurologic deficits can be correlated with different cardiovascular parameters. Suboptimum parameters may contribute to the development of vasospasm, cerebral ischemia, and neurologic deficits. The PWP alone does not provide information about the patient's neurologic status. A low PWP may indicate that the patient's intravascular volume is decreased. If a neurologic deficit is present, the patient may require an increase in intravascular volume or an increase in the PWP to reverse the deficit. Each patient has an individual optimal PWP. The optimal PWP is the PWP value below which neurologic deficits appear and above which the deficits are reversed.[25] Thus the optimal PWP to reverse a neurologic deficit varies from patient to patient.

Management of Neurologic Status and Cardiovascular Parameters

Protocols establish different cardiovascular and treatment parameters depending upon the patient's neurologic status.

When a neurologic deficit develops, a CT scan is always obtained to rule out cerebral edema, hydrocephalus, rebleeding of the unclipped aneurysm, or postoperative hematoma as possible causes for neurologic deterioration. Metabolic disturbances, such as hypoxia and hyponatremia, are also ruled out.

Vasospasm is suspected when the other possible causes of neurologic deterioration are ruled out. Protocols must be implemented immediately even prior to ruling out the other possible causes of neurologic deterioration. To be effective, the therapeutic management must be performed as soon as a deterioration in neurologic status is detected. Neurologic deficits are reversed by increasing the intravascular volume and increasing the PWP (assuming adequate CI) until the neurologic deficit disappears. To maintain the PWP, a high volume crystalloid infusion (DS 0.9 NaCl) is given at a rate greater than 100 cc/h. If the PWP falls or a neurologic deficit develops, the PWP is raised by administering colloid agents, such as hetastarch (Hespan), fresh-frozen plasma, or plasma fractionate (Plasmanate or 5% albumin). The maximum amount of hetastarch is 1500 mL per day.[25] Hetastarch may decrease clotting factors and fresh-frozen plasma is given to correct the clotting insufficiencies. Albumin 5% can be administered in 250 mL boluses every four to six hours. The amount of fluid bolus to be given and the rate of infusion are based on the PWP and the neurologic deficits.

When giving fluid boluses to increase intravascular volume, the patient may respond by diuresing large volumes. A vagal response increases urine output. Some authors have suggested the use of vasopressin to blunt diuresis, but the use of vasopressin carries a high risk of precipitating heart failure.[25] Other medications that can be used are Florinef (fludrocortisone acetate) and DDAVP (desmopressin acetate). These agents can also potentiate fluid overload and heart failure.

Administration of large volumes of colloid agents can alter serum lab values; the hematocrit and hemoglobin may change. Hemodilution reduces the viscosity of the blood and can be beneficial in reversing neurological deficits. It is important to maintain the hematocrit at 30% to 35%, because a decreased hematocrit will lower the oxygen-carrying capacity of the blood and lead to ischemia.

Guidelines for Treatments

SAH patients are placed into four categories:

1. Unclipped aneurysm with no neurologic deficit
   - PWP is maintained at 10 to 12 mm Hg
   - CI is maintained at 3 to 4 L/min/m²
   - BP is kept at a normal range or as low as neurologic status permits
2. Unclipped aneurysm with or developing neurologic deficits
   - PWP is raised until the deficit disappears
   - CI increases concomitantly
   - BP is kept normal or as low as the neurologic status permits
3. Postoperative patients with no neurologic deficits
   - PWP is kept at 12 to 14 mm Hg
   - CI is maintained at 3.5 to 4.5 L/min/m²
   - BP is kept at a normal level or as low as neurologic status permits
4. Postoperative patients with or developing neurologic deficits
   - Rapid fluid bolus is administered immediately after neurologic deficits develop
   - Infusion is continued until neurologic deficit disappears
   - PWP is raised to tolerable levels
   - BP is increased by using vasopressors[25]

Clinical observations from a study revealed that

1. neurologic deficit is preceded by a fall in PWP of about one hour
2. the less pronounced the deficit, the more easily it is reversed
3. a time lag of about one to two hours exists between increasing PWP and the disappearance of neurologic deficit
4. neurologic deficits related to acute hypotension, by contrast, are immediately reversed by raising blood pressure[25]

Current therapy for the treatment of vasospasm includes some form of hypertension or hypervolemia. In patients with unclipped aneurysm, caution must be used when raising the BP, because increased BP can cause rebleeding of the aneurysm. Maintenance of an optimal PWP can prevent hypotension and hypovolemia. When hypotension and hypovolemia do occur, raising the blood pressure and expanding the intravascular volume become necessary.[17]

If a patient develops a profound neurologic deficit, despite maximal intra-vascular volume status, vasopressors, such as dopamine hydrochloride (In-tropin) or dobutamine hydrochloride (Dobutrex), are used.

Surgical Intervention

Early intervention minimizes the risk of rebleeding but may increase cere-bral edema and precipitate intracerebral hemorrhage because of manipulation and retraction of compromised brain tissue.[26] Although further research in-volving balloon angioplasty is needed, there are several reported cases of successful treatment of vasospasm with this technique.

Previous research on the timing of surgery is voluminous and demonstrates the diversity of opinion among neurosurgeons. Vasospasm is the issue of conflict over the proper timing of surgery. Some neurosurgeons believe that early surgery may actually precipitate a vasospasm, while others believe that patients who are prone to developing vasospasm will do so regardless of the timing of surgery.[27] Regardless of the timing of surgery, most patients ini-tially are managed with a treatment protocol.

Patients in Grades I and II are taken to surgery as soon as possible, provided there is no significant vasospasm on angiography. Those with vaso-spasm, as seen on angiogram, are managed with a medical protocol in the ICU. When a repeat angiogram confirms the resolution of vasospasm, surgi-cal intervention is appropriate. Grades III to V are medically managed until they improve to Grades I, IA, or II. An angiogram prior to surgery will confirm the absence of vasospasm and give clearance to proceed to clip the aneurysm.

During surgery, the PWP, PADP, and CI are monitored and maintained at baseline values. Dobutamine or nitroprusside may be administered to main-tain BP as well as prevent myocardial depression related to the use of neuro-anesthetic drugs. Crystalloids, packed red blood cells, and colloids are used to maintain intravascular volume.

Mechanisms at Work in Treatment Protocols

There is only an approximate correlation between PWP/PADP and actual intravascular volume.[28] A low PWP is associated with low volume, but a higher PWP does not always correlate with increased intravascular volume. The higher PWP has clinical significance as an indicator of pulmonary edema. Small increases in PWP/PADP are sufficient to reverse neurologic deficits in the majority of patients, but is intravascular volume significantly raised?

There are no clues in the literature that relate left ventricular end-diastolic pressure, cardiac index, and cerebral blood flow. The close correlation between PWP and neurologic deficits associated with a high cardiac index and adequate blood pressure suggests that rheologic, humoral, or reflex factors are involved.[25] The exact role of PWP in reversing cerebral ischemia is unknown.

Medications

The incidence of seizures may increase following SAH. Patients should receive prophylactic anticonvulsant medication of phenytoin (Dilantin) or phenobarbital. Serum anticonvulsant levels should be monitored. Dexamethasone (Decadron) is administered to reduce cerebral edema and inflammation. Stress, catecholamine release, and steroid use can result in gastric deterioration. Histamine (H_2) receptor antagonist drugs, such as ranitidine or cimetidine (Tagamet), should be administered every six hours. Antacids can also be given.

Digoxin (Lanoxin) may be administered to patients with pre-existing heart disease or those prone to cardiac failure. In patients who require higher PWP values to reverse neurologic deficits, prophylactic doses of digoxin may be given to improve cardiac output and prevent complications from fluid overload.

Calcium channel blockers such as nimodipine have been found to be useful in controlling vasospasm, and their use is becoming the accepted standard with this patient population.

Nutritional Status

Nutritional status is important. Patients are given regular diets when they are alert and able to tolerate food. Patients who are drowsy and unable to eat due to their neurologic status receive tube feedings. Some patients receive peripheral parenteral nutrition. This nutrition is provided by a combination of 6.25% to 10% Travasol (a crystalline amino acid solution), a final dextrose concentration of 6.25% to 10% with appropriate electrolytes, and 20% Intralipid (an intravenous fat emulsion).

OUTCOME NARRATIVE

The outcome for D.S., the 56-year-old patient who suffered from a subarachnoid hemorrhage, is illustrated in Figure 2-4. As previously mentioned,

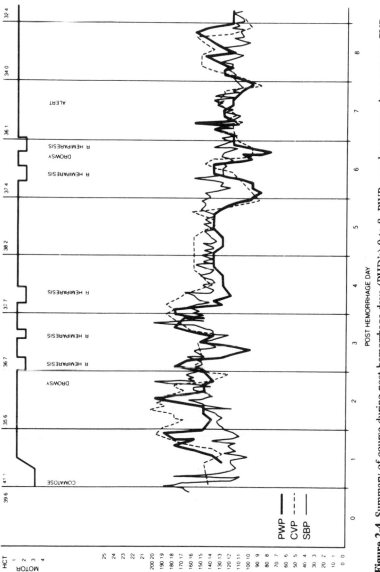

Figure 2-4 Summary of course during post-hemorrhage days (PHD's) 0 to 8. PWP = pulmonary wedge pressure; CVP = central venous pressure; SBP = systolic blood pressure; Hct = hematocrit (%). Motor scale: 1 = normal, 4 = hemiplegia. *Source:* Reprinted from "Observations on the Perioperative Management of Aneurysmal Subarachnoid Hemorrhage" by S. Finn, S. Stephensen, C. Miller, L. Drobnich, and W. Hunt with permission of the *Journal of Neurosurgery* (1986; 65:48–62), © 1986.

the patient was unresponsive to verbal stimuli and intermittently bilaterally decerebrate to nail-bed pressure. His pupils were equally reactive to 3 mm in diameter. His admission blood pressure (BP) was 180/110, pulse 120 beats per minute, and respirations 40 per minute with periods of apnea. The patient was electively intubated and mechanically ventilated.

Intravenous meperidine (Demerol) was administered in the emergency room and his BP decreased to 130/90 mm Hg and his pulse (normal sinus rhythm) to 100 beats per minute. He was transferred to the intensive care unit where a Swan-Ganz catheter was inserted. The initial pulmonary artery wedge pressure (PWP) was 16 mm Hg and the cardiac index (CI) was 3.9 L/min/m². The BP was controlled with hourly doses of intravenous meperidine (25 mg). Within 12 hours of admission, the patient was alert and following commands.

The PWP was maintained around 16 mm Hg. Three days following the SAH, the PWP fell to 12 mm Hg. The patient became drowsy and then developed a right hemiparesis. A 300 mL bolus of hetastarch was given to increase the PWP to 15 to 16 mm Hg and the deficit disappeared. That same day, another fall in PWP was followed by a right hemiparesis, which again resolved when the PWP was increased to 15 to 16 mm Hg.

Four days after the SAH, the patient again developed a right hemiparesis following a drop in PWP, but this resolved following an infusion of 300 mL fresh-frozen plasma. His systolic BP stabilized at 140 to 150 mm Hg. He was again responsive and without neurologic deficit. Administration of meperidine was reduced to every two hours as needed to control the BP and the patient's restlessness.

Six days following SAH, the PWP fell to 9 mm Hg. The patient became drowsy and the right hemiparesis returned. After a 200 mL bolus of hetastarch and 300 mL fresh-frozen plasma were administered, the PWP rose to 17 mm Hg. The hemiparesis disappeared. Another fall in PWP to 10 mm Hg was followed by the reappearance of the right hemiparesis. The cardiac index was 4.0 L/min/m². After a fluid bolus was given to raise the PWP, the hemiparesis disappeared. D.S. had an extended stay of 65 days in the intensive care unit. The aneurysm was successfully clipped 38 days after the hemorrhage without incident. The patient was a Grade II preoperatively.

Complications included pneumonia, urinary tract infection, fluid overload, and epidural hematoma. The pneumonia and urinary tract infections were successfully treated with antibiotics. Fluid overload was treated with mild diuresis and by reducing the hourly rate of the intravenous fluid. An epidural hematoma was detected two days postoperatively on a routine CT scan. The patient was taken to surgery following the CT exam and the hematoma was surgically evacuated. The patient had no change in neurologic status.

The patient had excellent recovery. He now leads a full and independent life without neurologic deficit.

NURSING CARE PLAN

The nursing care plan used to treat the patient in the case study in this chapter is outlined below.

1. Nursing Diagnosis: Potential for Altered Cerebral Tissue Perfusion Related to Vasospasm

Expected Patient Outcome

Cerebral tissue perfusion will be adequate as evidenced by:

1. normal or stable neurosurgical exam
2. CPP = 60–80 mm Hg

Nursing Interventions

1. Perform a thorough neurologic assessment every hour.
2. Obtain PWP every hour.
3. Record vital signs every hour.
4. Maintain BP within parameters.
5. Maintain PWP within parameters. Unclipped aneurysm: 10–12 mm Hg, clipped aneurysm: 12–14 mm Hg.
6. Obtain a CI every six hours and prn.
7. Notify neurosurgeon with a change in neurologic status, PWP or vital signs.
8. Promptly administer IV fluids as ordered.
9. Continue patient assessment: neurologic status, PWP, vital signs.

2. Nursing Diagnosis: Alteration in Comfort: Pain Related to Meningeal Irritation after SAH

Expected Patient Outcome

Patient will:

1. express a decrease in pain/discomfort
2. demonstrate reduced restlessness

Nursing Interventions

1. Assess level of consciousness and restlessness.
2. Administer intravenous meperidine (Demerol) every two hours and prn.
3. Premedicate before painful procedures.
4. Decrease environmental stimuli.
5. Provide a quiet, calm environment.
6. Elevate HOB 30 degrees to facilitate venous drainage.

3. Nursing Diagnosis: Alteration in Nutrition: Less Than Body Requirements Related to Level of Consciousness

Expected Patient Outcome

Patient will maintain adequate nutrition as evidenced by:

1. no weight loss
2. balanced intake and output
3. absence of negative nitrogen balance
4. maintenance of skin turgor

Nursing Interventions

1. Assess level of consciousness and ability to eat.
2. Nutritional consult; registered dietitian to make recommendations.
3. Administer tube feeding as ordered via feeding tube.
4. Check tube feeding residuals and bowel sounds every four hours.
5. Possess a thorough understanding of the use of total parenteral nutrition when utilized.

4. Nursing Diagnosis: Impaired Physical Mobility: Potential for Developing Deep Vein Thrombophlebitis (DVT) Related to Immobility and Bed Rest

Expected Patient Outcome

Patient will not exhibit complications as evidenced by:

1. absence of DVT
2. absence of pulmonary embolism

Nursing Interventions

1. Assess color, temperature, and presence of edema in lower extremities (LE) every shift.
2. Note any tenderness or pain in the lower extremities.
3. Measure calf and thigh; record every AM.
4. Apply external compression wraps to LE upon admission.
5. Use the external compression wraps continuously.
6. Turn every two hours.
7. Encourage leg exercises.
8. Use TED hose.

5. Nursing Diagnosis: Potential for Ineffective Patient and Family Coping Related to Lack of Knowledge regarding Disease Process, Procedures and Diagnostic Testing

Expected Patient Outcome

Patient and family will express an increased understanding of illness and demonstrate decreased anxiety.

Nursing Interventions

1. Educate patient and family about the disease process.
2. Explain all tests and procedures.
3. Inform patient and family of patient's daily status and upcoming procedures.
4. Assign a primary nurse to care for the patient.
5. Provide realistic encouragement.

6. Nursing Diagnosis: Potential for Infection Related to Ineffective Breathing Patterns (Pneumonia, Atelectasis), Invasive Lines, Indwelling Foley Catheter

Expected Patient Outcome

Patient will be free from infection as evidenced by:

1. no temperature
2. WBC within normal limits
3. no abnormal secretions or drainage
4. all cultures are negative

Nursing Interventions

1. Encourage alert patient to deep breathe and use volumetric exerciser every two hours.
2. Turn and reposition patient every two hours.
3. Intubated patients: suction every two hours and prn.
4. Suctioning should be brief: 6 to 10 seconds using sterile technique.
5. Note quality and characteristics of sputum.
6. Send sputum cultures prn.
7. All invasive line dressings are changed and the sites inspected every 48 hours; dressings to be occlusive and sterile.
8. Use sterile technique with Foley insertion.
9. Provide catheter care BID.
10. Pin or tape the catheter to prevent irritation traction on the meatus.
11. Note characteristics of urine (concentration, sediment).
12. Send urine cultures prn.
13. Administer antibiotics as ordered, monitor therapeutic drug levels.

IMPLICATIONS FOR NURSING

Maintaining the PWP (PADP) can prevent and reverse neurologic deficits associated with cerebral vasospasm. The nurse caring for the patient has a vital role in this protocol. The nurse must perform a thorough neurologic assessment every hour and be attuned to subtle changes. The blood pressure and PWP (PADP) are recorded every hour. The neurosurgeon must be notified immediately with any changes in neurologic status or PWP (PADP). Prompt action by the nurse will prevent neurologic deterioration.

The patient's physical, psychosocial and spiritual needs must be considered when planning care. Alterations in the function of the neurologic, cardiovascular, respiratory, gastrointestinal, renal, and musculoskeletal systems are incorporated in many care plans.[9,13,29]

Neurologic Status

A thorough hourly neurologic assessment is important in the continuous assessment of the patient. The neurologic assessment includes examination of the level of consciousness, pupillary response, motor response, and speech, as well as cranial nerve and sensory testing.

The nurse assesses eye opening in response to stimuli, reaction and equality of the pupils to light, and orientation to person, place, and time. The amount of stimuli to keep the patient awake is also noted. The patient's speech should be evaluated for aphasia (receptive or expressive) or slurring.

Motor response is tested with the patient's ability to follow commands (ie, hand grasp, dorsi-plantar flexion). All extremities are tested for motor strength. Equality and symmetry of movement is evaluated by comparing one side with the other. Testing for pronator drift will detect subtle weakness.

The nurse must also be aware of the number of days post-hemorrhage to identify the peak incidence of vasospasm. The site of the ruptured aneurysm and affected vessels should also be known. This will help identify the specific signs and symptoms that may be related to the cerebral ischemia resulting from vasospasm.

Pain control is very important. Agitation and restlessness can cause rebleeding of the aneurysm from acute elevations of BP. The nurse must administer narcotics, such as codeine, meperidine, and morphine sulfate, as ordered and as needed. It is also important to medicate the patient before painful procedures (ie, Swan-Ganz catheter and ICP needle insertion). Intramuscular injections should be avoided because they are painful. Pain can increase catecholamine release and blood pressure and cause aneurysm rerupture.

The amount of environmental stimuli must be reduced. Visitors may be restricted, and the length of the visit should be short. Noise must be kept at a minimum. Stressful conversation that may be heard by the patient should be avoided. Necessary treatments should be planned so the patient is disturbed as little as possible without becoming overtired.

The patient should be assessed for intensive care psychosis. Reorientation and emotional reassurance are important. Visits from family members and pictures of family and friends may help reduce the psychosis. A calendar, clock, and personal items may also be useful in orientating the patient.

Cardiovascular Status

The neuroscience nurse must possess knowledge of cardiovascular nursing. Nursing responsibilities include a thorough understanding of the use of the Swan-Ganz catheter. The nurse must know the Swan-Ganz waveforms. If the monitor displays a right ventricular pressure tracing, it is an indication that the catheter has moved back into the right ventricle. The catheter must be moved by the physician because of irritability to the ventricle. Proper wedging technique is important for consistency. The patient must be positioned at the same level (flat or the head of the bed elevated at 30 degrees) for the PWP reading. Consistency provides accuracy in obtaining the PWP value; the transducer should be placed at the level of the patient's right atrium. The balloon is slowly inflated until the waveform changes to the wedge waveform to prevent overwedging and an incorrect value. The PWP reading is recorded at the end of expiration.

The nurse must also be aware of the complications associated with the use of the Swan-Ganz catheter, such as balloon rupture, cardiac arrhythmias, hemoptysis, chest pain, and permanent catheter wedging. The balloon may become permanently wedged in the pulmonary artery. The Swan-Ganz catheter waveform will remain in the wedge waveform despite the release of air from the balloon. Pulmonary infarction can result. The physician must be immediately notified to adjust the placement of the Swan-Ganz catheter.

The nurse must also assess for complications of fluid overload, such as pulmonary edema, congestive heart failure, and myocardial infarction. Breath sounds, respiratory rate, arterial blood gases, and sputum production are assessed. Assessment also includes monitoring vital signs, EKG changes, cardiac index, presence of peripheral edema, and neck-vein distension. Bradycardia, a vagal response, can occur as a result of volume expansion. EKG changes and dysrhythmias may mimic or mask myocardial infarction and occur secondary to hypothalamic dysfunction and elevated levels of catecholamines. The dysrhythmias require treatment to prevent decreases in cardiac output and oxygenation. Strict monitoring of intake and output and daily weight is also important.

Digoxin (Lanoxin) levels should be monitored and the nurse must be aware of the side effects of this drug. The maximal rates of intravenous infusion and the side effects of dopamine and dobutamine must also be known. The serum potassium, sodium and other electrolytes, glucose, hematocrit, and hemoglobin values are monitored and corrected if abnormal.

The nurse must also monitor the coagulation factors that may be altered with hetastarch use. Slight alterations in clotting tests include prolonged partial thromboplastin time (PTT) and prothrombin time (PT) and decreased fibrinogen levels. Pancreatitis can also be associated with dexamethasone use. The signs and symptoms of pancreatitis include epigastric pain, abdominal rigidity, vomiting, low grade fever, and increased amylase.

Pulmonary and Renal Status

Nursing's most important contribution to the patient is the prevention of complications. Causes of sepsis can be related to pulmonary and urinary tract infections. These complications usually occur in patients who have extended stays in the intensive care unit.

Good pulmonary care is essential to prevent atelectasis and pneumonia. The alert patient should be encouraged to deep breathe and use a volumetric exerciser every two hours. The patient with an altered level of consciousness needs to be turned and repositioned every two hours or as needed. Intravenous lidocaine may be used to prevent violent coughing for patients who are intubated. Suctioning should be brief, lasting 6 to 10 seconds, and sterile technique should be used. The patient is hyperoxygenated with 100% oxygen before and after suctioning. The quantity and characteristic of sputum are recorded. Sputum cultures are obtained as necessary and antibiotic therapy is begun as ordered.

Urinary tract infections can be prevented by using sterile technique with Foley catheter insertion and Foley catheter care every shift. The characteristics of the urine are assessed. Urine cultures are obtained as necessary and antibiotic therapy is initiated as ordered.

Preventing Other Complications

Prolonged bed rest and immobility predispose the neurosurgical patient to deep vein thrombophlebitis (DVT) and pulmonary embolism. Low-dose heparin cannot be used because heparin can interfere with hemostasis and cause intracranial bleeding. All patients should be fitted with thigh-high external pneumatic compression leg wraps.

Psychosocial Needs of the Patient and Family

Hospitalization after SAH is a stressful time for the patient and family. Fear of death, disability, neurologic deficits, and an uncertain outcome produce anxiety. Frequent reassurance is essential.

Education for the patient and family is vital. The family's questions should be answered to the best of the medical and nursing staff's ability. The patient's status may change from day to day, and the final functional outcome of the patient may remain unknown up to one year or more after the SAH. This makes answering questions very difficult. Education should include the cause of SAH and vasospasm, the effects of vasospasm on the brain and their clinical manifestations, treatments for vasospasm, and possible complications.

The patient should be assigned to a primary nurse. The primary nurse can provide continuity of care as well as develop a trusting relationship with the patient and family during this stressful time. The family should be involved in the care of the patient as his or her condition permits.

CONCLUSION

Caring for a patient who has suffered a SAH and develops vasospasm is a very challenging experience. Various management regimens have been utilized with some success. Physicians and nurses become frustrated when neurologic deficits develop and poor patient outcomes result.

The neuroscience nurse must possess observation and assessment skills to detect subtle changes in neurologic status. Meticulous monitoring of the patient's neurologic status and prompt correction of suboptimal hemodynamic values have proven to be effective in preventing and reversing neurologic deficits in patients with subarachnoid hemorrhage.

NOTES

1. Raimond J, Taylor JW. *Neurological Emergencies: Effective Nursing Care.* Gaithersburg, Md: Aspen Publishers Inc; 1986:255–260.

2. Fisher CM, Roberson GH, Ojemann RJ. Cerebral vasospasm with ruptured saccular aneurysm—the clinical manifestations. *Neurosurg.* 1977;1(3):245–248.

3. Kassell NF, Sasaki T, Colohan ART, Nazar G. Cerebral vasospasm following aneurysmal subarachnoid hemorrhage. *Stroke.* 1985;16(4):562–567.

4. Hunt WE, Hess RM. Surgical risk as related to time of intervention in the repair of intracranial aneurysms. *J Neurosurg.* 1968;28(1):14–20.

5. Gary R. Cerebral vasospasm: process, trends and interventions. *J Neurosurg Nurs.* 1981;13(5):256–264.

6. Boullin D. Cerebral artery spasm. In: Crockard A, Hayward R, Joff J, eds. *Neurosurgery: The Scientific Basis of Clinical Practice.* London: Blackwell Scientific Publications; 1985:240–265.

7. Voldby B. Alterations in vasomotor reactivity in subarachnoid hemorrhage. In: Wood J, ed. *Cerebral Blood Flow: Physiologic and Clinical Aspects.* New York: McGraw-Hill Book Co; 1987:402–412.

8. Sano K, Asano T, Tamura A. *Acute Aneurysm Surgery: Pathophysiology and Management.* New York: Springer-Verlag; 1987.

9. Mitchell SK, Yates RR. Cerebral vasospasm: theoretical causes, medical management, and nursing implications. *J Neurosci Nurs.* 1986;18(6):315–324.

10. Gerk MK, Kassell NF. Cerebral vasospasm: update and implications. *J Neurosurg Nurs.* 1980;12(2):66–72.

11. Heros RC, Lavyne MH, Nelson PB. Treatment of cerebral vasospasm with sodium nitroprusside. In: Wilkins RH, ed. *Cerebral Arterial Spasm.* Baltimore: Williams & Wilkins; 1980:599–602.

12. Rosenstein J, Batjer HH, Samson DS. Use of the extracranial-intracranial arterial bypass in the management of refractory vasospasm: a case report. *Neurosurg.* 1985;17(3):474–479.

13. Finch K. Vasospasm secondary to subarachnoid hemorrhage: the current controversy, research, and nursing dilemmas. *J Neurosurg Nurs.* 1980;12(4):199–202.

14. Peck S. Calcium blocking agents for treatment of cerebral vasospasm. *J Neurosurg Nurs.* 1983;15(3):123–127.

15. Hickey JV. *The Clinical Practice of Neurological and Neurosurgical Nursing.* 2nd ed. Philadelphia: JB Lippincott Co; 1986:520–522.

16. Kassell NF, Peerless SJ, Durward QJ, Beck DW, Drake CG, Adams HP. Treatment of ischemic deficits from vasospasm with intravascular volume expansion and induced arterial hypertension. *Neurosurg.* 1982;2(3):337–343.

17. Kosnik EJ, Hunt WE. Postoperative hypertension in the management of patients with intracranial arterial aneurysms. *J Neurosurg.* 1976;45(2):148–154.

18. Fisher CM, Kistler JP, Davis JM. Relation of cerebral vasospasm to subarachnoid hemorrhage visualized by computerized tomographic scanning. *Neurosurg.* 1980;6(1):1–9.

19. DeWitt L, Wechsler L. Transcranial Doppler. *Stroke.* 1988;19(7):915–921.

20. Pritz MB, Giannotta SL, Kindt GW, McGillicudy JE, Prager RL. Treatment of patients with neurological deficits associated with cerebral vasospasm by intravascular volume expansion. *Neurosurg.* 1978;3(3):364–368.

21. Farhat SM, Schneider RC. Observations on the effect of systemic blood pressure on intracranial circulation in patients with cerebrovascular insufficiency. *J Neurosurg.* 1967;27(5):441–445.

22. Philbin DM, Roscow CE, D'Ambra M, Freis ES, Schneider RC. Hormonal changes during narcotic anesthesia and operation. In: Estafanous FG, ed. *Opioid in Anesthesia.* Boston: Butterworths; 1985:70–74.

23. Freye E. Cardiovascular effects of high dosages of fentanyl, meperidine, and naloxone in dogs. *Anesth Analg.* 1974;53(1):40–47.

24. Macharen Touissant GP, Burgess JH, Hampson LG. Central venous pressure and pulmonary wedge pressure in critical surgical illness. A comparison. *Arch Surg.* 1974;109(1):265–269.

25. Finn SS, Stephensen SA, Miller CA, Drobnich L, Hunt WE. Observations on the perioperative management of aneurysmal subarachnoid hemorrhage. *J Neurosurg.* 1986;65(1):48–62.

26. Handa Y, Weir B, Nosko M, Mosewich R, Tsuji T, Grace M. The effect of timing of clot removal on chronic vasospasm in a primate model. *J Neurosurg.* 1987;67:558–564.

27. Lloyd YSK, Tew JM. Saccular aneurysms, sub-arachnoid hemorrhage, and the timing of surgery. *Heart Lung.* 1985;14(1):68–74.

28. Baek S-M, Makabali GG, Bryan-Brown CW, Kusek JM, Shoemaker WC. Plasma expansion in surgical patients with high central venous pressure (CVP): the relationship of blood volume to hematocrit, CVP, pulmonary wedge pressure and cardiorespiratory changes. *Surgery.* 1975;78(3):304–315.

29. Oertel LB. The dilemma of cerebral vasospasm treatment. *J Neurosurg Nurs.* 1985;17(1):7–13.

Chapter 3

Arteriovenous Malformations

Evangeline Martin-Thomson and Susan M. Johnson

Traditionally the term arteriovenous malformation is used generically to describe most abnormal vascular malformations involving the parenchyma of the nervous system. McCormick has classified these congenital vascular malformations as (1) telangietasia (capillary angioma), (2) varix (dilated veins), (3) cavernous angioma (dilated sinusoidal vascular anomaly), (4) arteriovenous malformation, and (5) venous malformation.[1]

This chapter focuses on true arteriovenous malformations (AVMs). A case study will be presented to aid in discussion of assessment, diagnostic studies, and medical treatment for AVM patients. Nursing diagnosis will be used to plan nursing care.

The term arteriovenous malformation refers to a congenital malformation of blood vessels that has probably developed during embryonic life by no later than the eighth week. This lesion consists of one or more direct connections between the otherwise normal arterial and venous vessels without an intervening capillary bed. These malformations occur throughout the central nervous system but most often in the cerebral hemispheres. About 90% of cerebral AVMs are located above the tentorium, and the remaining 10% are in the posterior fossa. The majority involve the area supplied by the middle cerebral artery; those in the posterior regions of the hemispheres involve the area supplied by the anterior and posterior cerebral arteries.

AVMs appear as a coiled mass of dilated vessels, similar to a bag of worms. They vary in size from a few millimeters to essentially involving an entire hemisphere. The parenchyma adjacent to the AVM is not supplied with blood since there are no capillaries in the malformation. Blood flows into the AVM at an increased rate due to low peripheral resistance of the arteries. These arteries enlarge with time, as does the venous component of the malformation due to high flow volume and sustained increased venous pressure produced by the arteriovenous shunt.

Intracerebral steal occurs when blood is diverted from one cerebral area because of lowered vascular resistance in another. The AVM's flow capacity is so great that blood is shunted away from normal brain tissue surrounding the lesion causing ischemic damage, which may result in further neurological deficits. The deficits correlate anatomically with the area of decreased blood flow (ischemia).

The majority of AVMs become symptomatic before the patient reaches age 40. During the first two decades of the patient's life, AVMs undergo a gradual transformation from diffuse clusters of shunts to more discrete and larger foci diverting blood flow to an increased area of the brain. [2,3] As this occurs, AVMs become progressively more symptomatic, reaching a peak incidence of first symptoms early in the third decade of the patient's life. Most recent studies report no predilection for either sex and no familial predisposition. [4-6]

* * * * *

CASE STUDY

J.M. is a 20-year-old high school graduate who worked in a shipping and receiving department. He presented to the emergency room (ER) with expressive aphasia and a mild right hemiparesis. A CT scan showed a left frontal AVM with hemorrhage. He was admitted to the neurosurgical intensive care unit (see Figures 3-1 and 3-2).

He subsequently stabilized and a cerebral angiogram was performed. A left internal carotid, a right common carotid, and bilateral selective vertebral artery injections demonstrated a large left frontal AVM supplied by the branches of the left middle cerebral artery (see Figure 3-3).

He gradually improved neurologically and was discharged home with surgical excision scheduled. J.M. was seen in the neurosurgical clinic one month later. He had a mild drift of the right upper extremity and slow speech. His aphasia had markedly improved. He was able to speak in fluent sentences.

J.M. did well waiting for surgery until approximately two weeks later when he experienced increased left frontal headache, dizziness, and blurred vision prior to a syncopal episode of unknown duration. When he awoke his family reported that he remained confused and did not talk or think clearly. The patient had no recollection of the entire episode. He complained of headache and nausea in the emergency room. A CT scan revealed no acute bleed. It was believed that he had a seizure that morning and he was started on Dilantin to prevent further seizure activity. His loading dose was 500 mg in the ER, followed by another 500 mg two hours later. The next day he began taking Dilantin 300 mg every night. He was sent home with a follow-up appointment in the neurosurgical clinic.

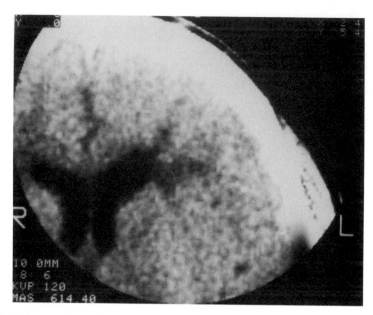

Figure 3-1 The unenhanced CT scan shows left frontal low density from previous hemorrhage.

At the clinic, J.M. was scheduled for a magnetic resonance imaging (MRI) study and given an admission date for surgery. The MRI showed multiple ser-piginous areas of absent signal in the left frontal lobe, which are characteristic of an AVM. There was a lobular large region of increased signal on the T_2 weighted image, most likely demonstrating an area of porencephaly that probably represented chronic old hemorrhage in the left frontal lobe resulting from the associated AVM.

J.M. was admitted to the hospital for elective surgical excision of his AVM. Routine laboratory studies were obtained preoperatively. These included a complete blood count (CBC), coagulation studies, urinalysis, electrolytes, and a Dilantin level. A chest x-ray, which was normal, was also obtained. The benefits and risks of the surgery were explained to the patient and his family by the operating surgeon. He consented to undergo a craniotomy for excision of his AVM.

Following an uneventful left frontal craniotomy with excision of the AVM, he arrived in the neurosurgical intensive care unit in satisfactory condition. His vital signs were stable and he was alert and oriented without discernable deficit, except for slow speech and response. He had an arterial line for the first two days post-op. As he became more awake, he complained of hypersensitivity as well as decreased coordination in his right arm (see Figure 3-4).

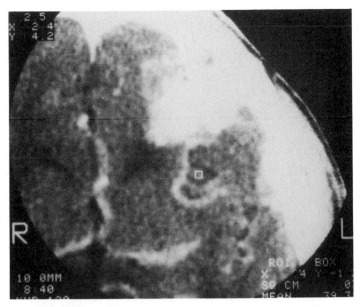

Figure 3-2 The unenhanced CT scan shows left frontal AVM with feeding vessels from middle cerebral artery.

The following day his protime decreased to 51% (normal is 80% to 130%) and he was given vitamin K 10 mg subcutaneously every day for three days. The next day he experienced a seizure lasting for three minutes. He was given ativan and phenobarbital intravenously and then had that dose repeated two hours later. Then phenobarbital 30 mg every eight hours was added to his prior anticonvulsant therapy.

He remained stable with only complaints of minor headache. He had occasional elevated temperatures between 101° and 102° that responded to Tylenol gr X. Five days after surgery he underwent a bilateral internal carotid angiogram. Prior to the angiogram, he was given a prep with Decadron 10 mg IVP. The cerebral angiogram showed no evidence for residual left frontal AVM. The intracranial distribution of both right and left internal carotid arteries was now unremarkable. A noncontrast head CT showed a left frontal craniotomy with adjacent postoperative changes. A left frontal lobe low density region and pneumocephalus was present. Mass effect was seen on the left.

He experienced a temperature spike to 102°. A fever workup included urine, blood, and cerebrospinal fluid. He continued to complain of headache and was started on Tylenol gr XV PO every four hours. The diagnosis of possible aseptic meningitis after surgery was made. He started on a 10-day course of antibi-

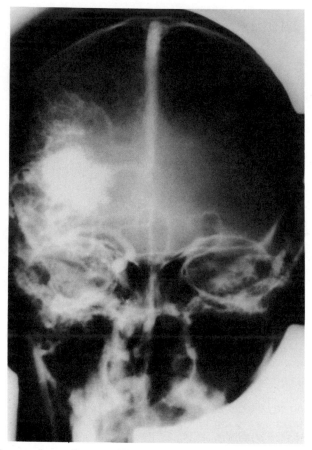

Figure 3-3 Preoperative angiogram (AP projection) shows left frontal AVM fed mostly by branches of the middle cerebral artery and draining into the superior sagittal sinus.

otics—ceftazidime 2 grams intravenously every six hours and vancomycin 750 mg IVPB every eight hours. All of his cultures came back negative. He was treated with cooling measures for temperature above 102°. His temperature came back to within normal range.

J.M. was discharged home to family two weeks after his operation. He was evaluated by speech therapy in early June and found to have mild to moderate cognitive impairment characterized by difficulty with short-term memory, deficits in abstract reasoning and judgment, difficulty with organizing responses, and difficulty with work-finding abilities.

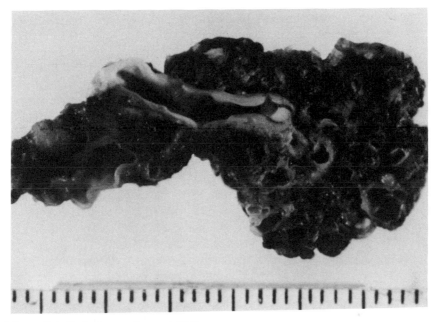

Figure 3-4 Brain tissue—dissected AVM.

He has continued to improve and now has no discernable aphasia. He is maintained on Dilantin and phenobarbital and has experienced no further seizure activity.

* * * * *

PRESENTING SYMPTOMS

The presenting symptom in adults with AVMs is usually either a seizure or a hemorrhage. These two types of presentation occur with about equal frequency. The average age of onset with seizure presentation is about 25, while onset with hemorrhage is about age 30.[7,8] Another 10% to 15% of patients present with intracerebral hemorrhage resulting in paralysis, and still another 10% to 15% have progressive hemiparesis. The remaining patients generally present with an uncomplicated subarachnoid hemorrhage (SAH). The 20-year-old case study patient experienced a SAH. Rarely, mental impairment secondary to hydrocephalus associated with repeat SAH is present. Large AVMs are twice as likely to cause seizures for presentation as compared with smaller AVMs, which are more likely to cause hemorrhage as their initial symptom.[9] The National Cooperative Study has reported that 10% of first-time bleeds from AVMs are fatal and the risk of recurrent bleeds after an initial bleed is about $3^1/2$% to 4% per year. The risk of death with the second hemorrhage is 13% and the risk is 20% with the third hemorrhage.[6]

About 50% of all patients have onset with a seizure. Seizures can be generalized or focal. The characteristics of seizures associated with cerebral AVMs relate to location and are not specific for the lesion. Seizures are especially likely to occur if the malformation is frontal or parietal in location. The seizures are usually readily controlled by anticonvulsant drugs, but may occasionally be intractable.

Intracranial or subarachnoid hemorrhage is the most alarming common presentation and approximately 50% to 70% of AVMs bleed at some time in their natural history. Generally there does not appear to be any correlation between the tendency to bleed and the site of the AVM or the age and sex of the patient. The incidence of hemorrhage may increase during pregnancy, labor, and the postpartum period.[10] Some reports suggest that the smaller AVMs are more likely to bleed than the larger ones.[11,12] Whether hemorrhage from an AVM is related to strenuous activity is not clear. The hemorrhage is typically parenchymal with extension into the subarachnoid space. Patients frequently present with severe headache, neck stiffness, photophobia, and a focal deficit; loss of consciousness may occur initially. The symptomatology related to the parenchymal hemorrhage is determined by the site of the hemorrhage.

Headache prior to the initial presenting symptom is present in 5% to 35%.[13,14] These recurrent or persistent headaches may appear during the second decade or later. They may be generalized, unilateral, focal, continuous, or intermittent, and not necessarily specific for an AVM. This may be due to mass effect as the lesion increases in size, displacing normal brain and resulting in increased intracranial pressure. With occipital AVMs, however, there does appear to be an increase in migraine-like headaches.[15] Our patient did have a history of headaches and continued to have headaches prior to surgery.

In children, hemorrhage is seven times more likely than a seizure to be the initial presenting symptom.[16] Another common presentation of an AVM in the neonatal period is a high output left ventricular cardiac failure.

DIAGNOSTIC STUDIES

High quality CT scanning has become an effective screening technique for diagnosis of cerebral AVMs. Recently, the development of magnetic resonance imaging (MRI) has enabled evaluation of AVMs without injection of contrast material, thereby lessening risk to the patient. The feeding arteries and draining veins and AVM itself are better visualized as compared with CT scanning. Both MRI and CT are useful for accurately defining the abnormal vasculature as it relates to normal brain anatomy. However, they do not provide the anatomical detail necessary for surgical planning and do not reliably disclose the presence of associated vascular anomalies, such as aneurysms. Performance of these imaging studies is ordinarily diagnostic of the site and size of the lesion that leads to performance of a cerebral angiogram. Cerebral angiography remains the definitive study for AVMs. Four-vessel angiography provides the most accurate and complete information that is essential for adequate planning of therapy and assessment of risks for the patient. The feeding arteries should be carefully inspected for associated aneurysms. Multiple projections may be useful to better delineate the lesion.

TREATMENT

Once the diagnosis of AVM has been made, several options for treatment are available. These include surgical excision, embolization, combination treatment with these two methods, stereotactic radiosurgery, and conservative management. Treatment is required for patients with intractable headaches, uncontrollable seizures, bleeding and increasing neurologic deficits secondary to ischemic steal.

Understanding the natural history of AVMs is essential prior to making treatment decisions. All cerebral AVMs are capable of bleeding and no common anatomic or other characteristic factor correlates with a propensity for bleeding. AVMs that have bled have approximately a 6% chance of rebleeding during the first year. After the first year, the incidence of rebleeding is about 3% per year. Generally, hemorrhage from AVMs is not as devastating as hemorrhage from intracranial aneurysms. Mortality rates of 6% to 30% after a first hemorrhage have been reported, with an average of about 15%. The average reported serious morbidity rate is about 30%.[17-19]

When the presenting symptom for an AVM is a seizure, the natural history is less well known. It has been estimated that there is a 25% chance of hemorrhage within 15 years.[7]

Recently there has been an increase in detection of totally asymptomatic AVMs. The risk of hemorrhage still seems to be 2% to 3% per year.[18,20]

When an AVM patient reaches middle age without a hemorrhage, the chance of hemorrhage in the future is less likely. Data indicate that at younger ages AVMs tend to grow and they seem to reach a stable size after middle age.

The role of surgery in treatment for a given patient is based on the probable natural history of the patient's future clinical course, the surgical risks, and the patient's age. Other key factors in establishing operability include location and size of the lesion and the pattern of venous drainage.[20]

If the AVM is accessible, surgical excision is generally the treatment of choice, with complete excision being the goal. Partial obliteration of the lesion has not been shown to reduce the risk of hemorrhage. Steroids and anticonvulsants are used routinely in preparation for surgery. Often prophylactic antibiotics are also used due to the prolonged nature of the procedure. Surgery is elective and performed after the brain has sufficiently recovered from the effects of subarachnoid hemorrhage. Neurologic deficits should be static prior to operation. Use of the operating microscope is essential. Excision is accomplished by first eliminating the large arterial feeders, or as many as possible, early in the operation, followed by the smaller vessels. Generally the veins are preserved until the end of the operation.

Use of lasers during surgery requires further development. They appear to be useful in defining the plane between the AVM and brain, coagulating the dural components of the AVM, and achieving hemostasis in the AVM bed after excision of the lesion. The laser has the ability to coagulate thin-walled vessels that cannot be coagulated by other methods.

Following excision of some large AVMs, the complication of normal perfusion pressure breakthrough (NPPB) may occur. This is characterized by severe, unexplained brain swelling with diffuse hemorrhage or focal deep hemorrhages in the parenchyma near the area of excision. There is massive dilation of vessels supplying the brain parenchyma adjacent to the AVM. When the AVM has been excised, blood flow that had been shunted through the AVM is now directed through the enlarged vessels at a normal perfusion pressure. These vessels have lost autoregulation, and blood flows without resistance into the capillary bed. This high pressure and high flow causes cerebral edema and/or hemorrhage.

NPPB is more likely to occur following excision of large AVMs (nidus greater than 4 or 5 cm) with large feeding vessels. Another predicting sign is found on cerebral angiography when there is preferential shunting into the lesion with lack of opacification of normal vessels to adjacent brain.

Management of NPPB involves prevention and intraoperative intervention. Staging removal of the AVM is thought to decrease incidence of NPPB. Staged treatment allows the brain to gradually adapt to the increased blood flow that previously supplied the AVM. Staged removal may be accomplished surgically or by embolization or by a combination of these procedures. However, even with staged excision of the lesion, hemorrhage and edema may occur. Treatment uses nitroprusside for blood pressure control intraoperatively and high dose steroids and intracranial pressure monitoring postoperatively.

Embolization is accomplished by inserting a catheter into the femoral artery and threading it to the AVM. A substance is then injected into the feeding vessels of the AVM. This procedure has become an important therapeutic adjunct to the surgical management of large AVMs.[21] In selected cases, embolization may be used to reduce the blood supply immediately prior to surgery. To date, the majority of AVMs cannot be totally occluded by embolization. However, as increased neuroradiologic techniques are developed, the use of embolization as sole treatment for AVMs is increasing. Generally, embolization does permit a staged preoperative decrease in size of the AVM, which produces significant circulatory readjustment and reduces the degree of NPPB following surgical excision of the lesion. Embolization, when available and practical, has largely replaced staged surgical occlusion of feeding arteries.

Feeder occlusion can frequently be accomplished by the percutaneous injection of liquid polymers, such as bucrylate, or solid particles, such as silastic spheres, metallic pellets, or Gelfoam, that are large enough to lodge in the feeders rather than traveling into the nidus of the AVM. When the feeders to the AVM are unreachable by this technique, intraoperative catheterization may be used.

Embolization may be useful as palliation for patients whose age or other medical condition makes surgical resection too dangerous. Complications occur when the embolization material does not stay lodged in proper position. The spheres may lodge in other vessels and cause cerebral infarction. Other complications include spontaneous hemorrhage or edema, especially if the venous channels are occluded prior to the feeding arteries.[22,23]

Conventional radiation therapy has occasionally been suggested for treatment of inoperable AVMs since radiation causes more injury to endothelium than to normal brain tissue, but in general this therapy has not been useful.

Stereotactic radiosurgery uses focused, high dose, ionizing radiation to initiate progressive vascular changes leading to complete occlusion of the lumen of the vessels. Currently, three methods are used. The stereotactic gamma unit or Leksell gamma knife provides multiple highly collimated cobalt sources of energy, all focused at a single point in space. Computed formatting takes data from images and allows positioning of the patient in the machine so that all energy sources are focused at the lesion. The proton beam is a noninvasive treatment that uses highly focused heavy particle radiation (Bragg peak) on a deeply placed target to shrink the AVM. The proton beam is generated by a cyclotron and administered stereotactically under local anesthesia. The third method is photon irradiation using linear accelerators. The use of linear accelerators in conjunction with stereotaxic frames provides a less expensive but perhaps equally effective method of stereotactic radiosurgery. The energy source travels through multiple arcs, much the way old tomographic x-rays were taken. Arcs have their focal point in the center of the lesion, as targeted by computer-derived coordinates taken from CT, MRI, and angiograms.

These treatments require one or two years to develop protection from hemorrhage.[24] Stereotactic radiosurgery is recommended for parenchymal lesions deep within the brain or those involving critical areas of brain tissue when the risks of surgery outweigh the risks of the natural history of the lesion. The advantages of therapy are less hospitalization time and shortened recovery time compared with conventional surgery. Complications are uncommon, but sudden neurologic deterioration may occur, as well as serious disability from radiation necrosis.

Conservative treatment is another alternative for selected patients. Since hemorrhage from AVMs is generally not as devastating as from cerebral aneurysms, many patients can live long and normal lives without disability from their AVM. When this approach is chosen, the surgeon should not overemphasize the danger of the lesion to the patient, and follow-up CT scans, MRIs, or angiograms are not necessary since these tests can cause anxiety but seldom increase the operability of an AVM. Seizures can usually be treated medically with good control. Future bleeding or increasing neurologic deficit are indications for reassessment of this treatment decision.

NURSING IMPLICATIONS

Once the diagnosis of cerebral AVM has been established, the role of the neuroscience nurse becomes essential. The nurse must act as a caregiver as well as a support for both the patient and family members. Questions must be answered clearly and simply as they arise. The patient, family, and neurosurgeon will make treatment decisions together. If conservative therapy is chosen, nursing care focuses on education. The patient must be taught the importance of anticonvulsant therapy along with side effects of the drugs and signs and symptoms of drug toxicity. Also signs of rebleeding must be discussed without inducing unnecessary fear in the patient. The medical team should not use phrases like "time bomb sitting in your head" to the patient.

When the patient is managed surgically, preoperative and postoperative teaching from the nurse is required. The patient is informed of what to expect in the immediate postoperative period. Frequently a tour of the intensive care unit is in order. Nursing care following surgery is standard postoperative craniotomy care, including frequent monitoring of neurologic vital signs and elevation of the head. Immediately upon arrival to the ICU the nurse does a complete assessment. Frequent evaluation of neurologic, cardiovascular, respiratory, and fluid and electrolyte status is performed. When doing neurologic assessment, it is also important that the nurse know the patient's preoperative neurologic status. Level of consciousness may change quickly following AVM resection and may be an early indication of increased intracranial pressure or hemorrhage. Cardiovascular assessment in the ICU is usually done using cardiac monitors and arterial lines. It is important to avoid hypertension so as to prevent hyperemia of the dysautoregulated chronically ischemic brain around the AVM bed. Blood pressure should not exceed the level at which hemostasis was obtained during surgery. Sometimes patients are maintained for a short period of time in barbiturate coma following surgery if NPPB is anticipated. Steroids are usually continued for five days or longer. One week postoperatively, the patient often undergoes cerebral angiography to confirm total excision of the lesion.

If embolization treatment is selected, frequently young healthy patients are seen one or two days prior to admission for lab studies, preoperative teaching, and preanesthesia interviews (although only standby anesthesia is expected). When embolization is performed, the patient is awake and requires continual education and support. The postprocedural care is similar to that given after cerebral angiography. The patient must be assessed for development of complications. If the transfemoral route has been used, the nurse must observe the groin for bleeding and check the leg for pulse and color. Routinely this is done every 30 minutes for the first two hours and then hourly for six hours. A pressure dressing is not used so as to facilitate observation of the catheter insertion site. Reversal of heparinization with protamine sulfate immediately following the procedure may help avoid excessive bleeding. Coagulation studies are usually obtained since heparin and protamine are used during the embolization procedure. The patient is maintained on bed rest for at least six hours, with the head of the bed elevated as per physician's order. Monitoring of neurologic vital signs is required to determine if signs and symptoms or cerebral ischemia have developed.

Following radiation treatment, patients must be observed for any neurologic changes. Hospitalization time and recovery time are lessened with these patients. The importance of long-term follow-up must be understood by the patient.

The following nursing diagnoses and standards of nursing care will assist the neuroscience nurse in planning care for this patient population.

NURSING CARE PLAN

The nursing care plan used for the patient described in the case study is presented below. The nursing diagnoses were made after a complete assessment of the patient, and the interventions were individualized for this patient.

1. Nursing Diagnosis: Potential or Actual Alteration in Cerebral Tissue Perfusion Related to Arteriovenous Malformation

Expected Patient Outcome

Cerebral tissue will be adequate, as evidenced by:

1. normal or stabilized neuro assessment
2. cerebral perfusion pressure $\geq$ 60 mm Hg

Nursing Interventions

1. Perform comprehensive neuro assessment every one to two hours.
2. Maintain vital signs within normal limits.
3. Monitor ICP and calculate CPP every one to two hours.
4. Avoid or minimize increased ICP by:
    • elevating HOB 30 degrees, maintaining body in neutral position
    • avoiding Valsalva type activities
    • cautious suctioning techniques (hyperventilation and hyperoxygenation prior to suctioning)
    • maintaining P_{CO_2} 25 to 30 mm Hg and P_{aO_2} saturation at $>$ 95 mm Hg
    • draining cerebral spinal fluid every hour as ordered
    • administering osmotic diuretics as ordered
    • administering pain medicines as necessary
    • sedating as needed if patient is restless or continuous posturing present
5. Review patient status and treatment with patient and family as needed.

2. Nursing Diagnosis: Potential for Injury Related to Seizure Activity Secondary to Arteriovenous Malformation

Expected Patient Outcome

The patient will be free of injury during his or her hospitalization.

Nursing Interventions

1. Assess for type and frequency of seizure.
2. Maintain seizure precautions at all times:
    • oral airway at HOB
    • siderails up and padded if needed

- bed at lowest position
- suction equipment available

3. Monitor anticonvulsant blood levels for therapeutic range (mcg/mL):
   - Dilantin (10-30)
   - phenobarbital (10-20)
   - Tegretol (8-16)
   - Valproate (50-100)
4. Administer anticonvulsant medication as ordered.
5. Review patient status and treatment with patient and family as needed.

3. Nursing Diagnosis: Potential or Actual Alteration in Respiratory Function Related to Postop Craniotomy Secondary to Arteriovenous Malformation

Expected Patient Outcome

The patient will experience adequate respiratory function, as evidenced by arterial blood gases within normal limits.

Nursing Interventions

1. Perform pulmonary assessment every one to two hours.
2. Monitor ABGs as ordered.
3. Adjust oxygen therapy as needed according to ABG data.
4. Suction and do chest physiotherapy every one to two hours.
5. Give respiratory treatments as needed.
6. Keep emergency equipment at bedside (Ambu bag, suction equipment, etc.).
7. Take aspiration precautions as needed.

4. Nursing Diagnosis: Alteration in Comfort, Pain As Related to Headache Secondary to Arteriovenous Malformation

Expected Patient Outcome

The patient will be free of pain, as evidenced by verbal statements from the patient.

Nursing Interventions

1. Perform comprehensive pain assessment every one to two hours as needed utilizing a pain scale (0-10) for intensity; also evaluate other characteristics, such as location, onset, relief measures used.

2. Identify and eliminate factors contributing to pain (ie, noise, stress).
3. Individualize drug therapy and monitor response to medications.
4. Utilize alternate method of pain control as needed:
   - massage
   - ice packs
   - diversional techniques (ie, breathing exercises, relaxation)

CONCLUSION

Although cerebral AVMs are congenital lesions, they seldom manifest themselves until later in life. Presenting symptoms include hemorrhage, seizures, and headaches. Treatment decisions are based on the natural history for AVMs and the risks of specific therapies. Brain AVMs, whether or not they have bled, carry a continuing risk of bleeding (approximately 3% per year). Every patient harboring a cerebral AVM must be treated individually. Recent innovations in surgical technique, the development of embolization procedures, better imaging modalities, and the introduction of stereotactic radiosurgery have revolutionized treatment for patients with cerebral AVMs and markedly improved mortality and morbidity.

NOTES

1. McCormick WF. The pathology of vascular ("arteriovenous") malformations. *J Neurosurg.* 1966;24:807–816.

2. Luessenhop AJ, Rosa L. Cerebral arteriovenous malformations. Indications for and results of surgery, and the role of intravascular techniques. *J Neurosurg.* 1984;60:14–22.

3. Walter W. Conservative treatment of cerebral arteriovenous angiomas. In: Pia HW, Gleave JRW, Grote E, Zierski J, eds. *Cerebral Angiomas, Advances in Diagnosis and Therapy.* New York: Springer-Verlag; 1975:271–278.

4. Aberfeld DC, Rao KR. Familial arteriovenous malformation of the brain. *Neurology.* 1981;31:184–186.

5. Michelson WJ. Natural history and pathophysiology of arteriovenous malformations. *Clin Neurosurg.* 1979;26:307–313.

6. Perret G, Nishioka H. Arteriovenous malformations. An analysis of 545 cases of craniocerebral arteriovenous malformations and fistulae reported to the cooperative study. *J Neurosurg.* 1966;25:467–490.

7. Forster DM, Steiner L, Hakanson S. Arteriovenous malformations of the brain. A long-term clinical study. *J Neurosurg.* 1972;37:562–570.

8. Stein BM, Wolpert SM. Arteriovenous malformations of the brain, I: current concepts and treatment. *Arch Neurol.* 1980;37:1–5.

9. Waltimo O. The relationship of size, density and localization of intracranial arteriovenous malformations to the type of initial symptom. *J Neurol Sci.* 1973;19:13–19.

10. Tuttelman RM, Gleicher N. Central nervous system hemorrhage complicating pregnancy. *Obstet Gynecol.* 1981;58:651–656.

11. Guidetti B, Delitala A. Intracranial arteriovenous malformations. Conservative and surgical treatment. *J Neurosurg.* 1980;53:149.

12. McCormick WF. Classification, pathology, and natural history of angiomas of the central nervous system. *Neurol Neurosurg Wkly Update.* 1978;1:3-7.

13. Pool JL, Potts DG. *Aneurysms and Arteriovenous Anomalies of the Brain: Diagnosis and Treatment.* New York: Harper & Row; 1965:326-373.

14. Svien HJ, McRae JA. Arteriovenous anomalies of the brain: fate of patients not having definitive surgery. *J Neurosurg.* 1965;23:23-28.

15. Lees F. The migrainous symptoms of cerebral angiomata. *J Neurol Neurosurg Psychiatry.* 1962;25:45-50.

16. Gerosa MA, Cappellotto P, Licata C, et al. Cerebral arteriovenous malformations in children (56 cases). *Childs Brain.* 1981;8:356-371.

17. Graf CJ, Perret GE, Torner JC. Bleeding from cerebral arteriovenous malformations as part of their natural history. *J Neurosurg.* 1983;58:331-337.

18. Sahs AL, Perrett GE, Locksley HB, et al, eds. *Intracranial Aneurysms and Subarachnoid Hemorrhage: A Cooperative Study.* Philadelphia: JB Lippincott Co; 1969.

19. Torner JC. Natural history of arteriovenous malformations. Paper presented at the American Association of Neurological Surgeons meeting; April 12, 1984; San Francisco.

20. Spetzler RF, Martin NA. A proposed grading system for arteriovenous malformations. *J Neurosurg.* 1986;65:476-483.

21. Debrun G, Vinuela F, Fox A, et al. Embolization of cerebral arteriovenous malformations with bucrylate. Experience in 46 cases. *J Neurosurg.* 1982;56:615-627.

22. Crowell RM. Aneurysms and arteriovenous malformations. *Neurol Clin.* 1985;3:291-312.

23. Cromwell LD, Harris AB. Treatment of cerebral arteriovenous malformations: a combined neurosurgical and neuroradiological approach. *J Neurosurg.* 1980;52:705-708.

24. Kjellberg RN, Hanamura T, Davis KR, et al. Bragg-peak proton-beam therapy for arteriovenous malformations of the brain. *N Engl J Med.* 1983;309:269-274.

SUGGESTED READING

Doolittle N. Arteriovenous malformations: the physiology, symptomatology, and nursing care. *J Neurosurg Nurs.* 1979;11:221-226.

Fode NC. Cerebral arteriovenous malformations: update for neuroscience nurses. *J Neurosurg Nurs.* 1984;16:319-322.

Garretson HD. Intracranial arteriovenous malformations. In: Wilkins RH, Rengachary SS, eds. *Neurosurgery.* New York: McGraw-Hill Book Co; 1984;2:1448-1458.

Malis LI. Arteriovenous malformations of the brain. In: Youmans JR, ed. *Neurological Surgery.* Philadelphia: WB Saunders Co; 1982:1786-1806.

Ojemann RG, Heros RC, Crowell RM. Arteriovenous malformations of the brain. In: *Surgical Management of Cerebrovascular Disease.* Baltimore: Williams & Wilkins; 1988:347-413.

Chapter 4

Carotid-Cavernous Fistulae and Intracavernous Aneurysms

Susan M. More and Jacques Dion

INTRODUCTION

Vascular disorders of the cavernous sinus include fistulae between the carotid artery and the cavernous veins (carotid-cavernous fistulae) and aneurysms of the intracavernous arteries. These relatively rare entities present with characteristic findings and offer the critical care nurse unique challenges of assessment and intervention. In addition, newer techniques of diagnosis and treatment have been developed recently, with which the critical care nurse must become familiar.

* * * * *

CASE STUDY

E.S., a 44-year-old woman, was involved in a motor vehicle accident four months prior to presentation. At that time the patient sustained head trauma with loss of consciousness, rib fractures, and a left hip fracture. She was treated and released from the hospital with no neurologic sequelae. Two months after the accident she noted the onset of a continuous swishing sound in the left side of her head. This sound gradually worsened, and she presented for neurologic evaluation.

The patient's past medical history was remarkable for a history of mild bilateral diplopia on extreme lateral gaze, which was thought to be due to strabismus, had been present for 15 years, and was unchanged since the accident. Otherwise, the patient had been in excellent health. A detailed review of systems was otherwise negative.

On examination, she was a well-developed, well-nourished, pleasant female in no acute distress. Examination of the head, eyes, ears, nose, and throat revealed left exophthalmos with mild periorbital swelling and an auscultated bruit over the left orbit. Fundi were visualized with disks sharp bilaterally. Visual acuity was

20/20 bilaterally. The neck was supple, and the carotid arteries had 2+ pulses without bruits. Mental status exam revealed the patient to be awake, alert, and oriented, with fluent speech and intact language and cognition. Cranial nerve testing was remarkable for a slight limitation of left lateral movement with visual fields remaining full, consistent with a mild left sixth cranial nerve paresis. Diplopia was noted bilaterally at the limits of horizontal movement. Pupils were 3 mm, round and reactive to light bilaterally. Motor exam was unremarkable except for some difficulty in movement of the left lower extremity proximal musculature related to her prior hip fracture. Sensory exam was intact to all modalities. Reflexes were symmetric at 2+ on a scale of 4 in upper and lower extremities, and plantars flexed bilaterally.

The patient was given a clinical diagnosis of posttraumatic left carotid-cavernous sinus fistula, which was verified by cerebral angiography (Figure 4-1). It was felt that this particular fistula could be managed by the newer technique of transarterial balloon occlusion.

The patient was admitted to the hospital for this procedure. A small catheter was inserted into the femoral artery, threaded up the aorta into the left carotid artery, and finally into the internal carotid. A balloon was inflated and wedged into the fistula, thereby occluding it (Figures 4-2 and 4-3). The patient tolerated the

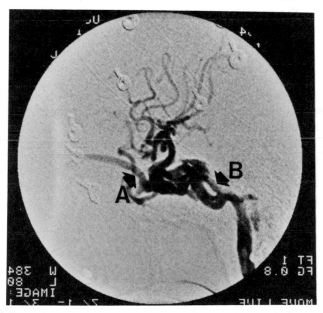

Figure 4-1 Internal carotid angiogram. This early arterial phase shows an abnormal fistulous communication to the cavernous sinus with venous drainage into the superior ophthalmic vein, **A**, and the petrosal veins, **B**.

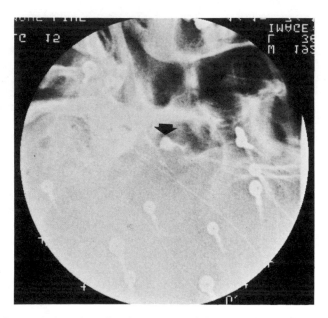

Figure 4-2 Lateral scout view after placement of a 0.5 mL detachable silicon balloon (arrow) at fistula site.

procedure well without any complications. She was monitored overnight in the neurologic intensive care unit and then transferred to the floor until discharge, two days after balloon embolization. At this time, the patient no longer had a bruit, and at a two-week follow-up examination, the exophthalmos had resolved. A mild left sixth cranial nerve palsy persisted.

* * * * *

PATHOPHYSIOLOGY AND ETIOLOGY

In order to understand vascular disorders of the cavernous sinus, a basic awareness of the anatomy of the sinus is necessary. The cavernous sinuses lie just posterior to the orbits, one on each side of the pituitary gland in the middle cranial fossae at the base of the skull. The floor of each sinus is the periosteum of the sphenoid bone. Medially, there is a layer of dura mater that separates the sinus from the pituitary gland. Laterally, a fold of dura mater extends from the sphenoid wing down to the floor of the middle cranial fossa, thus forming the roof of the lateral wall of the sinus. The relationship of the

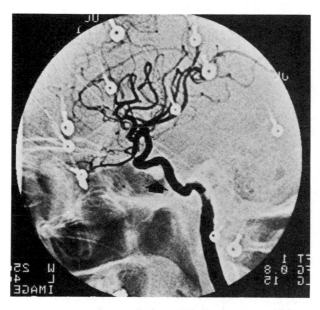

Figure 4-3 Internal carotid angiogram, lateral projection after balloon placement. The carotid-cavernous fistula is occluded with preservation of the internal carotid artery. The balloon is seen at the fistula site (arrow).

cavernous sinus to the base of the skull is summarized in the coronal cross section shown schematically in Figure 4-4A.[1]

In order to understand the clinical manifestations of disorders of the cavernous sinus, it is important to appreciate its contents. The cavernous sinus contains the internal carotid artery, a plexus of veins, and the abducens (sixth cranial) nerve. The internal carotid artery enters the sinus posteriorly, then exits through the anterior roof. The abducens nerve roughly parallels the course of the artery. An extensive plexus of veins fills the remainder of the sinus, enveloping the artery and nerve (Figures 4-4A and 4-4B).[2]

Contained within the dura mater of the lateral wall of the sinus are several other cranial nerves: the oculomotor (III), trochlear (IV), trigeminal ganglion, and the ophthalmic (V_1) and maxillary (V_2) divisions of the trigeminal (V) nerve (Figure 4-4B). Increased pressure within the cavernous sinus from an intracavernous aneurysm or a carotid-cavernous fistula can result in dysfunction of any or all of the nerves listed.[3]

Carotid-cavernous fistulae are classically thought of as abnormal connections between the carotid artery and one of the veins of the venous plexus within the sinus. This classic type is also known as a direct fistula. However,

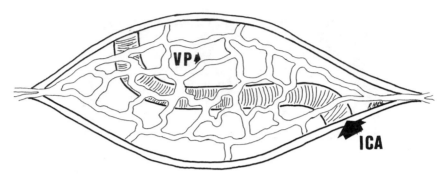

Figure 4-4A Coronal section through the cavernous sinus, indicating its relationship to the base of the skull and the pituitary gland.

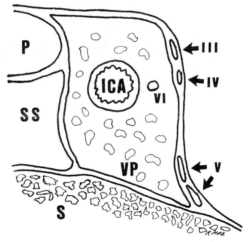

Figure 4-4B Schematic diagram of the cavernous sinus, showing the relationship of the internal carotid artery and the venous plexus. P—pituitary gland; SS—sphenoid sinus; S—sphenoid bone (part of base of skull); ICA—internal carotid artery; VP—venous plexus; cranial nerves indicated by Roman numerals, ie, III—oculomotor, IV—trochlear, V—1st and 2nd divisions of trigeminal, and VI—abducens.

---

instead of the carotid artery being involved, the fistula may originate from an artery of the dura mater; this is known as an indirect fistula.[3] The dura mater constitutes the walls and roof of the sinus. The arteries of the dura mater originate from either the internal carotid or external carotid artery, or sometimes both. Thus, the ultimate source of blood to a carotid-cavernous fistula can be the internal and/or the external carotid artery.

Carotid-cavernous fistulae have been classified according to their pathogenesis as either posttraumatic or spontaneous. Posttraumatic fistulae can arise from a penetrating foreign object (eg, a stab wound to the orbit), a severe closed head trauma, a basilar skull fracture, or after surgery. Spontaneous fistulae form in the absence of any traumatic event. They can arise from a ruptured aneurysm of the internal carotid artery or a dural artery. More commonly, they can arise from a ruptured arteriovenous malformation (AVM) in the dura mater. Carotid-cavernous fistulae secondary to AVMs of the dura mater typically occur in middle-aged females. Posttraumatic fistulae are about three times more common than spontaneous ones.[3]

An intracavernous aneurysm is an aneurysm of the intracavernous portion of the internal carotid artery. These aneurysms may rupture either spontaneously or after trauma, sometimes forming a carotid-cavernous fistula. More commonly, they do not rupture, and only become symptomatic when they enlarge. When these aneurysms do enlarge, they can produce increased pressure in the cavernous sinus, and thereby produce signs and symptoms that are similar to those found with carotid-cavernous fistulae. These signs and symptoms will be described in detail later in the chapter.

CLINICAL MANIFESTATIONS

The signs and symptoms secondary to carotid-cavernous fistulae and intracavernous aneurysms are often related to increased pressure within the cavernous sinus. In the case of a fistula, high blood flow exists between the artery and the venous plexus, with increased pressure due to the resultant venous engorgement.[3,4] With an intracavernous aneurysm, increased pressure can be secondary to either expansion of the aneurysm or bleeding if the aneurysm ruptures.[3]

The most common presenting symptom of a carotid-cavernous fistula is the patient's sensation of a bruit behind the eye socket. This is due to the high flow through the fistula, and the patient will often describe this as either a swishing or humming sound. Another common symptom is headaches, which are often due to vessel wall distention (either arteries or veins), and may resolve after the vessels accommodate to the distention.[3]

A less common symptom is diplopia (double-vision), which is due to ophthalmoplegia (impaired movement of the eye). There can be two causes of ophthalmoplegia. The first is due to poor venous drainage of the eye, since the ophthalmic veins communicate with the venous plexus of the cavernous sinus. Increased pressure in the sinus can thus cause venous engorgement of the eye and result in mechanical restriction to eye movement. The other cause of ophthalmoplegia is paresis of cranial nerves III, IV, and VI secondary to pressure on the nerves in the cavernous sinus. Finally, an infrequent symptom can be facial numbness due to paresis of cranial nerve V.[3]

A frequent sign of fistula is an audible bruit when the stethoscope is placed against the patient's closed eyelid. A palpable thrill can sometimes be felt if the fistula has large flow.[5]

Impaired venous return from the ophthalmic vein due to high pressures in the sinus causes the eye to become engorged. Chemosis can result, which is edema of the bulbar and palpebral conjunctiva. Severe retroorbital venous engorgement can result in exophthalmos, which is an abnormal protrusion of the eye from its socket. The direction of protrusion is usually inferior and lateral, since the veins are superiorly located. Severe exophthalmos may prevent closure of the eyelids, causing damage to the cornea. The entire eye may pulsate, which can be seen and palpated. Rarely, the venous engorgement can lead to nosebleeds.[3]

Impaired venous return from the retinal vein can cause papilledema, retinal hemorrhages, decreased visual acuity, and, as a late effect, retinal atrophy. Thus, funduscopic examination is important in all of these patients. Impairment of the retinal artery due to high sinus pressures can result in blindness, which fortunately is an uncommon presenting sign.

As discussed above, diplopia can result from two different mechanisms. Mechanical restriction of movement due to eye engorgement results in poor motion in all directions. Ophthalmoplegia due to cranial nerve paresis results in specific deficits, depending on the nerve involved. Careful cranial nerve examination is important. If the VI nerve is involved, lateral deviation will be impaired (lateral rectus muscle), with diplopia noted at the extremes of lateral motion. This is the most common type of cranial nerve palsy seen, since the VI nerve is the most susceptible to pressure injury in the cavernous sinus.[3] If the IV nerve is involved, inferior/medial gaze will be impaired (involvement of the superior oblique muscle). And if the III nerve is involved, the eye will tend to gaze inferior and lateral, since all muscles are weak except lateral rectus and superior oblique. Naturally, paresis of all three nerves can occur, limiting motion in each direction.[3]

One interesting aspect of these disorders is that bilateral symptoms can result from a unilateral fistula or aneurysm. This is because there are venous connections between the two cavernous sinuses, so that increased pressure in one sinus may cause venous engorgement on the contralateral side.[3]

DIAGNOSIS

The diagnosis of a carotid-cavernous fistula or an intracavernous aneurysm is usually readily apparent, due to the characteristic signs and symptoms that are associated with these disorders, as described in the preceding section.[4] The patient presented in the case report had several of these signs and symptoms: swishing sound in the left head, left exophthalmos, periorbital swelling, and a mild VI cranial nerve paresis with associated diplopia on left lateral gaze.

The diagnosis of these disorders is confirmed by cerebral angiography. As is true for the patient discussed above, the most common entry site for the catheter is the femoral artery. With newer contrast agents and better radiographic equipment, the incidence of complications following angiography has declined in recent years. However, one must still watch for bleeding from the artery used for access, renal insufficiency, and allergic reactions to the contrast dye.[1]

Computerized tomography (CT) has limited usefulness for the evaluation of carotid-cavernous fistulas. However, CT scanning is helpful for suspected bleeding from intracavernous aneurysms to ascertain the extent of hemorrhage.[3]

TREATMENT

The natural history of carotid-cavernous fistulae is still incompletely understood. While spontaneous closure has been reported, most authors feel that treatment is indicated to prevent irreversible changes.[3] Recently, Halbach and colleagues identified several clinical and angiographic characteristics associated with increased morbidity and mortality from carotid-cavernous fistulae that indicate the need for emergent treatment. These characteristics include increased intracranial pressure, rapidly progressive proptosis, diminished visual acuity, hemorrhage, transient ischemic attacks, and radiographic evidence of severe venous congestion.[1]

Treatment of carotid-cavernous fistulae can be via transarterial embolization of the fistula or by direct surgical packing of the sinus. Transarterial embolization has been used for a number of years, but a significant advancement occurred in the early 1970s when Serbinenko developed the detachable balloon.[6] The detachable balloon has significantly improved the success rate of embolizations, as exemplified in the case report described in this chapter. Fistulae between the internal carotid artery and venous plexus (direct fistulae) can usually be managed by balloon embolizations, although Debrun and coworkers showed that the success rate is higher with larger fistulae.[4,7] If this fails, then a frontotemporal craniotomy to pack the sinus surgically can be performed.[8] Fistulae between the dural arteries and venous plexus (indirect fistulae) are usually fed from both the internal and external carotid artery circulations. Transarterial embolization of the external carotid feeder branches can be attempted, but it is only 50% successful. Surgical packing may be necessary.[8]

Following either transarterial or surgical treatment of these fistulae, a deterioration in the neurologic status can occur. These patients need close monitoring in the intensive care unit following these procedures.

Treatment of intracavernous aneurysms is similar. Balloon occlusion of the aneurysm is often successful. Should this fail, the surgical options are internal carotid ligation or clipping of the aneurysm.[3] The postembolization monitoring of these patients is the same as for patients with fistulas.

NURSING IMPLICATIONS

A patient diagnosed with a carotid cavernous fistula requires a detailed assessment. Eye examinations, including visual field testing, ocular movement evaluation, pupillary response, and general description, should be performed and documented by every nurse caring for the patient. Subtle manifestations of increasing orbital venous pressure need to be detected. The physician should be notified immediately if the patient complains of decreasing visual acuity or pain, or if he or she develops increased orbital swelling or bleeding. Early treatment to prevent further deterioration can then be initiated.

Patient symptoms require specific medical and nursing interventions planned for each individual. Problems known to be associated with cavernous sinus fistulae as well as nursing management of these problems are reviewed below. It is important to remember that these are nursing management suggestions. Creative problem solving for each patient is the primary nurses' ultimate goal.

NURSING CARE PLAN

Potential for Infection

The sclera of the exophthalmic eye may become dry, red, and prone to infection secondary to difficulty in closing the eyelid. Eye ointment and raised eye shields (nonvented to maintain moisture) help prevent the sclera from drying out. Frequency of application depends on the severity of the problem and needs to be assessed by the nurse.

In the case of E.S., lubricating antibiotic eye ointment was prescribed every four hours for treatment of her conjunctival inflammation. Because complete closure of her eyelid was maintained, an eye shield was unnecessary.

1. Nursing Diagnosis: Potential for Infection Related to Exophthalmos

Expected Patient Outcome

The patient will not develop an eye infection as evidenced by pink conjunctiva, clear nonirritated sclera, and lack of purulent drainage or itching.

Nursing Interventions

1. Examine eyes to assess for swelling, redness, dryness, drainage, and eyelid closure.
2. Perform eyecare using sterile technique.
3. Apply eye ointments as prescribed and assess for adequacy of prescription.
4. Use cupped plastic eyeshields to maintain moisture to exposed exophthalmic eyes.
5. Teach patient regarding unnecessary touching of the eye.

Alteration in Auditory Input

Patient E.S. had a disturbing bruit that caused her to seek medical consultation. She was able to tolerate the pulsing sound during the daytime, but required a sleep medication at night.

2. Nursing Diagnosis: Auditory Sensory/Perceptual Alteration Secondary to Pulsating Sound of Cavernous Sinus Fistula Bruit

Expected Patient Outcome

The patient will demonstrate decreased perception of bruit as evidenced by ability to perform daily activities, interact with others, and sleep comfortably through the night.

Nursing Interventions

1. Provide activities to divert attention from the bruit.
2. Address the patient on the unaffected side.
3. Offer prescribed sleep medication for sleep disturbances and assess the adequacy of the prescription.

Alteration in Vision

Ocular movement dysfunction and diplopia cause the obvious problem of difficulty in seeing. E.S. had a cranial nerve VI disturbance manifested by a slight limitation of lateral movement of the left eye. She also described diplopia when moving her eye horizontally to follow an object to the left. E.S. stated that she had diplopia for 15 years prior to the onset of the fistula, but that the diplopia was slightly increased on left lateral gaze. With nursing assistance, she learned to turn her head slightly to the left to increase her visual field.

3. Nursing Diagnosis: Visual Sensory/Perceptual Alteration Secondary to Cranial Nerve Dysfunction

Expected Patient Outcome

The patient will demonstrate ability to independently and safely function in hospital room setting by identifying placement of items, including the nurse call button.

Nursing Interventions

1. Monitor extraocular movements and visual acuity every shift. Report any deterioration in vision immediately.
2. Place call button and other necessary items nearby on patient's unaffected side. Orient patient to the location of these items.
3. Orient patient to room setting. Maintain this setting and keep pathways clear.
4. Address patient in intact visual field.
5. Teach patient to increase field of vision by changing position of head.

Pain

Headache pain related to a cavernous sinus fistula may be persistent until the fistula is treated. After treatment, patients also experience headache pain due to edema or a craniotomy incision site. Patient E.S. experienced mild headache pain for two days after embolization. She was treated with acetaminophen every four to six hours. This regimen was effective in relieving her pain.

4. Nursing Diagnosis: Pain Related to Headache

Expected Patient Outcome

The patient will remain comfortable as evidenced by lack of pain in expressions and decreased verbalization of pain on a pain scale.

Nursing Interventions

1. Decrease environmental stimuli.
2. Administer prescribed analgesics as needed and assess for adequacy of prescription.

Alteration in Tissue Perfusion

Complications of intracranial hemorrhage and retinal ischemia can develop as a result of a cavernous sinus fistula. Postembolization, the patient is at risk for developing cerebral ischemia. Frequent neurologic assessments to determine changes in level of consciousness, motor or speech functions, and visual acuity are necessary. The neurologic nursing assessment is the primary indicator to clues that a hemorrhage or ischemic event is occurring. Consistent well-documented assessments provide important patient status information and may help to prevent permanent damage from these potential problems.

E.S. was assessed routinely before and after embolization for evidence of hemorrhage or ischemia. These were potential problems for her that did not develop.

5. Nursing Diagnosis: Potential for Alteration in Cerebral Tissue Perfusion Related to Ischemia or Intracranial Bleeding Secondary to Cavernous Sinus Fistula, Embolization, or Surgery

Expected Patient Outcome

The patient will be neurologically stable as evidenced by lack of neurologic deterioration from baseline status.

Nursing Interventions

1. Determine baseline neurologic status.
2. Assess for changes in neurologic exam every two to four hours. Report any deterioration to the physician immediately.

Anxiety

After receiving the diagnosis of cavernous sinus fistula, patients and their families experience anxiety about the impending procedure. Preoperative or preprocedure teaching to provide information about the procedure will help to reduce unnecessary anxiety. The patient and her family should have realistic expectations of the procedure and postprocedure care.

E.S. was assessed preembolization by the nurse on the neurosurgery ward and found to be knowledgeable about the procedure, which was explained to her in detail by her physician. The nurse reinforced the physician's efforts and explained to her that she would be in the intensive care unit after the embolization. This prospect disturbed her at first, but an explanation of the nursing rationale for this move helped her to relax and expect close observation postprocedure.

6. Nursing Diagnosis: Anxiety Related to Impending Embolization for Cavernous Sinus Fistula

Expected Patient Outcome

Coping mechanisms will be strengthened as the patient becomes more knowledgeable about the procedure and postprocedure care as evidenced by:

1. a restful night before the procedure
2. verbalization related to ability to cope

Nursing Interventions

1. Assess the patient's knowledge of the impending procedure.
2. Provide information about the procedure and recovery.
3. Encourage the patient to ask questions.
4. Provide reassurance for the patient and family.

Potential for Hemorrhage

The arterial catheter approach, usually femoral, which includes continuous heparin flush during the embolization, puts the patient at risk for hemorrhage after the procedure. Frequent observations of vital signs, puncture site, and peripheral pulse to assess for indications of hemorrhage are needed postembolization.

When E.S. was admitted to the ICU postembolization, her blood pressure was monitored frequently and found to be stable with a systolic range of 108 to 120 mm Hg. Her pulse was stable at a rate of 60 to 70 beats per minute. Posterior tibial pulses and dorsalis pedis pulses remained equal and palpable. Her left femoral artery catheter insertion site remained without bleeding, swelling, or hematoma. She was flat in bed for six hours after the procedure to prevent unnecessary stress from activity to the puncture site. Pressure bags were not applied to the puncture site.

7. Nursing Diagnosis: Potential for Hemorrhage Related to Arterial Catheter Insertion Site and Heparinization

Expected Patient Outcome

Patient's catheter insertion site will remain free of hemorrhage as evidenced by stable blood pressure and pulse and lack of puncture-site bleeding or hematoma.

Nursing Interventions

1. Check blood pressure and pulse rate every 15 minutes until stable.
2. Check catheter insertion site for bleeding or enlarging hematoma.
3. Check peripheral pulses every 15 minutes × 4, then every 30 minutes × 4, then every hour × 4.
4. Maintain bed rest for six hours.
5. If bleeding or enlarging hematoma are noted, apply direct pressure to site and call physician immediately.
6. Call physician immediately if peripheral pulses are not palpable.

OUTCOME NARRATIVE

The patient recovered rapidly and satisfactorily from the cavernous sinus fistula occlusion procedure. Her bruit resolved immediately postembolization. Two weeks postembolization her exophthalmos had resolved. Decreased lateral movement of her left eye persisted, but long-term improvement of this cranial nerve palsy was expected.

E.S. was admitted to a neurologic nursing unit for preparation of her cavernous sinus embolization. Postembolization she was admitted to a neurologic intensive care unit for 24 hours before returning to the other unit. Her nursing care plan was a collaborative effort between both staffs.

E.S.'s comprehensive plan of nursing and medical care provided a smooth course of treatment and recovery that led to successful resolution of the fistula.

NOTES

1. Halbach VV, Hieshima GB, Higashida RT, and Reicher M. Carotid cavernous fistulae: indications for urgent treatment. *Am J Neuroradiol*. 1987;8:627–633.

2. Last RJ. *Anatomy, Regional and Applied*. New York: Churchill Livingstone; 1978.

3. Mullen S. Carotid-cavernous fistulas and intracavernous aneurysms. In: Wilkins RH, Rengachary SS, ed. *Neurosurgery*. New York: McGraw-Hill Book Co; 1985.

4. Debrun GM, Vinuela F, Fox AJ, Davis KR, Ahn HS. Indications for treatment and classification of 132 carotid-cavernous fistulae. *Neurosurgery*. 1988; 22(2):285–289.

5. Leslie DJ, Kammer KS. Carotid cavernous fistula: a case study and subject review. *J Neurosurg Nurs*. 1984;16:68–73.

6. Serbinenko FA. Balloon catheterization and occlusion of major cerebral vessels. *J Neurosurg*. 1974;41:125–145.

7. Debrun G, LaCour P, Vinuela F, Fox A, Drake CG, Caron JP. Treatment of 54 traumatic carotid-cavernous fistulae. *J Neurosurg*. 1981;55:678–692.

8. Hakuba A, Matsouka Y, Suzuki T, Komiyama M, Jin TB, Inoue Y. Direct approaches to vascular lesions in the cavernous sinus via the medial triangle. In: Dolenc VV, ed. *The Cavernous Sinus, A Multidisciplinary Approach to Vascular and Tumorous Lesions*. New York: Springer Verlag Wien; 1987.

Chapter 5

Guillain-Barré Syndrome

Kathleen Thomas

INTRODUCTION

Guillain-Barré syndrome (GBS) is an inflammatory autoimmune disorder of the peripheral roots and nerves. It was first identified by Landry in 1859. Other names of GBS include: acute polyradiculoneuropathy, polyneuritis, Landry's acute ascending paralysis, ascending transverse myelitis, schwannosis, and Landry-Guillain-Barré-Strohl syndrome. The annual incident rate of GBS is 117 per 100,000 population.[1] The incident rates are higher among men than women, among whites than blacks, and among persons over 39 years of age.[2] There is no apparent seasonal variation and GBS occurs in all parts of the world.[3]

The peripheral nervous system is composed of the sensory, motor, and autonomic components of the cranial and spinal nerves. These nerves have axons that carry impulses away from the cell body. A myelin sheath covering the axon increases the speed of impulse conduction. Some axons are more heavily myelinated than others, and therefore conduct impulses more rapidly. Myelin sheaths covering axons are able to regenerate after injury.

The major pathological finding with GBS is segmental demyelination of the peripheral nerves.[3] This action interferes with saltatory conduction so that nerve impulse transmission is slowed or lost (Figure 5-1).

This process may occur rapidly over the course of a few days, causing either minor symptoms, paresthesia, or, in the more extreme case, complete paralysis. The patient is often frightened as he experiences loss of body function while his level of consciousness and cognitive abilities are not affected. Some patients fear impending death.

The etiology of the syndrome is unclear, but it is considered to be idiopathic. Several cases have been reported to follow an upper-respiratory tract infection, gastrointestinal illness, measles, mumps, rubella, influenza A and B, cytomegalovirus, and Epstein-Barr virus. Vaccinations for smallpox,

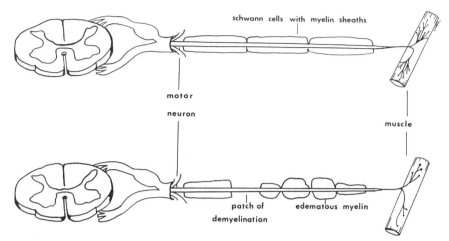

Figure 5-1 Demyelination of axon. *Source:* Drawing courtesy of Ann Label, Westlake, CA.

influenza, tetanus, and measles have been associated with the syndrome as well.

It is believed that the acute illness or immunological event that precedes the onset of symptoms is the stimulus that causes the T-cell to have a deleterious effect on the myelin sheaths of the peripheral nerves. [1]

* * * * *

CASE STUDY

Mr. B., a 71-year-old retired chauffeur, was in good health until he began noticing tingling sensations in his feet. This gradually spread upward to involve his lower extremities up to his knees. A few days later, he noted similar sensations in his hands, at which time his feet and lower extremities were numb. The following day he began experiencing difficulty walking, especially upstairs in his home. This led him to seek medical advice and his eventual hospitalization.

His past medical history was negative for recent vaccinations, upper-respiratory tract infection, or gastrointestinal illness. Recent exposure to toxins or chemicals was negative as well.

Mr. B. was born in Budapest but had lived the last 42 years in California. He was living with a female friend prior to hospitalization. He had never smoked cigarettes or abused drugs and rarely used alcohol.

As previously described, upon admission Mr. B.'s symptoms consisted of paresthesia involving lower extremities more so than upper extremities. His dorsiflexion and hip flexion were graded 2/2 on a scale of 5 and he became extremely ataxic. He was unable to walk without the use of a walker and was unable to arise from a seated position. On the fourth day of hospitalization, the weakness progressed to the point that he was unable to move his legs and could only move his upper extremities against gravity. Electromyogram showed delay in the nerve conduction velocities of the peroneal nerves. F-waves were also present. There was dampening in the amplitude of the muscle action potentials. He was areflexic in all extremities. A spinal fluid examination revealed an elevated protein of 102 mg/dL (normal range is 15 to 40 mg/dL) and white blood cell count of 1/mm^3 (normal range is 4.5 to 10.0/mm^3).

By the seventh day of hospitalization, he was having difficulty swallowing and some shortness of breath. Vital capacity had decreased from 4.5 liters to 2.0 liters (normal > 60 to 80 cc/kg) of ideal body weight. A chest x-ray reported elevation of the right hemidiaphragm. There were scattered rales throughout the lung fields on auscultation. Arterial blood gases were within normal range. He was transferred to the intensive care unit for close observation. A nasogastric tube was inserted and he was maintained on tube feedings of half strength at 75 cc/h. Over the next seven days, vital capacity and minute ventilation were recorded every four hours. There was some fluctuation over that period of time, but on the fourteenth day of hospitalization, vital capacity had decreased to 560 mL and he was unable to maintain adequate oxygenation and ventilation on his own. A tracheostomy was performed and he was placed on mechanical ventilation with settings of AC 10, Fio$_2$ 40%, TV 750, and PEEP 0.

At this point, he had complete paralysis of all muscles except that he was able to close his eyes and slightly nod his head. He did not receive plasmapheresis treatment due to the rapid onset of paralysis early in the course of his illness. With the paralysis, he lost the ability to control his bladder and bowel. Therefore, an indwelling Foley catheter was inserted. He was periodically incontinent of stool.

Over the course of four weeks, he developed atrial fibrillation with rapid ventricular response at 160/minute, which often occurs in patients with GBS.[4] He was treated with digoxin and converted to normal sinus rhythm at a rate of 84/minute. He also developed pneumonitis and was treated with antibiotics. Chest x-rays first revealed slight fluid infiltrates at the bases of his lungs with pleural effusions. These were probably due to atelectasis. Repeated chest x-rays over the course of the following 12 days showed clearing of the atelectasis. A sputum culture revealed *Acinetobacter* infection, which required antibiotics. Also, a urinary tract infection of *E. coli* required seven days of intravenous antibiotics. Mr. B. developed a fecal impaction related to his immobility and decreased sensation. He was placed on daily stool softeners, which prevented a reoccurrence.

He was gradually weaned from the ventilator during the sixth week of hospitalization (Table 5-1). At the time he was weaned, he was able to lift his extremities against gravity and the sensory disturbances were beginning to subside. He was then transferred from the intensive care unit to a medical floor. During the seventh week, he was able to swallow without difficulty and maintain bowel and bladder control. As he gradually regained increased strength, occupational and physical therapy improved both his active and passive range of motion. He had been maintained with splints and hand rolls to carefully maintain proper body

Table 5-1 Indications for Weaning

Weaning is indicated when the patient is able to maintain his ABGs and the following parameters are reached:

Pao_2	60 mm Hg on $Fio_2 \leq 40\%$
Spontaneous respiratory rate	< 30/min and > 10/min
Tidal volume	greater than 5 cc/kg body weight
Vital capacity	$1.5-2.0 \times$ tidal volume
$Paco_2$	35–45 mm Hg
Cardiovascular status	stable

alignment and prevent foot drop or contracture. During the eighth week of hospitalization, he was able to stand for brief moments with assistance, even though paresthesia in the legs persisted. He was transferred to a rehabilitation setting at the ninth week of hospitalization. He continued to have slight paresthesia in the lower extremities, and he required a walker to ambulate.

Incomplete recovery occurred with Mr. B., since the duration of his maximum symptoms lasted beyond 18 days. He required mechanical ventilation for approximately four weeks and had severe paralysis lasting 20 days. His final outcome, after extensive rehabilitation, consisted of mild weakness of lower extremities and paresthesia of his feet.

* * * * *

CLASSIC FEATURES

The severity of this syndrome is determined by the clinical presentation and may vary greatly from patient to patient. The onset is most often sudden and includes weakness, usually beginning symmetrically in the legs. The term ascending paralysis reflects weakness that begins in the legs and progresses to the arms. Distal sensory symptoms with mild associated sensory loss may be prominent early in the illness.[4] Areflexia is almost always present in paretic limbs after several days of illness. Patients may present with motor deficits ranging from mild weakness to flaccid symmetrical paralysis. As a result, they may demonstrate difficulty in walking, climbing stairs, and arising from a seated position and ataxia. Cranial nerves may also become involved, causing weakness of facial muscles, tongue, and the muscles of deglutition, which may result in aspiration. Autonomic dysfunction is common and may present with tachycardia or other arrhythmias. However, pulmonary, acid-base, and electrolyte imbalances may also produce arrhythmias. While arrhythmias are observed in many hospitalized patients with GBS, mortality related specifically to these arrhythmias appears to be uncommon.[5] Fluctuating blood pressure, ileus, or urinary retention may also result from autonomic dysfunction. Atonic bowel may cause abdominal cramping, but bladder or bowel incontinence is rare.

Symptoms may progress up to 48 days, with the duration of maximum symptoms approximately ten days. Recovery period may range from two weeks to 24 months with infrequent relapses. Incomplete recovery may be predicted if the duration of maximum symptoms is greater than 18 days. Residual weakness is more likely to occur in severe cases in which there is disruption of the axon and not just demyelination of the sheath.[4]

SYSTEMS ASSESSMENT

Cardiovascular System

During the acute stage of the illness, in the fourth week of hospitalization, the patient developed sudden onset of atrial fibrillation with rapid ventricular response at rates of 130 to 140 per minute. Blood pressure was 118/68. There was no jugular venous distension. There were no murmurs or gallops. Dorsalis pedis and anterior tibial pulses were palpable bilaterally. There was no peripheral edema.

Pulmonary System

Continuous mechanical ventilation was maintained with settings of assist control/10, Fio_2 45%, tidal volume 700 cc. Breath sounds revealed scattered rales and ronchi throughout. There were some rhonchi that cleared after suctioning large amounts of thick yellow sputum. Pao_2 saturation was maintained at $>95\%$.

Genitourinary System

A Foley catheter was maintained, draining cloudy, yellow, and foul-smelling urine. Urine cultures reported *E. coli* growth. Urinary output was adequate.

Gastrointestinal System

There was a maximum caloric intake of 3700 calories per 24 hours via nasogastric tube. Diminished bowel sounds were auscultated in all four quadrants. Abdomen was somewhat distended. X-rays of the abdomen reported a pronounced fecal impaction. This is related to the immobility and decreased sensation. Atonic bowel from ileus can be a major complication if not detected.

Musculoskeletal System

The patient was maintained on a low air loss bed. Foot drop boots were in place as well as splints and hand rolls. Physical therapy provided range of motion to all extremities on a daily basis. As the patient's strength improved, range of motion exercises were increased.

Nervous System

The patient was alert but unable to respond verbally due to a tracheostomy. He was oriented to person and place, but at times disoriented to time. There was weakness of cranial nerves V, VII, IX, XI, and XII. Flaccid paralysis and areflexia were present in all extremities. There was patchy sensory loss to pinprick and touch sensation over both lower extremities and forearms. Cerebellar testing was not possible due to paralysis.

DIAGNOSTIC PROCEDURES

Cerebrospinal fluid (CSF) protein elevation with normal cell count, termed albuminocytologic disassociation, is the most significant laboratory finding in GBS. After the first week of symptom onset, the CSF protein will be increased, with 10 or less mononuclear leukocytes present. Presence of diffuse symmetrical flaccid paralysis with minimal sensory changes and areflexia, along with preceding infectious process, may be correlated with the changes in spinal fluid. Electrophysiologic abnormalities are also associated with GBS and will demonstrate a delayed nerve conduction velocity. F-waves are the first abnormality and the most classical finding for early diagnosis. Another feature of GBS with electrophysiological testing is the dampening in amplitude or absence of the muscle-action potentials from stimulating a peripheral nerve. This may occur in the proximal portion or distally in the nerve.[4] Somatosensory-evoked potentials are typically abnormal in peripheral nerves as well. There is usually a lengthy interval between clinical improvement and normalization of electrophysiological studies.[4] Ba-

sically, the diagnosis of GBS is most evident by the clinical picture. The acute onset with progressive weakness and paralysis of both proximal and distal extremities with areflexia are the most important features of GBS. The increase in CSF protein without an increase, or only a slight increase, in the cell count may not be evident in the spinal fluid until 7 to 10 days after symptom onset. The nerve conduction velocities are slowed only after paralysis develops.[4]

TREATMENT

There is no specific treatment for GBS, other than supportive care. The quality of daily nursing care the patient receives while in the intensive care unit is the major factor in patient outcome. The use of steroids and adrenocorticotropic hormone (ACTH) is still somewhat controversial. Clinically significant improvement in patients with acute GBS treated with ACTH has not been demonstrated.[6] However, plasmapheresis, also termed therapeutic plasma exchange (TPE), has been shown to benefit GBS patients based on the results of a multicenter randomized clinical trial that compared TPE to supportive care.[7] Benefits have been seen with severe disease when TPE has been initiated early in the course of illness, preferably within the first two weeks of symptom onset. TPE may shorten duration of ventilatory assistance if the first plasma exchange is performed prior to ventilator support. Therapeutic plasma exchange has been recommended for GBS patients who display, at a minimum, severe weakness at the time of the first plasma exchange. Severe weakness is defined as inability to walk without support. Patients who are able to walk without support may not benefit from TPE.[7]

Plasmapheresis is performed by removing blood, separating formed elements from the plasma, and reinfusing the formed elements with the plasma replacement (Table 5-2). Unwanted substances and antibodies or other immunologically active substances are removed from the plasma. With GBS, autoimmunity is believed to play a role in the process. The ability to remove these antibodies and immunologically active substances, as well as nonspecific factors, such as mediators that cause inflammation and lymphokines that contribute to the severity of GBS, may have beneficial effects.

Benefits of using TPE with GBS have been demonstrated using a schedule of 40 to 50 cc/kg per exchange (approximately one plasma volume) for a total of three to five exchanges over a 7 to 14 day period.[7] The volume, frequency, and number of exchanges needed to achieve optimal benefit remains to be established. It is recommended that TPE be done in hospitals staffed with personnel who are experienced in the procedure of TPE.

Table 5-2 Mechanisms of Therapeutic Plasma Exchange

Remove	Provide
Antibody (Auto or Allo)	Deficient Plasma Factor
Immune Complex	
Toxin (Protein Bound)	
Paraprotein	

Possible Effects
Alteration of AG:AB Ratio
Alteration of Inflation or Immune Response
Improved Clearance of Immune Complexes
Placebo

Source: Reprinted from NIH Consensus Development Conference, Utility of Therapeutic Plasmapheresis for Neurological Disorders, Washington, D.C., June 1986.

Risks of Therapeutic Plasma Exchange

Fifty fatal reactions associated with TPE between 1978 and 1983 have been reported worldwide; 16 of these were cardiac-related and 14 were respiratory-related deaths.[7] Other reported deaths resulted from anaphylaxis, pulmonary thromboembolism, vascular perforation, hepatitis, systemic hemorrhage, and disseminated intravascular coagulation and sepsis. The risk factors that have been identified are classified as either device-related or procedure-related. The device-related risk factors that are potentially severe include red cell hemolysis, overheating of blood, and inaccurate delivery of anticoagulant or replacement fluids. The procedure-related risk factors that are considered to have potential for severe complications include citrate-induced hypocalcemia; replacement fluids that are depleted of coagulation factors, proteins, or electrolytes; replacement fluids containing plasma that have the capacity to transmit infection, such as hepatitis, cytomegalovirus and human immunodeficiency virus (HIV); allergic reactions, urticaria, and anaphylaxis; hemorrhage secondary to systemic anticoagulants; activation of coagulation, complement, fibrinolytic cascades, or aggregation of platelets, and fluid imbalance (Table 5-3).[7]

PROGNOSIS

The mortality rate of GBS is 4% to 5%, usually occurring from paralysis of the respiratory muscles, with or without terminal bronchopneumonia.

Table 5-3 Complications of Therapeutic Plasma Exchange

Vascular	Procedural	Delayed
Local hemorrhage	Vasovagal reaction	Depletion of clotting factor
Vein sclerosis	Hemolysis	Thrombocytopenia
Thrombosis/embolism	Anaphylaxis	DIC/thrombosis
Catheters:	Acute pulmonary edema	Infections:
Perforation	Hypoproteinemia	Bacterial (sepsis)
Infection		Viral (hepatitis)
Shunts/fistulas:	Citrate:	
Surgical procedure	Tremors, paresthesias	
Thrombosis	Tetany	
Infection	Cardiac arrhythmia	
Circulatory interference	Volume changes:	
	Hyper- or hypovolemia	

Source: Reprinted from NIH Consensus Development Conference, Utility of Therapeutic Plasmapheresis for Neurological Disorders, Washington, D.C., June 1986.

There have been rare cases of ileus causing death from obstruction. Complete recovery occurs in 75% of the patient population.[4] There is no association between cerebrospinal fluid protein values and severity, mode of onset or progression, or recovery from disease.[4]

NURSING CARE PLAN

Since there is no specific treatment for GBS, the quality of daily nursing care is of utmost importance to the patient outcome. The astute nurse must be very sensitive in assessing the patient for any possible complications that may arise. The respiratory status of the patient may change drastically within a few hours. The O_2 saturation via pulse oximeter may be the first clue that respiratory status has suddenly changed dramatically and the patient may require intubation. If the patient does eventually require mechanical ventilation, careful attention to pulmonary assessment and chest physiotherapy needs to be a priority. Due to the nutritional demands of the patient in acute care, a nutritionist should be consulted so that appropriate caloric needs may be provided. For the patient who is immobile, careful assessment of skin condition and positioning is important to prevent complications such as contracture, foot drop, decubiti, and peroneal palsy. Long-term effects from these complications can be disastrous for patients who may have otherwise recovered from GBS. Assessment of changes in motor strength is important so that increased range of motion, both passive and active, can be initiated.

The following is a patient-outcome-based nursing care plan that details the most important nursing interventions.

1. Nursing Diagnosis: Impaired Gas Exchange Related to Inadequate Chest Expansion

Expected Patient Outcome

The patient will experience adequate gas exchange as evidenced by normal values for arterial blood gases.

Nursing Interventions

1. Assess pulmonary status every two hours as needed.
2. Monitor arterial blood gas values and pulse oximeter as ordered.
3. Stimulate coughing of tenacious secretions by instilling 5 cc normal saline down tracheostomy tube every two hours.
4. Perform chest physiotherapy and suction every two hours as needed, being sure to oxygenate with 100% oxygen for one minute prior to and following suctioning.
5. Perform tracheostomy care every eight hours to maintain patency of tube.

2. Nursing Diagnosis: Alteration in Nutrition, Intake Less Than Body Caloric Requirements, Related to Tracheostomy and Healing Process

Expected Patient Outcome

Patient will have adequate nutrition as evidenced by:

1. daily caloric intake of 3000 calories/day
2. normal protein and albumin levels
3. weight loss less than 1% total body weight

Nursing Interventions

1. Consult with nutritionist regarding appropriate caloric needs.
2. Monitor albumin and electrolytes.

3. Check placement of nasogastric tube prior to administration of feedings. If residual is greater than 60 cc, then hold tube feeding and recheck residual after one hour; resume feeding if there is no residual.
4. Weigh patient every other day.
5. Monitor intake and output every hour.

3. Nursing Diagnosis: Impaired Physical Mobility Related to Paralysis

Expected Patient Outcome

Patient will be free of complications from immobility, such as contracture, foot drop, decubiti, and peroneal palsy.

Nursing Interventions

1. Turn and position patient every two hours with elevation of upper extremities as needed. If possible, provide kinetic bed.
2. Perform passive range of motion every four to six hours. Assess motor strength of extremities daily and increase range of motion activities as strength improves. Consult occupational and physical therapy.
3. Provide pulsatile hose for lower extremities.
4. Apply foot and hand splints as needed.

4. Nursing Diagnosis: Potential for Impaired Skin Integrity, Related to Immobility

Expected Patient Outcome

Patient's skin will be free of decubiti as evidenced by physical inspection.

Nursing Interventions

1. Provide adequate hydration and nutrition.
2. Protect skin by providing air mattress, elbow and heel protectors, and positioning devices. Provide hand and foot splints as needed.
3. Massage reddened pressure areas over skin and turn patient every two hours.

5. Nursing Diagnosis: Potential Fluid Volume Deficit Related to Physical Immobility

Expected Patient Outcome

Patient's fluid and electrolyte balance will be maintained, as evidenced by:

1. normal serum electrolytes
2. balanced intake and output
3. adequate urine output
4. normal blood urea nitrogen (BUN) and creatinine

Nursing Interventions

1. Maintain accurate intake and output.
2. Monitor electrolytes, blood urea nitrogen, and creatinine.
3. Monitor vital signs.
4. Assess skin turgor and mucous membranes.
5. Maintain intravenous fluids and nasogastric feedings.
6. Monitor body weight every other day.

6. Nursing Diagnosis: Sensory Perceptual Alterations Related to Intensive Care Unit

Expected Patient Outcome

Patient's sensory perception will be maintained, as evidenced by:

1. periods of rest and sleep
2. continuous orientation

Nursing Interventions

1. Provide uninterrupted periods of rest and sleep.
2. Decrease background noise in environment.
3. Coordinate visiting time to decrease number of unwanted interruptions.
4. Monitor light in room to provide reminder of day and night cycles.
5. Provide clock and calendar.
6. Orient patient frequently to surroundings.

7. Nursing Diagnosis: Altered Patterns of Urinary Elimination Related to Atonic Bladder

Expected Patient Outcome

Patient's urinary elimination will be maintained, as evidenced by patient being free of distention or overflow incontinence.

Nursing Interventions

1. Monitor intake and output.
2. Maintain indwelling Foley catheter.
3. Provide catheter care daily.

8. Nursing Diagnosis: Alterations in Bowel Elimination, ie, Constipation Related to Immobility and Decreased Sensation

Expected Patient Outcome

Patient's bowel elimination will be adequately maintained, as evidenced by:

1. normal bowel movement every one to two days
2. absence of fecal impaction

Nursing Interventions

1. Assess bowel sounds.
2. Maintain fluid intake at 3500 cc over 24 hours.
3. Maintain bowel regimen with use of stool softeners or laxatives to promote evacuation.

9. Nursing Diagnosis: Potential for Aspiration Related to Loss of Gag and Swallow Reflexes

Expected Patient Outcome

Patient will be free of aspiration as evidenced by:

1. normal breath sounds in lung fields
2. normal chest x-ray

Nursing Interventions

1. Auscutate lung fields every two hours.
2. Provide frequent suctioning as needed.
3. Check for gastric residuals prior to nasogastric feedings.
4. Elevate head of bed 30 degrees.
5. Monitor ET or track tube cuff pressures.

10. Nursing Diagnosis: Potential for Multisystem Infection Related to Immobility, Tracheostomy, and Invasive Procedures

Expected Patient Outcome

Patient will be free of infection as evidenced by:

1. clear breath sounds
2. normal chest x-ray
3. normal temperature
4. negative sputum, urine, and blood cultures
5. normal white blood cell count

Nursing Interventions

1. Monitor vital signs and auscultate lung fields every two hours and as needed.
2. Provide tracheostomy care daily using sterile technique.
3. Maintain strict hand-washing and aseptic technique while caring for patient.
4. Obtain urine, sputum, and blood cultures as ordered.
5. Administer antibiotics as ordered by physician and monitor patient's response.

11. Nursing Diagnosis: Impaired Verbal Communication Related to Paralysis and Tracheostomy

Expected Patient Outcome

Patient will be able to communicate his needs to others, with minimal frustration, as evidenced by effective communication.

Nursing Interventions

1. Establish system for communication, ie, word board, electronic keyboard, picture cards, or pen and pencil.
2. Allow time for patient to verbalize in whatever form he is able and listen attentively.
3. Anticipate patient's needs frequently.
4. Establish trust with patient by carrying out planned activities on a regular schedule.

12. Nursing Diagnosis: Potential Ineffective Individual Coping Related to Lack of Knowledge of Disease Process

Expected Patient Outcome

Patient's coping skills will be adequate as evidenced by patient's verbalization of fears, feelings, and decreased anxiety.

Nursing Interventions

1. Assess level of anxiety and ability to cope.
2. Encourage patient to verbalize his feelings.
3. Allow time for patient and family to share feelings, fears, and concerns.
4. Communicate openly with patient and family members, providing information according to patient's and family's readiness or responsiveness.
5. Provide explanation regarding illness as self-limited with a good prognosis.
6. Involve patient and family in decision-making and planning of care.
7. Obtain psychological consult, if needed.

CONCLUSION

Most deaths from GBS are a result of respiratory complications or infections. Therefore, careful monitoring for potential infection and respiratory complications is a priority in nursing care. The nurse must also remember that GBS does not affect the patient's cognitive abilities. If the patient's level of consciousness or cognitive abilities are affected, secondary complications must be investigated. The patient with GBS who is dependent on a ventilator and unable to move may feel helpless and may even fear death.

The intensive care unit setting alone can cause changes in sensory perception. These patients require uninterrupted periods of rest and sleep. Visiting hours must be coordinated to decrease the time and number of interruptions and yet provide emotional support from family and friends. While on mechanical ventilation, the patient needs a system for communication. Establishing trust and providing reassurance and encouragement are two of the most important responsibilities of the nurse providing day-to-day bedside care for these patients. Nursing care alone may prevent the complications of GBS and significantly impact the prognosis of the patient.

The case study patient with GBS who became quadriplegic within a matter of days, dependent on mechanical ventilation, and spent two and a half months in an acute care facility followed by three months in a rehab setting will long remember the nurses who provided daily care, anticipated his needs, and prevented complications.

NOTES

1. Hickey JV. *The Clinical Practice of Neurological and Neurosurgical Nursing*. 2nd ed. Philadelphia: JB Lippincott; 1986:595–596.

2. Mobley WC, Wolinsky JS. *Progress in Clinical Biological Research: Therapeutic Apheresis and Plasma Perfusion*. New York: Liss; 1982:162.

3. Ashbury AK, Arnason BG, Adams RD. The inflammatory lesion in idiopathic polyneuritis. *Medicine (Baltimore)*. 1969;48:173.

4. Ropper AH, Kennedy SF. *Neurological and Neurosurgical Intensive Care*. 2nd ed. Gaithersburg, Md: Aspen Publishers Inc; 1988:253–265.

5. Greenland P, Griggs R. Arrhythmic complications in Guillain-Barré syndrome. *Arch Intern Med*. 1980;140:1055.

6. McQuillen MP, Sivick AM. ACTH in Guillain-Barré syndrome (letter). *Lancet*. 1978;2:1209.

7. National Institutes of Health. Consensus development conference: utility of therapeutic plasmapheresis for neurologic disorders. *JAMA*. September 12, 1986;256(10):1334.

SUGGESTED READINGS

Ashbury AK, Arnason BGW, Karp HR, et al. Criteria for diagnosis of GBS. *Ann Neurol*. 1978; 3.

Blanco K, Cuomo N. From the other side of the bedrail: a personal experience with Guillain-Barré Syndrome. *J Neurosurg Nurs*. December 1983;15(6).

Brettle RP, Gross M, Legg NJ, et al. Treatment of acute polyneuropathy by plasma exchange (letter). *Lancet*. 1978;2:8099.

Gajdos PH, et al. Long-term results of plasma exchange and immunosuppressive therapy in two cases of chronic inflammatory demyelinating neuropathy. *Plasma Therapy*. 1985;6(3).

Hughes JE, Newsum-Davis JM, Perkin GD, Pierce JM. Controlled trial prednisone in acute polyneuropathy. *Lancet*. 1978;2:8104–8105.

Kealy SL. Respiratory care in Guillain-Barré Syndrome. *Am J Nurs*. 1977;77(1).

Matthews WB, Miller HH. The Guillain-Barré Syndrome. In: *Diseases of the Nervous System.* London: Blackwell Scientific Publications; 1979.

Newsum J, Smith R, Crocker D. Intubation for acute respiratory failure in Guillain-Barré Syndrome. *JAMA.* 1979;242(15).

Perseghin P, et al. Guillain-Barré Syndrome with autoimmune hemolytic anemia following acute viral hepatitis. *Ital J Neurol Sci.* 1985;6.

Prydun M. Guillain-Barré Syndrome: disease process. *J Neurosurg Nurs.* February 1983;15(1).

Taylor J, Ballenger S. *Neurological Dysfunctions and Nursing Interventions.* New York: McGraw-Hill Book Co; 1980.

Tikkanen P. Landry-Guillain-Barré-Strohl Syndrome. *J Neurosurg Nurs.* April 1982;14(2).

Weintraub MI. Autonomic failure in Guillain-Barré Syndrome—value of Swan-Ganz catheter (letter). *JAMA.* 1979;242(6).

Chapter 6

Spinal Cord Injury

Lorena A. Gaskill and Carol F. Holt

INTRODUCTION

Spinal cord injury (SCI) is one of the most catastrophic medical conditions experienced. Its consequences impact not only on patients physically but emotionally, socially, and economically as well. Because of the resultant loss of sensory and/or motor function below the level of injury, long-term rehabilitation is required and a total change in the patient's life style may be needed. This injury affects every aspect of the patient's life, including family, friends, and the community in general.

Each year approximately 10,000 to 12,000 people suffer spinal cord injuries.[1,2,3] Spinal cord injury frequently occurs in young age groups, with the mean age being 33 years. Males constitute 82% of the spinal cord injured population, with 50% of injuries resulting from motor vehicle accidents (MVA). Other causes of spinal cord injury include falls (16%), sports injuries (16%), and penetrating wounds (12%).[3]

Although the incidence of spinal cord injury is relatively low, the required intensity of acute care followed by the life-long duration of rehabilitation of these young people makes this a high cost disability.

During World War II, the life expectancy after the initial injury of these patients was only 6 to 12 months.[3] Now with aggressive treatment in the acute care setting and rehabilitation, these patients can live near to their full life expectancy. Ten percent of those who survive resuscitation succumb to cardiopulmonary complications within three months of injury.[3] The goal of acute care is to prevent life-threatening complications and additional neurologic deterioration.

The authors of the chapter on spinal cord injury would like to thank Tom Wyper for his generous support and professional art work.

Because of its permanence, prevention is the only safeguard against spinal cord injury. Laws, such as the 55 mile-per-hour speed limit, seat belt restrictions, and water and safety standards, attempt to create guidelines of prevention for the community, while educational programs attempt to increase the general public's awareness of this preventable catastrophe. Once a spinal cord injury has been incurred, health professionals depend on secondary prevention that focuses on early detection and treatment to prevent any further injury. Finally, tertiary prevention involves restoring the patient to the fullest rehabilitation potential and avoiding complications.

This chapter focuses on a case presentation of a spinal cord injured patient in the critical care setting. Examination of the initial assessment, diagnosis, and treatment allows one to better understand the importance of nursing diagnosis and its role in the planning of care and in the patient's final outcome.

The presentation and nursing care of SCI vary depending on the type and level of injury. To illustrate this, a case study of an individual spinal cord injury patient is presented.

* * * * *

CASE STUDY

L.C., a 28-year-old male, was brought to the hospital by paramedics after involvement in a motor vehicle accident. He was a passenger in the front seat of the automobile when it was struck by an oncoming vehicle. Since he was not wearing a seat belt, he was thrown from the vehicle. At the scene, emergency personnel suspected spinal cord injury and immobilized his spinal column by placing him in a cervical collar with sandbags. L.C. was transported while securely strapped to a backboard.

Due to a loss of sympathetic innervation, which is often seen in SCI, he arrived at the emergency room with a blood pressure of 90/60 and a sinus bradycardia rhythm of 58. His skin was warm, dry, and flushed, and he had a temperature of 96.4. The attending nurse noted that L.C. was taking shallow breaths at a rate of 28 with a decreasing tidal volume and abdominal breathing. After assessment of arterial blood gases, L.C. was nasally intubated to prevent further respiratory compromise. L.C. was placed on a ventilator with a tidal volume of 750, rate of 12, on intermittent mandatory ventilation at 50% oxygen. As per standard trauma emergency protocol, a Foley catheter, nasogastric tube, and large bore intravenous lines were promptly inserted. His initial neurologic assessment showed gross movement of the upper extremities only, but no sensation or movement below the C6 dermatone. Diagnostic studies, including lateral c-spine, showed a C6 subluxation confirming the neurological exam. His vital signs were stabilized in the emergency room and he was transported to the intensive care unit (ICU). In the ICU, cervical traction was applied, confirmation of cervical realignment was obtained, and thus the patient was removed from the cervical collar and back-board, then placed on a kinetic therapy bed.

* * * * *

ASSESSMENT

Primary Mechanisms of Injury

Up to 25% of spinal cord injuries that lead to permanent neurologic damage are the result of improper handling of a spinal fracture.[1] Thus initial management of patients with spinal injury is focused on immediate immobilization of the head, neck, and back. Movement of the spine is prevented by using a semirigid cervical collar and a backboard.

The vertebral column is a circumferential bony ring that houses the fragile spinal cord and nerve roots. It is designed to withstand low velocity penetrating injuries and contusions. The intervertebral articulations are weak points in rotational extension and flexion injuries.

The degree and type of force exerted upon the vertebral column and spinal cord when the initial injury occurs will determine the extent of initial damage. There are a variety of primary mechanisms of injury that can result in cord damage. Among these are extension, flexion, rotation, compression, and penetrating injuries. Stress from these mechanisms causes fractures and dislocations at points where relatively mobile portions of the vertebral column meet a relatively fixed segment.

Extension injuries of the cervical spine are incurred through a severe head back motion (as seen in Figure 6-1A). This type of injury usually occurs after a forward fall, and the resulting damage is primarily anterior and lateral. Surgical intervention may be required for instability and it usually involves a posterior fusion. Often this injury is seen in the elderly with cervical spondylosis. Hyperextension during general anesthesia causes a small percentage of these injuries.

Flexion injury results from a chin-to-chest action with compression of the anterior bones and stretching or rupture of the posterior ligaments, as seen in Figure 6-1B. A fracture dislocation often occurs in one or more of the articular processes. Motor vehicle accidents are the most common cause of flexion injuries, in which the head is thrown forward with great force after impact from behind. This was the situation in the case presentation. A direct blow to the back of the head also causes flexion injuries.

Rotational injuries result from a blow to the head while the head is turned, as seen in Figure 6-1C. These injuries usually manifest themselves in the cervical region and often occur in conjunction with flexion forces. If rotation and flexion occur simultaneously, one facet can slide over and above the other. This action can result in a locked facet and severe ligamentous injury to the joint capsule.

Compression fracture is a shattering of the vertebral body produced by a force to the skull with the spine in a neutral position, as seen in Figure 6-1D. The vertebral body may burst, shooting bone fragments and disk materials into the canal and causing neurologic damage. The most frequent cause of thoracic lumbar injury is via compression fractures. This mechanism has been noticed after a high velocity blow to the top of the head from a long distance fall or a diving accident. Surgical intervention entails removing bony fragments from the canal and stabilizing the column with bone grafts and/or instrumentation.

Penetrating injuries as a result of stabbing or gunshot wounds creates a different kind of injury. The projectile enters the canal slightly lateral of the midline; this is attributed to the protection offered by the spinal lamina. This mode of entrance can cause hemisection or damage of the cord laterally or posteriorly.

All of these mechanisms of injury may cause a variety of bony injury: simple, compression, burst, dislocation, or subluxation. Commonly, in a simple fracture, the vertebrae remain aligned and the spinal cord remains intact. Location of the fracture is often at the spinous processes or through the facets or pedicle. In a compression or wedge fracture, the vertebral column is crushed, but a cord injury may or may not occur, depending on involvement of the canal. A shattering of the vertebral body is known as a burst fracture or a comminuted fracture. Dislocation of the vertebral column occurs when one vertebrae overrides another with misalignment of the facets. Subluxation is a partial dislocation, and it was the injury seen in the diagnostic studies for L.C.

Secondary Mechanisms of Injury

Even with immobilization of the spinal column, injury to the cord may continue to occur. When the spinal cord is torn or contused, there is damage to the nerve fibers and microvasculature. Edema of the nerve fiber and surrounding tissues results in the disintegration of the axon matter and myelin. Small hemorrhages then develop within the central gray matter. The amount of hemorrhages increases in number and volume and causes a decrease in spinal cord blood flow, which results in hypoxia and edema and a vicious cycle of edema, hypoxia, cell injury, and more edema. Several hours

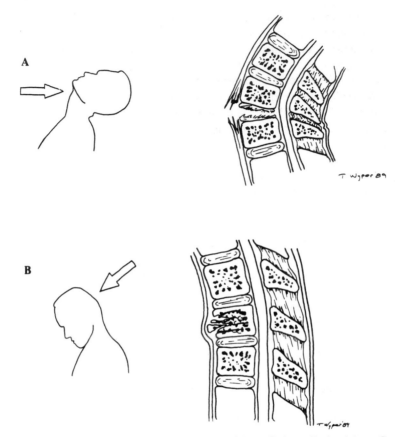

Figure 6-1 Mechanisms of injury. **A**, hyperextension injury; **B**, hyperflexion injury; **C**, rotational injury; **D**, compression injury.

after injury, there is central hemorrhagic necrosis of the gray matter and adjacent white matter. The central gray and white matter continues to necrose up to 24 hours until only the rim of the white matter remains. The edema in the area peaks between approximately the third and sixth day after initial injury.[4,5] Any damage to vessels in the area exacerbates spinal cord hypoxia. The release of catecholamines stimulated by the hypoxia may also contribute further to hemorrhage and necrosis. Cord swelling can actually enlarge the region of traumatic injury. There is argument over the exact pathophysiology of cord injury, but the final pathology is well understood.[4,5]

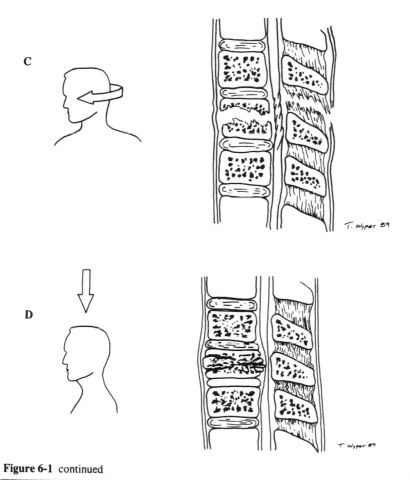

Figure 6-1 continued

Classification of Cord Injury

Not all cord injuries result in the same type of deficits. The functional abilities may vary from patient to patient depending upon whether the spinal cord injury is complete or incomplete. A complete spinal cord injury results in complete loss of neurologic function below the level of injury. Partial cord injuries may result in a variety of incomplete cord syndromes. Incomplete injuries are more frequent than complete injuries. As seen in the case presentation, L.C.'s assessment revealed that he had no neurologic function below the level of injury. This finding suggested a complete spinal cord injury.

Complete

Complete cord injury is rare and results in a total disruption of ascending and descending tracts below the level of the lesion. The signs and symptoms of a complete block, as in the case of L.C., include spinal shock, flaccid paralysis, loss of sensation, and absence of reflexes below the level of injury. The patient will experience loss of vasomotor tone and exhibit no perspiration below the level of injury. Disruptions in fecal and bladder continence also occur. Signs and symptoms can last from a few days to several months. Reflexes may return even if neurologic function does not. This can lead to spasticity or hyperreflexia.

Incomplete

Incomplete cord injury occurs when there is preservation of some sensory and/or motor function below the level of the lesion. Careful assessment must be conducted to detect any evidence of cord preservation. Subtle evidence, such as rectal tone, found on examination may suggest sacral sparing. Certain signs of preservation, such as the presence of the bulbocavernosus reflex, do not necessarily indicate an incomplete lesion. If sensory function is detected at least three levels below the level of cervical injury, the patient has a 50% chance of being able to walk again. If motor ability is detected, the percentage increases to 90%.[2] Incomplete injuries are categorized according to the area damaged. Partial cord syndromes can cause an interruption of the cord function, which results in a mixed loss of motor and sensory function below the level of injury.

Central cord syndromes occur in 70% of incomplete cord injuries.[2,6] Damage to the central portion of the spinal cord results from cellular damage attributable to edema or hemorrhage, as seen in Figure 6-2. In central cord syndromes, motor ability is impaired more in the upper rather than the lower extremities and sensory loss varies. This syndrome results commonly from extension injuries and occurs frequently in older patients with cervical arthritis.

Anterior cord syndromes account for 20% of incomplete cord injuries.[2,3] This injury usually occurs when there is a loss of blood supply via the anterior spinal artery or compression to the anterior portion of the cord, thus sparing only the posterior column, as seen in Figure 6-2. The injury results in motor paralysis and loss of pain and temperature sensation below the level of injury, but touch, motion, position, and vibration senses are preserved. Anterior cord syndromes are frequently seen in flexion injuries with a cervical cord lesion.

Brown-Séquard syndrome has been noted in 8% of incomplete injuries.[2] With this syndrome, there is a disruption in one side of the spinal cord

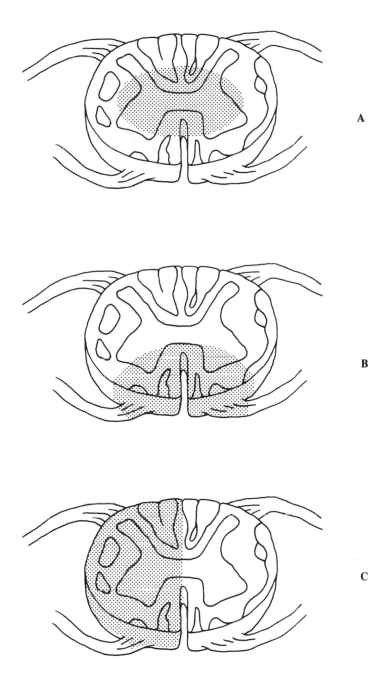

Figure 6-2 Incomplete spinal cord injuries (cross section of spinal cord). **A**, central cord syndrome; **B**, anterior cord syndrome; **C**, Brown-Séquard's syndrome.

(Figure 6-2). The patient suffers from ipsilateral paralysis and loss of touch, pressure, vibration, and proprioception below the level of injury. Contralateral impairment consists of loss of pain and temperature sensation below the lesion. Patients exhibiting Brown-Séquard syndrome are frequently victims of gunshot wounds or other penetrating injuries.

Not all incomplete spinal cord injuries fit specifically into one of these syndromes. Some patients will present with mixed motor and sensory findings that do not fall into any one of these categories.

Level of Injury

When documenting the level of injury, the patient's last functioning level of the spinal cord is identified, not the first level that is absent. The higher the lesion on the spinal cord, the greater the motor and sensory impairment. It is important to note that the vertebral level of injury does not always correspond exactly to the spinal segment injured. For example L.C.'s vertebral injury was documented at the level of C6; therefore, his spinal function should reflect that of a C6 to C8 injury. Cervical spine injuries occur more frequently because the neck is an area of greatest mobility and is less protected than the rest of the spine. The descriptions below reflect the level of spinal cord lesions and their resulting motor and sensory ability (see Figure 6-3).

C1-C3

Usually with a C1 to C2 vertebral fracture, there is no neurologic involvement.[2] However, with spinal cord damage at these levels, significant motor loss occurs, including respiratory function secondary to diaphragmatic and accessory muscle impairment. Therefore, these injuries are usually fatal without immediate resuscitation. If the patient does survive he will remain ventilator dependent.

C4

The muscle function remaining at this level includes the scapular elevators and diaphragm, thus allowing respiratory independence. The patient is usually dependent on others for activities of daily living but can achieve some degree of independence with the use of special adaptive devices and rehabilitation.

C5

Muscles left innervated at this level include the deltoids, trapezius, levator scapulae, and partial biceps. With innervation of C5, the patient may have

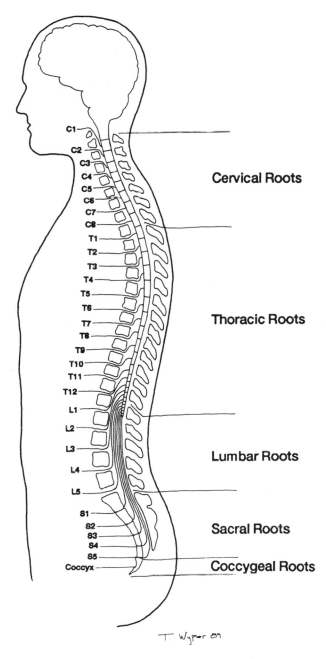

Figure 6-3 Levels of spinal cord injury.

some movement of the arms with contraction of the shoulder muscles. This patient requires assistance with all activities of daily living; ambulation with an electric wheelchair is possible, and the patient can feed himself with special devices.

C6

At the C6 level of injury, muscle innervation includes the deltoids, biceps, and brachio radialis muscles. As was true with L.C., these patients will be able to abduct their arms and have some thumb control. There is also the possibility of functional recovery of the triceps. Sensation remains intact over the lateral aspect of the arms. These patients can be independent in most of their activities of daily living, such as independently driving a car with hand controls.

C7

With injury at the level of C7, innervation allows the patient to make gross arm movements in the region of the forearms and have pincer function. Motor function includes elbow extension made possible by triceps function. Sensory assessment will reveal sensation over the posterior aspect of the middle finger. The patient has the potential for independent living without assistance.

C8

Injury at the level of C8 leaves movement of the lateral aspect of the hand and last two fingers. The latissimus dorsi and trapezius muscles are strong enough to allow the patient to sit up. Sensory sensation will include the posterior aspect of the little finger. These patients should achieve independent living.

Thoracic

Thoracic injuries produce varying levels of responses. With T1 to T6 injuries, there is a loss of motor ability and sensation at the mid-chest level. There is some intercostal impairment. The lower the thoracic lesion, the less respiratory involvement. T4 injuries are associated with sensation at the nipple line and T10 with the umbilicus. These patients have increased sitting balance.

Lumbar

In this region there is a loss of motor function of the legs and pelvis with a lack of sensation to the lower abdomen and legs. There also can be a deficit in bowel or bladder control. These patients can achieve independence with wheelchairs and possibly learn to walk with braces.

Sacral

Areas of involvement with sacral lesions include loss of plantar flexion and loss of sensation to part of the legs, perineum, anal area, scrotum, and the glans penis. Bowel and bladder function will be impaired. Ambulation should be normal, but the patient might require assistance with braces or canes. Bowel evacuation can be produced by manual stimulation or straining while bladder evacuation can be achieved by Credé's maneuver or straining.

Physical Assessment

The initial diagnosis is based upon a complete and accurate accident history, general clinical condition, and physical assessment. The assessment gives the practitioner baseline data with which to determine subsequent improvement or deterioration.

An accurate accident history should include the mechanism of injury, the intensity of the force involved, treatment received at the site, and transportation to the hospital. The type of accident such as a fall, motor vehicle accident, or gunshot wound can provide information about the mechanism of injury. The handling of the patient at the scene of the accident and the mode of transportation to the hospital are pertinent data for the baseline assessment.

Often the spinal cord injured patient presents as a multiple trauma victim. All trauma patients, particularly those complaining of neck pain, loss of consciousness, or head injury, must be assessed for spinal cord injury. The initial assessment for the patient with actual or potential spinal cord injury must focus on the ABCs: airway, breathing, and circulation. A patent airway, adequate respiratory effort, and circulation are the primary concerns in the initial evaluation. Alteration in the patient's level of consciousness will make an accurate assessment more difficult.

Preexisting medical conditions, such as ankylosing spondylitis or rheumatoid arthritis, may be significant because these disorders influence the likelihood of a cord injury.

Respiratory

For patients with spinal cord injuries, respiratory insufficiency is the most serious threat. Breathing difficulties will vary depending on the level of SCI.

The abdominal, intercostal, accessory, and diaphragm muscles are required for normal ventilation. Innervation of the phrenic nerve is at the level of C3 to C5. Damage to this area will result in compromised diaphragmatic movement leading to respiratory insufficiency. The patient with injury at or above the level of C4 will be ventilator dependent.

The patient with injury at C5 and above will not retain function of the diaphragm. Intercostal muscles are innervated in the thoracic region; therefore, patients with lesions above this area and below C5 must rely on the diaphragm as their major respiratory muscle. The diaphragm normally contributes 50% to 60% of normal vital capacity in quiet breathing. Function of the diaphragm can be greater on one side or the other. Respiratory function can deteriorate if the diaphragm fatigues; this can lead to hypoventilation.

Respiratory function may also deteriorate if edema and hemorrhage ascend to higher cord levels and interrupt intact nerve function. Hypoxia from altered respiratory status can only lead to further damage of the injured cord tissue.

When assessing the respiratory status of the patient, inspect the rate, depth, and type of respiration. Also note the muscle groups used for breathing. Other factors, such as gastric distention, that diminish lung expansion can alter pulmonary function. When completing an assessment also consider preexisting pulmonary disease.

Pulmonary function tests should include tidal volume, negative inspiratory force, and vital capacity. Alterations in pulmonary function tests can alert the practitioner to deterioration of respiratory status. Further evaluation involves auscultation of lung fields and percussion. X-rays and arterial blood gases should be routinely monitored.

Respiratory complications include aspiration, pulmonary edema, pulmonary emboli, and pneumonia. Aspiration can occur at the time of trauma from emesis of stomach contents or water ingestion after or during a diving accident. Pulmonary edema can occur iatrogenically from overzealous fluid volume replacement during resuscitation, especially in patients with shock symptoms. Pulmonary emboli from the dislodgement of a deep vein thrombosis is common in SCI and can further compromise respiratory function. Pneumonia is too often seen because of poor chest expansion in the dependent areas of the lungs exacerbated by immobility and paralysis of respiratory muscles.

Cardiovascular

Initial cardiovascular evaluation will reflect signs and symptoms related to the loss of sympathetic function. Patients with injuries at the level of T5 to T6 and above will experience an interruption in sympathetic outflow, which typically results in hypotension, hypothermia, and bradycardia. Venous pooling and decreased venous return caused by vasodilation result in a decreased cardiac output. Blood loss must be ruled out before attributing the hypotension to loss of sympathetic innervation. Hypotension from sympathetic nervous system disruption can often be distinguished from volume loss hypotension by the absence of the reflex tachycardia associated with hypovolemia. The patient's skin will remain pink and warm because of vasodilation, even in the face of severe hypotension when normal reflex would cause vasoconstriction. There will also be lack of perspiration below the level of the injury.

Fluid volume replacement to combat hypotension should be used judiciously to prevent fluid overloading, although resuscitation procedures may require large fluid replacement. Hemodynamic monitoring and vasoactive drugs such as dopamine are often required in the face of hypotension and shock. It is important to prevent hypoxia, which can increase cardiac stress.

An acute syndrome called autonomic dysreflexia is a hyperactive response to stimuli that causes an excessive autonomic response. Autonomic dysreflexia occurs when sensory receptors below the level of injury are stimulated. A stimulus is transmitted up the spinal cord, which stimulates the sympathetic nervous system. The impulse is blocked at the level of injury; therefore, the message is not received by the brain, and no parasympathetic feedback is transmitted. This blockage results in a sympathetic surge uninhibited by a parasympathetic response. This syndrome is more likely to occur in patients with injuries at the T6 level and above. It is also more likely to occur if the spinal cord has been transected completely and is seen rarely in incomplete injuries.

There is a loss of temperature regulation in spinal cord injuries above the thoracolumbar outflow of the sympathetic nervous system. With diminished ability to vasoconstrict, the patient also suffers a loss of the ability to shiver for warmth and sweat to dissipate heat below the level of injury. Therefore, these patients tend to assume the temperature of their environment; this is called poikilothermy.

Neurologic

The purpose of the neurologic exam is to evaluate the presence and level of injury. The exam also establishes the completeness of the lesion and the type of cord syndrome if the lesion is incomplete.

Inspection of the back or neck should be done for any obvious signs of hematoma, deformity, or localized pain. Motor evaluation can be performed by asking the patient to move all major motor groups beginning with the deltoids. Each group is assigned a numerical value, which is assessed on a scale of 0 to 5. A value of 5 signifies full strength while 0 indicates no movement whatsoever.

The following is an example of a muscle strength scale:

0—complete paralysis
1—visible or palpable flicker of muscle contraction
2—weak contraction
3—normal range of motion against gravity only
4—normal range of motion with some resistance
5—normal range of motion with full resistance

In order to facilitate a consistent motor assessment, the nurse should test resistance once the joint is set, not throughout the range of motion. Muscle strength should be assessed with the same test bilaterally for comparison. When performing this part of the examination, remember to keep in mind the age and overall condition of the patient.

Sensory assessment is performed with an understanding of the dermatome system (see Figure 6-4). With a toothpick and a cotton swab, all dermatones can be tested for pinprick and light touch. A change in the quality of sensation should be noted and documented. While determining sensory function, there may be a level of dull sensation before the level of anesthesia. This should be recorded as a relative sensory level. Often the sensory level left intact is one or two levels below the motor level. Sacral sparing must be evaluated by testing rectal tone. This is the most caudal representation of cord function.

Superficial and deep tendon reflexes should also be tested to determine sensory or motor sparing. The absence of reflexes initially does not indicate complete cord injury. Spinal shock will prevent the transmission of reflexes and reflex arcs, which will result in temporary areflexia or sluggish reflexes. This state can last from two weeks to six months; the return of reflexes suggests the resolution of spinal shock. In the unaltered spinal cord, the neurons are maintained in a state of excitability by impulses from the brain. Spinal shock is generally considered to be caused by the sudden loss of these impulses and loss of this excitation state.

Neurologic findings should be documented on a form that allows the practitioner the opportunity to evaluate trends or changes in the patient's condition at a glance. Many facilities have specific neurologic flow sheets that are used to serially document muscle strength, motor level of function, and sensory level of function. Since the practitioner bases decisions for treatment and procedures on deterioration or stabilization of neurologic status, clear documentation is vital.

Musculoskeletal

The human body is constructed for movement. People usually spend at least two thirds of their time erect or sitting.[7] The immobilized patient is at risk for thrombus formation arising from loss of vascular and muscle tone, prolonged bed rest, fluid and electrolyte changes, and other trauma-related injuries. Initially, trauma to the spinal cord can cause a loss of sympathetic nervous system control with the resultant loss of tone in peripheral blood vessels. This causes vasodilation and decreased arterial blood pressure. It is most pronounced initially and stabilizes with time. This vasodilation can cause hypotension and venous stasis. Normally, the extension and flexion of muscles assist in venous return. Additionally, prolonged bed rest impedes the efficiency of metabolic functions and results in a variety of complications, including altered blood viscosity. With bed rest, the gravitational effects of a head-to-foot loading along the axis is altered, which can further lead to venous stasis. Many spinal cord injury patients have other traumatic injuries that compound their problems of immobility and can lead to thrombus formation.

Thrombus development is stimulated by local trauma, stasis in the venous system, continuous contact of the skin to the bed, loss of pain perception, and immobilization. Signs and symptoms of thrombus formation include: pain, swelling of the involved limb, local redness, increased skin warmth, and a possible systemic rise in temperature. With a neurologic deficit, the patient may not be able to detect the most common signs of deep vein thrombosis—pain and discomfort. These peripheral forming clots can dislodge and lead to pulmonary embolus.

With any spinal cord injury, a patient experiences to some extent temporary or permanent immobility. Immobility itself is the main factor that leads to complications commonly manifested in spinal cord injury patients. These complications can be minimized through aggressive anticipation, assessment, and intervention by the critical care nurse. In fact, because of the autonomous nature of nursing care as it relates to immobility, nurses are provided with the unique opportunity of almost complete responsibility for prevention of complications.

The immobility resulting from spinal cord injury leads to many threats to the integrity of the skin. Externally, the skin is subject to friction, heat, moisture, and prolonged pressure. Internally, skin can be compromised by chemical imbalances, nutritional deficits, or cardiovascular complications. Prevention is the best form of care to maintain skin integrity. As the first line of defense, skin acts as a barrier to protect the patient from foreign organisms and toxins.

Pressure to any one area of skin over a prolonged period of time results in poor tissue perfusion. Because of a decreased supply of nutrients and oxygen

A

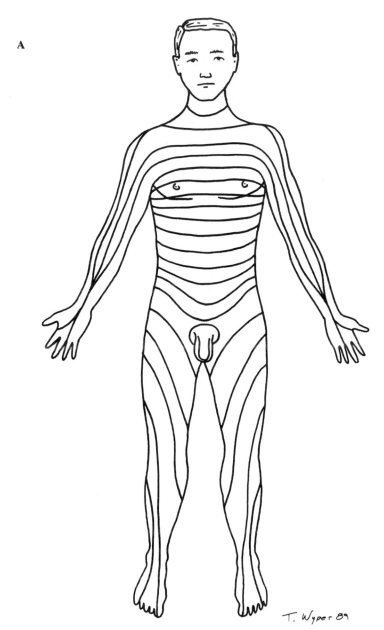

Figure 6-4 Dermatomes of body. **A**, anterior view; **B**, posterior view.

B

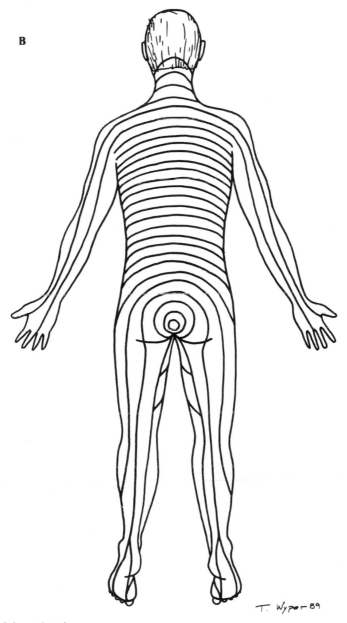

Figure 6-4 continued

to the area, integrity of the tissue can become compromised. With prolonged pressure comes congestion and induration followed by loss of the superficial epidural layers of skin. The site could develop progressively to deeper layers, causing necrosis and ulceration extending to deeper fascia, muscle, and bone. The process of deterioration is enhanced by the previously mentioned internal and external factors. Decubitus ulcers lead to prolonged hospitalization, limited patient activity level, increased risk for infection, increased medical costs, and increased morbidity and mortality.

Another concern for the immobilized patient is contracture. Muscle shortening from disuse can begin to develop within three days of immobilization. Inactivity results in changes in the size and fiber types of muscle groups, with further stiffening and limited mobility of the joints.

Specialized beds are designed to allow personnel to care for the patient with a spinal cord injury without moving the spinal cord. The five goals of these specialty beds are to (1) maintain correct spinal alignment, (2) assess for improvements or deterioration in condition, (3) facilitate progressive mobility, (4) prevent complications of decreased mobility, and (5) prevent loss of vertebral alignment and additional mechanical insult to the spinal cord.[1] Kinetic therapy also allows continuous movement of the patient, thereby decreasing any risks of immobility (see Figure 6-5).

Gastrointestinal

Gastric complications are a common occurrence in the spinal cord injured patient. Gastrointestinal paralysis from spinal shock is due to loss of sympathetic innervation and uninhibited parasympathetic action. This state of atony or paralytic ileus starts within 24 hours and may last up to seven days. A paralytic ileus is more likely to occur in patients with cervical injuries.

With paralytic ileus, gastric secretions can build up and put the patient at risk for vomiting and aspiration. Patients with a cervical injury may be unable to turn their heads and thus have an increased risk for aspiration. Abdominal distention can also put pressure on the diaphragm and cause respiratory compromise.

There is also an increase in the acidity of the gastric contents that puts the patient at risk for stress ulcers. This situation is aggravated by the use of steroid therapy. Antacids are normally administered for a gastric pH of less than 4.0 and H_2 antagonists are administered routinely.

Though intestinal tract absorption and digestion appear to proceed normally, alterations in bowel patterns will often depend upon the level of spinal cord injury. In the spinal cord injured patient the intrinsic bowel contractile response remains intact. With upper motor lesions, the defecation reflex remains intact. With lower motor lesions, the reflex for defecation is destroyed and there is a loss of anal tone.

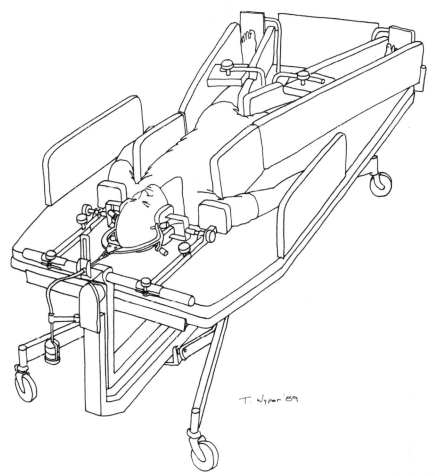

T. Wyper '89

Figure 6-5 L.C. on a Roto Rest bed in Trippe-Wells tongs. Trippe-Wells tongs can be placed on the patient in the emergency room to provide cervical traction.

Genitourinary

Urinary elimination. Since the bladder is controlled by the autonomic nervous system, the degree of loss of innervation will depend on the level of injury. Upon initial injury, the bladder is atonic and areflexic. After spinal shock resolves, the full extent of bladder involvement can be evaluated.

With upper motor neuron lesions, the reflex arc is intact at the S2 to S4 spinal segment. When the bladder wall is stretched, the detrusor muscle is stimulated to contract, resulting in an involuntary voiding response.

Lower motor neuron lesions cause a flaccid bladder with lack of motor involvement to provide contraction. The bladder will fill until it overflows and incontinence occurs.

Two tests easily performed at the bedside will provide the nurse with information as to the type of neurogenic bladder the patient has. The bulbocavernosus reflex is elicited by squeezing the clitoris or glans penis and watching for a contraction of the anal sphincter. The anal reflex is initiated by stroking the perianal skin causing the anal sphincter to contract. Positive results of these tests indicate an upper motor neuron lesion and an intact reflex arc.

Renal complications in the cord-injured patient include urinary tract infections, renal calculi, urethral diverticula, and possibly renal failure. Infections are the most common complication and are usually related to the inability to completely empty the bladder. Renal calculi, which are also common sequela to SCI, result from increased serum calcium arising from immobilization and subsequent bone demineralization.

Sexual. Sexual function is an important part of the assessment of the cord-injured patient. The degree of the alteration in sexual function depends on the type of spinal cord injury.

In males, two types of erection are possible depending on the location of the lesion. Psychogenic erections are a result of mental sexual arousal. This response is obviously impaired whenever the lesion interrupts the path of higher cortical stimulation. Reflexogenic erections are involuntary responses to a stimulation of the penis and surrounding area. Most cord-injured patients are able to obtain erection through this response since it requires no higher cortical stimulation. Reflexogenic erections are a result of the sacral reflex arc, a parasympathetic response, which is located at the S2 to S4 cord segment. If the sacral segment is not intact then the patient is unable to have reflexogenic erections. The higher the cord lesion, the greater the likelihood of reflexogenic erections. The lower the lesion on the cord, the greater likelihood the patient can ejaculate, since this is a sympathetic response. Male patients may have changes in fertility, such as decreased sperm count, poor sperm motility, and difficult or absent ejaculation.

After spinal shock resolves, the sacral segments can be tested to evaluate sexual reflex activity. Using Cormarr's Classification of Sex, three areas are tested.[8] The external anal sphincter is tested by digital examination. Pinprick and light touch sensation is tested in the penile, scrotal, and perianal skin. The final criterion is the patient's ability to voluntarily control the external anal sphincter. Research has shown that the presence of intact bilateral pinprick sensation offers the best prognosis for psychogenic erections.

In female patients, sensation is lost below the level of injury. Since the organs of sex are included, females may not experience orgasm but can participate in sexual intercourse. They may have amenorrhea for some time after injury but are capable of becoming pregnant. However, they are unable to detect uterine contractions and are at risk of autonomic dysreflexia during labor.

DIAGNOSTIC STUDIES

Even with today's technology, the best diagnostic tool is still the patient's accident and medical history coupled with a complete physical exam. Other diagnostic procedures used to confirm or rule out SCI include a complete spinal series, computerized tomography (CT), myelogram, magnetic resonance imaging (MRI), and somatosensory cortical evoked potential (SSEP). Care should be taken during all procedures to avoid movement that could cause further neurologic damage.

A complete spinal series is the most frequently performed procedure to visualize the spinal column. C-spine films must provide visualization of all seven cervical vertebrae, including the C7 to T1 junction. Lateral, anterior-posterior, and open mouth views are necessary to definitively rule out or identify a fracture. The open mouth view is taken specifically to visualize C1 and C2. If all the cervical spine is not clearly imaged, injuries at the level of C7 to T1 junction can be missed. The lower cervical vertebrae may be difficult to view in a patient with broad shoulders or a muscular neck. To help facilitate visualization, the patient's arms can be pulled down to the side. The swimmer's position can be used to visualize the complete set of cervical vertebrae. In this procedure, stretch one arm above the patient's head while the other arm is placed at the patient's side with the hand down.

An examination with multidirectional CT scanning can be used for questionable cases. This is used to obtain more information regarding the extent of bony injury by allowing cross-sectional views of the vertebral column.

Myelogram studies can be performed in conjunction with CT studies to enhance visualization of the subarachnoid space. These studies are done to determine the presence of pressure on the cord, which could be caused by hematomas or ruptured disks that may be surgically reduced. A C1 to C2 level puncture is made, and dye is injected while the patient is supine. The dye flows down the column and across the level of injury to indicate the presence of a subarachnoid block. Some practitioners use this procedure only if a patient demonstrates increasing deficits, but it is rarely done in critically ill patients.[5]

Magnetic resonance imagery can provide clear and concise images of the central nervous system. The main advantage of MRI, outside of its remarkably clear views, is that the patient receives no radiation.

Somatosensory-evoked potential (SSEP), although used more for prognosis than diagnosis, deserves mentioning in this section. It is used in the acute phase to determine the neurologic level of injury and completeness of lesion. SSEP is measured by using a peripheral nerve below the level of injury. The nerve is stimulated and the response of the cerebral cortex is measured by scalp electrodes. An altered response is characteristic of an incomplete injury, while no response is indicative of a complete lesion. SSEP in the acute care setting can be too time-consuming and the results difficult to interpret since spinal shock can mimic a complete lesion and have no prognostic value. The value of this procedure is questionable when one considers that a thorough physical exam yields the same results.

Diagnosis of SCI is based upon a multidimensional approach that includes an accurate medical and accident history, complete physical exam, and appropriate diagnostic procedures.

MEDICAL/SURGICAL TREATMENT

Medical

Progressive pathological changes can lead to irreversible cord destruction hours after the injury has occurred. Rapid intervention is required to preserve the vulnerable spinal cord tissue and function. Treatment of SCI may involve a combination of drug therapies, stabilization of the spine, and, in some cases, surgical intervention.

The focus of medical treatment is to prevent secondary damage caused by inadequate spinal cord perfusion and edema. Controversy surrounds the use of drug therapies, such as steroids, although it is generally an accepted practice.[3]

Steroids are the most common medication used initially and in the acute phase after stabilization. Their mechanism of action is unclear in these patients. Steroids are believed to prevent depletion of potassium at the cellular level. Therefore, they may prevent edema from the inflammatory response by stabilizing membranes, preserving lysosome integrity, and preventing the release of phagocytic enzymes. Even though the degree of positive effects of steroids is unclear, it is generally thought that the effects are beneficial. Cortisone continues to be administered, but evidence is mounting that corticosteroids have no effect on reducing morbidity in SCI patients.[9]

Osmotic diuretics, such as mannitol, are used in an attempt to decrease swelling in the area of injury. Mannitol is thought to decrease fluid volume in the cord by increasing plasma osmolality and pulling fluid into the vascular system, thus inducing diuresis. This is not a definitive practice since there are no controlled human studies supporting this form of treatment and the effects are considered to be transient.[5]

Naloxone and thyroid-releasing hormone (TRH) are both currently under investigation for their opiate and antagonistic qualities. They are thought to minimize the histopathologic effects produced by endogenous opiates released after SCI. Current research suggests that TRH is superior to naloxone in improving neurologic function.[2,9]

Another area of research is in the effects of hypothermia on the injured cord. It is thought that hypothermia has a protective influence by decreasing edema, inflammatory response, oxygen demands, and metabolic activity of the tissue. Studies on humans to examine the effects of surgically cooling the spinal cord are in the nascent phase so the exact mechanisms are unknown. The outlook for hypothermia treatment is not promising. It involves a large amount of equipment and surgery, and must be completed within four to eight hours of injury in order to be effective.[5,9]

L.C.'s diagnosis of C6 subluxation with rupture of the posterior longitudinal ligaments and complete cord transection was based upon accident history, physical exam, c-spine x-rays, and CT scan with intrathecal contrast.

Procedures

Stabilizing procedures involve the use of tongs and traction to realign the spinal column and reduce pressure on the cord by impingement of bony fragments. The patient is left in traction for about one week to reduce the site of fracture and allow the cord swelling to subside. The decision is then made whether the treatment will consist of surgery, a brace, or prolonged traction and a brace. Cervical traction is applied to immobilize and align the spine and to relieve cord compression. This is achieved by the use of Trippe-Wells (Figure 6-5), Gardener-Wells, or Crutchfield tongs. L.C. was placed in Trippe-Wells tongs, which have the advantage of being placed in the emergency room and allowing for the use of halo traction without further manipulation. Gardner-Wells tongs may be placed at the bedside but do not fit the halo frame.

Traction was applied to L.C's tongs via a rope-and-pulley system. Weights in five-pound increments were added until reduction of the injury was accomplished. A rule of thumb to determine the amount of weight needed is that every level above the injury requires five pounds of traction. The amount of weight will vary depending upon the reduction needed. The literature has reported the use of up to 100 pounds of traction to reduce a locked fracture. Since the spinal cord and vertebral arteries are sensitive to pulling forces, the least amount of weight possible to achieve the desired effect is preferred.[2,4,5]

X-rays should be taken and neurologic assessment should be performed with every traction adjustment (in 5- to 10-pound increments) to ensure vertebral alignment. Traction should be freely hanging and pin insertion sites should be cleaned regularly. Halo braces and jackets are becoming increasingly popular for stabilization of c-spine and upper thoracic fractures. They allow more mobility but subject the patient to greater risk of decubitus ulcers in inadequately padded areas of the hard jacket. They also require ready access to wrenches in order to release the brace in the event that cardiopulmonary resuscitation is necessary.

Nonsurgical immobilization in acute thoracic and lumbar injuries is done using proper alignment, supports, padding, and bed rest.

Surgical

Surgical intervention has historically been controversial and remains so today. In general, the goal of surgical intervention is to minimize complications of immobility by stabilization of the spinal cord and by allowing early mobilization. There are no absolute criteria for the decision to operate. However, some general indications for surgical intervention include patients with complete or incomplete cord injury and obvious operative pathology, ie, bony fragments in the canal; unstable dislocations; and evidence of cord compression. A more compelling indication for surgical intervention is deterioration of neurologic function. Patients with questionable need for surgery include those exhibiting neurologic improvement, those with complete cord injury with no operative pathology, and those with central cord syndromes. Central cord syndromes sometimes improve spontaneously.

Decompression laminectomy is the main neurosurgical procedure performed. Whether the surgical approach is anterior or posterior depends on the site of cord compression and clinical findings. Laminectomy involves the removal of the vertebral arch (lamina) and is performed to remove pressure on the cord posteriorly. In the cervical spine, a posterior approach may be indicated for fractures of the lamina. An anterior approach may be utilized if there is an anterior compression of the cord by disk or bone fragments. A posterior decompression in these cases could create further instability. Tracheostomies are initially avoided because they would interfere with the anterior approach.

In the thoracic and lumbar regions, the posterior approach is the most common while the lateral approach is less common. Harrington rods are especially useful for spinal stabilization. Harrington rods are metal rods attached to the vertebral body or laminae, two or three levels above and below the level of injury.

For unstable fractures, spinal fusions are created using bone grafts taken from the iliac crest or from the bone bank.

NURSING CARE PLAN

Ineffective Breathing Pattern

If the respiratory status of the patient is adequate, intubation should be avoided, since subsequent weaning of the patient from the ventilator is difficult. Patients breathing independently should receive continuous close observation of their respiratory status regarding muscle fatigue or neurologic deterioration. If intubation does becomes necessary, as it was with L.C., it should be performed nasally. This route avoids neck extension and allows a patient to communicate by mouthing words.

Aggressive pulmonary toilet is essential even with adequate ventilation in order to prevent the retention of secretions and the development of pneumonia. Suctioning, chest percussion, incentive spirometry, aerosol breathing treatments, assisted coughing, and turning (as permitted) are all measures employed to ensure adequate airway clearance and lung expansion.

The nurse performs an assisted cough by placing the fist or heel of a hand between the patient's umbilicus and xiphoid process. Then she applies firm, quick pressure up toward the chest during the patient's expulsion effort of his cough.

L.C. was treated aggressively with frequent suctioning, breathing treatments, and chest physiotherapy as a result of his aspiration of emesis at the time of the accident. He was also placed on antibiotics for aspiration pneumonia. Four days later, he was successfully weaned from the ventilator. At this time, incentive spirometry and assisted coughing were added to his care plan. L.C.'s respiratory rate was 22, his arterial blood gases were within normal limits, and his pulmonary function studies were adequate. He had rhonchi audible over the larger upper airways, and his x-ray showed resolving pneumonia.

1. **Nursing Diagnosis: Ineffective Breathing Pattern Related to Decreased Respiratory Effort, Fluid Overload, Ineffective Secretion Clearance, and Pneumonia**

Expected Patient Outcome

Patient will experience adequate breathing as evidenced by lack of respiratory distress, freedom from preventable complications, normal arterial blood gases (ABGs), and optimal pulmonary function.

Nursing Interventions

1. Maintain patent airway by suctioning, positioning, and postural drainage.
2. Assess respiratory function, including quality and quantity of respirations, breath sounds, and strength of cough every one to two hours.
3. Encourage deep breathing with incentive spirometry and coughing 10 to 15 times each hour.
4. Assess arterial blood gases and pulmonary function studies serially.
5. Monitor input and output.
6. Administer heparin therapy as ordered for the prevention of pulmonary embolus (deep vein thrombosis).
7. Teach patient the significance of pulmonary toilet and the potential preventable complications.
8. Administer intermittent positive-pressure breathing to expand and humidify underventilated areas of the lungs every four to six hours.

Alteration in Cardiac Output

Nursing concerns related to cardiac output involve the close monitoring of the blood pressure and pulse for the first few days since cardiovascular instability is a potentially fatal complication. Though the patient will remain slightly hypotensive and bradycardic for the rest of his life, the stability of this system will return over the next few days to weeks.

The patient should be turned slowly and positioned with care to avoid orthostatic hypotension. Hypotension occurs because of the loss of vasomotor tone and blood pooling in the dependent areas. Loss of tone and pooling can result in a decreased venous return and decreased cardiac output. Any alteration in cardiac output may cause an inadequate perfusion of vital organs. Inadequate cardiac output can affect other body systems and result in altered mental status, complaints of dizziness, and decreased urinary output. These signs and symptoms should alert the nurse to a potential or actual problem.

Autonomic dysreflexia is an acute situation and requires immediate intervention. The signs and symptoms include headaches, blurred vision, reddened face, hypertension, nausea, bradycardia, goose flesh, nasal congestion, and diaphoresis above the level of injury. The only definitive treatment is to find and remove the noxious stimulus.

Potential precipitating factors include:

- bowel stimulus—distention, impaction, rectal stimulation
- bladder stimulus—distention, urinary tract infection

- uterine contractions, ejaculations
- suctioning—endotracheal, nasotracheal
- skin involvement—turning, pressure sores
- pain—ingrown toe nail, surgical incisions
- tight clothing—shoes, support hose

The patient with spinal cord injury might complain that he feels cold even though his temperature is normal or elevated. With higher levels of injury, patients exhibit more severe effects of loss of thermoregulation.

L.C. was hypotensive and bradycardic but remained asymptomatic; therefore, no vasoactive medications were administered. His mentation was clear and his urinary output was sufficient. His vital signs were stable even on the Roto Rest bed. He had a peripheral intravenous line at 75 cc per hour, which was discontinued when he was able to take fluids orally. His skin remained pink and dry, and even though his temperature was 98.8°F (oral) he was complaining of feeling cold.

2. Nursing Diagnosis: Decreased Cardiac Output Related to Loss of Vasomotor Tone

Expected Patient Outcome

Patient will demonstrate stable cardiovascular system as evidenced by adequate blood pressure and pulse. The patient will maintain normothermia.

Nursing Interventions

1. Monitor vital signs every one to two hours, or more frequently if on vasoactive medications.
2. Monitor patient's level of consciousness and orientation every one to two hours.
3. Monitor urinary output every hour.
4. Assess for signs of autonomic dysreflexia, such as hypertension, diaphoresis, bradycardia, and headache.
5. If autonomic dysreflexia is present:
   - elevate head of the bed
   - seek and remove noxious stimuli
   - administer antihypertensives as ordered
   - continue to monitor and treat blood pressure closely
6. Assess trends in hemodynamic monitoring when appropriate.
7. Keep atropine at bedside.

8. Continually monitor the temperature via a rectal probe.
9. Alter the patient's environment to help maintain a normal temperature. Utilize a fan or warming blanket.

Sensory Perception Alteration

The spinal cord injured patient can have a deficit of tactile sensation that alters his sensory perception. This patient needs to be assessed for sensory deprivation, including lack of social support and physical isolation. Sensory overload in the critical care environment from noise and lights coupled with fear, pain, and anxiety can affect the patient's sensory perception.

L.C. had difficulty in the intensive care unit adjusting to the environment and the routine. His sleep was interrupted frequently and he expressed irritation with the staff. As L.C. stabilized, the need for frequent interruption decreased and he was able to achieve longer periods of sleep. L.C. had limited areas for tactile stimulation. He made frequent requests of staff and family to rub his shoulders and to reposition his arms. This helped supply some sensory stimulation.

3. Nursing Diagnosis: Sensory Perception Alteration Related to Changes in the Amount and/or Pattern of Incoming Stimuli

Expected Patient Outcome

The patient will express and demonstrate decreased symptoms of sensory overload. The patient will be protected from further bodily injury, such as deterioration in neurologic status.

Nursing Interventions

1. Maintain proper spine alignment, continuously assess alignment, and maintain immobilization techniques.
2. Instruct the patient concerning proper body position.
3. Provide a nurse call-light system, such as a mouth sip-and-puff call light.
4. Monitor the environment, ie, temperature, noise, and light, in order to assimilate day and night patterns and provide an environment that is comfortable to the patient.
5. Encourage diversional activities, such as visitors, television, or talking books.

6. Alter the patient's environment to best facilitate a stimulating environment. Use prism glasses or position the rotating bed so that one side allows a view of the window.
7. Provide tactile stimulation to areas where the patient has sensation.
8. Orient the patient to procedures during care.
9. Assist the patient to recognize patterns of pain and provide stimuli, such as massage, position changes, or diversional activities.

Alteration in Tissue Perfusion

Nursing interventions that focus on the prevention of deep vein thrombosis (DVT) include scheduled turning, position changes, and a range of motion exercises that can help to reduce venous pooling. L.C. had thigh-high elastic stockings and intermittent inflatable stockings that increased venous return. These devices were removed for 30 minutes after each eight-hour period. Although controversial, some practitioners use low-dose heparin therapy or Trendelenburg periodic positioning to reduce thrombus formation. Other preventive measures include daily monitoring of leg circumferences by measuring 20 cm above the upper border of the patella and 10 cm below the tibial prominence. During range of motion exercises (ROM), L.C.'s skin was assessed for subtle changes indicating DVT. Rapid identification and intervention by critical care nursing staff can prevent such complications as loss of limb or pulmonary embolus. L.C. exhibited no signs of DVT and was transferred out of the ICU without complications.

4. Nursing Diagnosis: Potential for Alteration in Tissue Perfusion Related to Sluggish Venous Return Secondary to Loss of Sympathetic Control and Immobility

Expected Patient Outcome

Patient will not experience DVT or other adverse effects of venous stasis.

Nursing Interventions

1. Apply elastic and pneumatic compression stockings and remove for 30 minutes each eight-hour period.
2. Turn patient every two hours, provide ROM, avoid restrictive clothing, and eliminate pressure points on limbs with pillows and sheepskin.
3. Unless otherwise contraindicated, place patient in Trendelenburg 15 degrees for one hour in each eight-hour period.

4. Assess extremities for redness, swelling, warmth, and low-grade temperature indicative of DVT.
5. Observe for tachypnea, dyspnea, tachycardia, and elevated temperature indicative of pulmonary embolus.
6. Assess coagulation studies as needed.
7. Administer anticoagulants as ordered, with awareness of implications and contraindications of the drug.
8. Begin patient teaching as early as possible.

Potential for Impaired Tissue Integrity

Signs and symptoms of altered skin integrity are reddened areas, commonly over bony prominences, and other changes in skin color. Precipitating factors include exposure to moisture, pressure, shearing effects, and wound drainage. Factors that increase the risk of developing skin breakdown are advanced age, excess weight, poor nutritional status, poor skin turgor, preexisting breakdown, and underlying medical problems.

Nursing interventions for L.C. began with regular skin assessment: careful assessment of bony prominences and sites exposed to stressors, such as inadequately padded areas of the Roto Rest bed and later the halo jacket. Skin was kept clean and dry and protected from body fluids. Incontinence pads were not used since they keep moisture next to the skin. Proper nutritional support with increased calories and protein intake was initiated upon the return of L.C.'s bowel sounds to promote adequate skin integrity.

Nursing research has shown that the best solution for wound cleansing is normal saline—not betadine or hydrogen peroxide.[10] Donuts used on the coccyx have also been shown by nursing research to be counterproductive.[11]

L.C. was taught daily skin inspection and pressure-relief measures. The nurses informed L.C. of causes and symptoms of excessive pressure. The nurses emphasized to L.C. that he was responsible for regular skin care. Family members were included in skin care instruction. He was also taught that skin breakdown can be prevented if a skin care routine is followed.

5. Nursing Diagnosis: Potential for Impaired Tissue Integrity Related to Immobility

Expected Patient Outcome

Patient will maintain skin integrity as evidenced by no skin breakdown.

Nursing Interventions

1. Provide skin care every eight hours. Keep skin dry, clean, and free of body fluids.
2. Monitor bony prominences and other sites of pressure for signs of breakdown with each turn and bath.
3. Pad all pressure points. Pay close attention to special orthopedic devices, such as halo vests and antiflexion orthotics.
4. Avoid shearing effects of bed linen by turning patient carefully with the proper assistance.
5. Avoid extreme temperatures in bathwater.
6. Determine turn schedule and follow it. Document each turn.
7. Document pressure sores that develop and chart description of wound daily in nurses' notes.
8. Perform pin care and wound care with normal saline as ordered.
9. Begin patient teaching when appropriate as early as possible.

Impaired Physical Mobility

Contracture preventive measures should be initiated immediately. Passive range of motion exercises done every two hours, which alternately flex and extend the patient's hips, knees, and elbows, can reduce the risk of contracture. Splints, padded with sheepskin, are used to prevent flexion contracture. Permanent disability and deformity can result if such interventions are not employed. Physical and occupational therapy was immediately initiated for L.C. Both these services, as well as nursing, provided range of motion exercises at scheduled intervals to provide L.C. with exercise every three to four hours while he was awake. He enjoyed these treatments, saying, "It's good to feel me move." He was fitted with splints to prevent flexion contractures. These were removed for a half hour every four hours, usually during his range of motion treatments.

The commonly used methods to manage spinal cord injuries are log-rolling on a regular bed, a Roto Rest bed, or a Stryker bed. Log-rolling is done in order to maintain alignment while repositioning the patient to prevent complications. Log-rolling can be used for patients with cervical tongs and halos. To log roll a patient, nurses cross the patient's arms over the chest and keep the patient's legs extended with feet together. The patient is lifted and turned as an even unit by three or more staff members. One mover supports the base of the head and neck with both hands while the others support the patient at the level of the shoulder and buttocks. The nose should remain in alignment with the sternum. When log-rolled, the patient's shoulder pain can be alleviated by tucking a small pillow under the axilla prior to turning. The side-back side-back sequence should be avoided since the patient ultimately spends more time on the back.

The Stryker bed consists of an anterior and posterior frame that allows positioning from supine to prone. The advantages of this bed are that it provides accessibility to all body parts and it enables the nurse to place the bed in the Trendelenburg position. It is also easy to use. Turning in these beds is done by sandwiching a patient between two frames. Halfway through the turn, a patient is positioned vertically, which can cause severe compression and postural hypotension. While the patient rests in the prone position, his vision is severely limited and he may feel as if he were falling or claustrophobic. Suctioning on the ventilator is much more difficult for patients in the prone position, and when the patient is being turned, the ventilator must be temporarily disconnected.

The Roto Rest bed, which L.C. was on, is a specialty bed that slowly and continuously rotates the patient side to side 60 degrees to 60 degrees from left to right. It also has three back hatches for access to the patient's back and buttocks. This bed prevents pressure sores, respiratory complications, bone demineralization, muscle wasting, urinary stasis, and calculi. Additionally, the patient is turned 200 times a day in comparison to 12 times a day. Some patients complain of nausea, claustrophobia, or motion sickness. Viewing the patient posteriorly can also be difficult unless the bottom hatches are opened. When the bed parts are moved, care should be taken to assess for skin pressure sites and pinching of skin or digits between pads. Roto Rest beds can also have a small television attached to them, which will rotate with the patient's bed.

When using specialty beds, try to position the bed in the room so that, at one position, the patient is allowed an outside view. The bed should be set in such a way that space to work is left around the bed. If the patient is supine, prism glasses will enable him to watch TV. These glasses can be irritating to look through for some patients. For quadriplegics, a sip-and-puff call-light system should be set up immediately to allow the patient to call for assistance. Improper use of any of these specialty beds can potentially result in increased neurologic damage.

6. Nursing Diagnosis: Impaired Physical Mobility Related to Loss of Motor Function Related to Spinal Injury

Expected Patient Outcome

Patient's extremities will remain free of contractures.

Nursing Interventions

1. Perform and document comprehensive neurologic assessment, including detailed motor and sensory function, each day.
2. Perform range of motion four times a day on all joints.
3. Maintain spinal alignment during all turns and transfers by log-rolling, proper positioning, and maintenance of traction or other stabilizing devices.
4. Assess need for antiflexion orthotics or other physical therapy devices during patient care conferences.
5. Position call device for ready use by patient.
6. Begin patient teaching and rehabilitation services as early as possible.

Alteration in Bowel Elimination

Initially L.C. was on "nothing by mouth" status and a nasogastric tube was inserted to decompress the stomach. His gastric pH was checked every four hours and treated with antacids for a value of less than five. The nurse monitored his abdomen for distention and auscultated bowel sounds every four hours. Upon the return of bowel sounds, fluids were initiated and feedings advanced as tolerated. Increased fiber, adequate calories, and sufficient fluids help to regulate bowel movements. Long-term use of laxatives and enemas is discouraged.

To initiate bowel training, the nurse discussed L.C.'s preinjury bowel habits with him. L.C. was put on a regular schedule of every other day bowel evacuation. His bowels were stimulated at the same time and with the same method each day.

It is advantageous to stimulate the bowel 30 minutes after meals in order to utilize the gastrocolic reflex. Massaging the abdomen from right to left and down can stimulate the large intestines.

7. Nursing Diagnosis: Alteration in Bowel Elimination Related to Loss of Voluntary Control and Potential for Paralytic Ileus

Expected Patient Outcome

Patient will establish an effective bowel program as evidenced by regular bowel movements and lack of incontinent episodes. The patient will have active bowel sounds with no abdominal distention.

Nursing Interventions

1. Assess patient's previous bowel habits and establish mutual goals for bowel program as early as possible.
2. Monitor present elimination patterns for number and characteristics each shift.
3. Auscultate bowel sounds and assess abdomen for distention every eight hours.
4. Promote adequate hydration and nutrition. Consider dietary consultation.
5. Insert and manage nasogastric tube when ordered.
6. Monitor gastric pH and administer antacids as ordered.
7. Administer laxatives, stool softeners, and suppositories as needed.

Alteration in Urinary Elimination

Bladder management considerations in the acute care phase involve maintaining function and sterility of the system, establishing a means of bladder evacuation, and initiation of a bladder training program.

Function of the urinary tract system can be assessed by hourly outputs, laboratory values, and observation of urinary odor, color, and clarity. Since there is an increased risk of bacterial entry with catheter placement, the catheter and meatus area should be cleaned every eight hours. Indwelling catheters or intermittent catheterization can be used as a way of evacuating the bladder in the acute care setting. L.C. had reflex voiding, which was advantageous when bladder training was initiated. As spontaneous voiding occurs, the frequency of intermittent catheterization can be decreased. Catheterization is necessary, however, to evaluate the presence of residual urine, which can lead to urinary tract infections. Patients who have flaccid bladders will learn to rely on regular interval catheterization to keep their bladder empty. If the bladder is overextended, damage to the detrusor muscle can occur and the patient can become incontinent. L.C.'s bladder training was initiated after his discharge from the intensive care unit.

8. Nursing Diagnosis: Functional Incontinence Related to Loss of Voluntary Control

Expected Patient Outcome

The patient will establish an effective urinary elimination pattern as evidenced by lack of retention, incontinence, signs and symptoms of urinary tract infection, or renal calculi.

Nursing Interventions

1. Monitor intake and output every eight hours.
2. Palpate for bladder distention every six hours.
3. Insert Foley catheter if needed, maintaining sterility.
4. Monitor urine for color, odor, clarity, and specific gravity.
5. Assess lab values: BUN, creatinine, and white blood count.
6. Ensure adequate fluid intake.
7. Tape the Foley catheter in male patients to the abdomen to avoid urethral scrotal fistulas.
8. Clean the catheter and meatus every eight hours.

Sexual Dysfunction

Initiation of sexual evaluation and counseling is an important factor in the recovery process. As with any teaching, the nurse should assess the patient for readiness. Behaviors indicating readiness can include sexual overtures to staff or comments about relationships. The nurse should consider that some patients will avoid conscious consideration of sexuality or will be fearful of the information they may receive. Developing a trusting relationship and allowing the patient the freedom to discuss sex can promote a communicative environment. When providing sexual counseling, nurses need to consider the experiences and cultural values of themselves and the patient as well.

L.C. was eager to find out if he could have sex again. Although he had no intimate person at this time, he was young and sexually active up until the time of his accident. The nurses utilized time during baths and Foley catheter care to talk about his sexual future. The intimate nature of bathing and the private environment allowed L.C. to talk about his concerns and fears. It also provided the nurse with a comfortable, appropriate setting to provide L.C. with information and support.

9. Nursing Diagnosis: Sexual Dysfunction Related to Alteration in Sensation and Changes in Motor Function

Expected Patient Outcome

The patient will express an understanding of his or her own sexuality. The patient will explore his or her alteration in sexuality and appropriate coping mechanisms.

Nursing Interventions

1. Create an environment in which sexuality and sexual function can be discussed.
2. Evaluate and recognize the sexual needs of the patient and grant permission to talk about concerns.
3. When the patient is ready, begin sexual counseling, with a complete sexual history to determine sexual interest and values prior to injury.
4. Explain to the patient alterations in sexual function and alternative expressions of sexuality.
5. Sexual counseling should focus on emotional adaptation and provide information about physical changes and problems associated with sex.
6. Educate the patient about available resources, such as the National Spinal Cord Injury Foundation.
7. Refer to a qualified counselor as needed.

Anxiety

During the immediate hospitalization, attention is focused on physical survival. This catastrophic event overwhelms the patient and family with fear and anxiety. Since the trauma is unexpected, the family and patient do not have time to prepare emotionally. There will be confusion and concern over the patient's future. There are a wide variety of emotional needs and responses patients and families may exhibit, which must be taken into consideration.

The individual's anxiety can be exhibited through the grieving process. This patient may express denial of his disability. Frequently, anger is exhibited and the patient may be preoccupied with his physical condition. The prospect of long-term dependency and fears of abandonment can overwhelm these patients. There are alterations in self-concept, role function, and interdependence that can undermine a patient's sense of self-worth.

The nurse should be aware of the manifestations of these psychological responses. The patient can exhibit verbal and nonverbal behaviors, including hostility, noncompliance, verbal abuse, and self-destructive behaviors. Opening lines of communication and nonjudgmental responses are conducive to helping these patients grieve and cope with their anxieties.

During L.C.'s ICU stay he had periods of anger and crying, especially when his mother was present. He eventually was able to discuss his fears and anxiety with his family and the nursing staff.

10. Nursing Diagnosis: Anxiety Related to Loss of the Ability To Walk and/or Use of Arms, Physical Changes, Unknown Prognosis, Dependency, Inability To Deal with Chronicity of Illness and/or Grieving

Expected Patient Outcome

The patient will be able to describe his anxieties and past effective coping defenses. The patient will use effective coping strategies to manage anxiety over changes in life.

Nursing Interventions

1. The nurse will assess the patient for:
   - previous patterns of coping
   - patient's and family's current knowledge base
   - dynamics between patient and significant others
   - comments and responses to others over situation
   - signs of grieving (shock, denial, anger, depression)
2. The nurse will provide accurate information concerning prognosis, treatment, and alterations in life style.
3. Encourage expressions of grief, fear, guilt, and anger.
4. Include the significant others in problem-solving and planning.
5. Consult social supports, such as chaplains or social services.
6. Allow the patient choices and participation in his care when possible.
7. Decrease sensory stimulation when possible; provide time for resting, speak calmly and slowly, and convey a sense of empathy.
8. Be available to listen and discuss patient's fears. In discussions, talk in language that is understandable to the patient and significant others.

Knowledge Deficit

The goal of patient teaching is to increase the patient's understanding about future needs, assist the patient and family to make positive choices towards future actions, and provide positive feedback and reinforcements. There needs to be teaching in all aspects of care. Keep in mind that the patient and family cannot digest all of this information at once; incremental information should be provided. Including the family in the patient's care and teaching can strengthen the patient's support group and ease fears of dependency and abandonment. L.C. was always eager for information from the staff. He expressed many misconceptions about spinal cord injury that the staff corrected.

11. Nursing Diagnosis: Knowledge Deficit Regarding Spinal Cord Injury, Prognosis, and Alterations in Life Styles

Expected Patient Outcome

The patient's and his significant others' knowledge level will reflect adequate understanding of spinal cord injury and alterations in life styles.

Nursing Interventions

1. Be available to listen and provide information factually and honestly.
2. When teaching, initiate new information slowly and allow time for questions and for the patient or significant others to comprehend.
3. Explain reasons for procedures and symptoms the patient is experiencing.
4. Allow the patient some environmental control, involve the patient in the plan of care, and encourage the patient to assist when feasible.
5. Explore with the patient his information needs and the effects of the spinal cord injury on him and his significant others.
6. Provide written material and/or videos.

OUTCOME NARRATIVE

L.C. was treated in the intensive care unit for a total of five days. His stay was uneventful, with the exception of his aspiration pneumonia. After the halo frame was applied, he was transferred out of the intensive care unit to a neurology nursing unit with no complications and no improvement in his neurological status. L.C.'s occupational and physical therapy continued for one week until his transfer to a spinal cord rehabilitation facility.

L.C.'s ICU nurses provided him with comprehensive physical, psychological, and social support, which helped him achieve optimum health during his rehabilitation stage. This is the ultimate goal for a patient with spinal cord injury.

NOTES

1. Metcalf J. Acute phase management of persons with spinal cord injury: a nursing diagnosis perspective. *Nurs Clin North Am.* 1986;21:589–591.

2. Cerullo L, Quigley M. Management of cervical spinal cord injury. *J Emerg Nurs.* 1985;11:182–187.

3. Cardona V, Hurn P, Mason P, Scanlon-Schilps A, Veise-Berry S. *Trauma Nursing.* Philadelphia: WB Saunders Co; 1988.

4. Nikas D. Resuscitation of patients with central nervous system trauma. *Nurs Clin North Am.* 1986;21:693–704.

5. Bloch R, Basbaum M. *Management of Spinal Cord Injuries.* Baltimore: Williams & Wilkins Co; 1983.

6. Hanak M, Scott A. *Spinal Cord Injury.* New York: Springer Publishing Co; 1983.

7. Sandler H, Vernikos J. *Inactivity: Physiological Effects.* New York: Academic Press Inc. 1986.

8. Cormarr E, Cressy J, Letch M. Sleep dreams of sex among traumatic paraplegics and quadriplegics. *Sexuality and Disability.* 1983;6:25–29.

9. Janssen L, Hansebout R. Pathogenesis of spinal cord injury and newer treatments. *Spine.* 1989;14:23–32.

10. Thomas C. Wound healing with the use of providone-iodine. *Ostomy/Wound Management.* Spring 1988:30–33.

11. Romeo J. Spinal cord injury: nursing the patient toward a new life. *RN.* 1988;51:31–35.

SUGGESTED READINGS

Agee B, Herman C. Cervical logrolling on a standard hospital bed. *Am J Nurs.* 1984;84:314–318.

Allen M. Nursing care of the spinal cord patient with recurrent pressure sores. *Rehabil Nurs.* 1984;9:34–36.

Bloch R, Basbaum M. *Management of Spinal Cord Injuries.* Baltimore: Williams & Wilkins Co; 1983.

Bourdon S. Psychological impact of neurotrauma in the acute care setting. *Nurs Clin North Am.* 1986;21:629–639.

Brackett T, Condon N, Kindelan K, Bassett L. The emotional care of a person with a spinal cord injury. *JAMA.* 1984;252:793–795.

Canelas C. The nervous system risk game. *Rehabil Nurs.* 1984;9:32–33.

Cardona V, Hurn P, Mason P, Scanlon-Schilps A, Veise-Berry S. *Trauma Nursing.* Philadelphia: WB Saunders Co; 1988.

Carpenito L. *Nursing Diagnosis: Application to Clinical Practice.* 2nd ed. Philadelphia: JB Lippincott Co; 1987.

Cormarr E, Cressy J, Letch M. Sleep dreams of sex among traumatic paraplegics and quadriplegics. *Sexuality and Disability.* 1983;6:25–29.

Cerullo L, Quigley M. Management of cervical spinal cord injury. *J Emerg Nurs* 1985;11:182–187.

Elliott F. A nursing protocol for anxiety following catastrophic injury. *Rehabil Nurs.* 1983;8:18–20.

Finnegan D. Positive living or negative existence? *Nursing Times.* 1983;79:51–54.

Hanak M, Scott A. *Spinal Cord Injury.* New York: Springer Publishing Co; 1983.

Hanlon K. Maintaining sexuality after spinal cord injury. *Nursing 75.* May 1975:58–62.

Howlett M, Stevens J. Recognizing the symptoms of autonomic dysreflexia. *Can Nurs.* 1985;81:40–41.

Hudak CM, Lohr TS, Gallo BM. *Critical Care Nursing.* 3rd ed. Philadelphia: JB Lippincott Co; 1982.

Janssen L, Hansebout R. Pathogenesis of spinal cord injury and newer treatments. *Spine.* 1989;14:23–32.

Luce MJ. Medical management of spinal cord injury. *Crit Care Med.* 1985;13:126–131.

Maher AB. Dealing with head and neck injuries. *RN.* 1985;48:43–46.

McGuire A. Issues in the prevention of neurotrauma. *Nurs Clin North Am.* 1986;21:549–553.

Metcalf J. Acute phase management of persons with spinal cord injury: a nursing diagnosis perspective. *Nurs Clin North Am.* 1986;21:589–591.

Niederpruem MS. Autonomic dysreflexia. *Rehabil Nurs.* 1984;9:29–31.

Nikas D. Resuscitation of patients with central nervous system trauma. *Nurs Clin North Am.* 1986;21:693–704.

Pepper G. The person with spinal cord injury: psychological care. *Am J Nurs.* 1977; 77:1330–1335.

Richmond ST, Craig M. Family-centered care for the neurotrauma patient. *Nurs Clin North Am.* 1986;21:641–651.

Romeo J. Spinal cord injury: nursing the patient toward a new life. *RN.* 1988;51:31–35.

Ruby E. Advanced neurological and neurosurgical nursing. St. Louis: CV Mosby Co; 1984.

Rusk H, Scott A. *Spinal Cord Injury.* New York: Springer Publishing Co; 1983.

Sandler H, Vernikos J. *Inactivity: Physiological Effects.* New York: Academic Press Inc; 1986.

Segatore M, Villenueve M. Spinal cord testing: development of a screening tool. *J Neurosci Nurs.* 1988;20:30–33.

Thomas C. Wound healing halted with the use of povidone-iodine. *Ostomy/Wound Management.* Spring 1988:30–33.

Toth L. Spasticity management in spinal cord injury. *Rehabil Nurs.* 1983;8:14–17.

Weinberg JS. Human sexuality and spinal cord injury. *Symposium on Sexuality and Nursing Practice.* 1982;17:407–419.

White EJ. Appraising the need for altered sexuality information. *Rehabil Nurs.* 1986;11:6–9.

Chapter 7

Glioblastoma Multiforme

Maureen A. Mielcarek

INTRODUCTION

Cancer is a general term that describes a disorder that affects the normal patterns of growth and function of cells. It is universal in that it can affect any of the body's cells and can disrupt single or multiple organ systems. The disorder is carried on through succeeding generations of cells causing a disruption in the normal replication of deoxyribonucleic acid (DNA). The rate of proliferation varies widely among the various types of cancer growths.

The diagnosis of cancer carries with it ominous connotations for those afflicted with this disease. It is the second leading cause of death in the United States, second only to cardiovascular disease in adults and trauma in children. To quantify this picture, cancer causes more than 350,000 deaths annually in the United States.[1]

Two percent of these deaths occur from cerebral tumors. In 1986, according to the American Cancer Society, 10,900 cases of central nervous system (CNS) tumors were diagnosed and 8,500 deaths resulted from brain tumors in this country. An additional 67,000 patients have primary tumors in other parts of the body that metastasize to the brain.[2]

Cerebral tumors vary according to their histologic characteristics, rate of growth, and location. Improvement in the early diagnosis, care, and treatment of patients with cerebral neoplasms has positively affected the prognosis of many of these patients.

Cerebral tumors have two distinct peaks of incidence in patients—from 5 to 10 years of age and from 45 to 70. In children, tumors have a propensity for infratentorial locations (brain stem, pons, medulla, cerebellum, and upper spinal cord), while in adults they are more common at supratentorial sites (cerebral hemispheres, sellar, pineal, and upper brain stem regions). Pedi-

145

atric tumors also have a tendency to be better differentiated (having functional cells) than adult tumors.

Causes for the spontaneous eruption of cerebral neoplasms are unknown. There is some evidence that correlates immunosuppression with CNS tumors. A transplant patient is 350 times more at risk for developing a central nervous system lymphoma than the general population.[3] The mechanism for this phenomenon is not understood. There is also an increased risk for patients that have contracted the Epstein-Barr virus. This gives rise to a possible viral implication in the development of brain tumors. Other areas of possible catalysts are physical and chemical carcinogens, genetic predisposition, high protein and/or fat diets, radiation, and trauma. Endocrine influences may also have an effect since the incidence of CNS tumors decreases in both males and females after age-related reductions of sexual hormones.[3] To date, there is no concrete evidence of a direct cause-and-effect relationship between these factors and the development of cerebral neoplasms.

TYPES OF CEREBRAL TUMORS

Gliomas

Gliomas are a broad category of brain tumors that arise from neuroectodermal origins and involve neuroglia, the cells that form the supporting structure of the central nervous system. Over 95% of gliomas in adults are unifocal.[4] As they proliferate, they either invade or displace adjacent brain tissue. Approximately 40% to 60% of intracranial tumors are gliomas.

This category is further subdivided according to the particular cells of the neuroglia that are involved. There are three primary cell types: astrocytes, oligodendroglia, and ependymal.

Astrocytomas

Astrocytes make up the majority of brain tissue cells and function to support the neurons, although the specific relationship is unclear. Tumors arising from these cells are termed astrocytomas and they range from benign to highly malignant. Astrocytomas are the second most common gliomas, comprising 30% of this category. They are commonly located in the white matter of the cerebral hemispheres, but they can originate in any area of the central nervous system. Generally astrocytomas are confined to one hemisphere.

The malignancy of tumors is graded from I to IV depending on the degree of anaplasia (lack of differentiation) present. Astrocytomas grades I and II are considered benign. They comprise 6% to 10% of all CNS tumors. These are usually well encapsulated and if located in a surgically resectable area, the prognosis is good. They can, however, advance to a higher grade over time. Median survival length for patients with a subtotal resection or recurrent tumors of this type is four to five years.

Astrocytomas grades III and IV are considered highly malignant. They are also termed anaplastic astrocytomas. An astrocytoma is considered anaplastic if it displays one or more of the following features: mitosis, vascular endothelial proliferation, cellular or nuclear pleomorphism (the assumption of diverse forms), or secondary growth structures.

An anaplastic astrocytoma is termed a glioblastoma if it contains areas of necrosis within the tumor. The incidence of glioblastoma before age 30 is rare. Fifty-six percent of glioblastomas occur in males, and the frontal lobes are the areas most often involved. A grade IV glioblastoma with marked anaplasia that grows across myelinated white matter, such as the corpus callosum, is known as a glioblastoma multiforme. It has a characteristic butterfly appearance due to this migration across the corpus callosum and proliferation bilaterally into the cerebral hemispheres. Glioblastoma multiforme comprises 25% of all adult intracranial tumors. There is a 2:1 incidence in males over females. Median survival length for a glioblastoma multiforme patient with treatment is approximately one year.

Oligodendrogliomas

Oligodendroglia cells are satellite cells involved in the myelination process of neurons in the central nervous system. Tumors arising from these cells are slow-growing neoplasms that develop in women more often than in men, and they generally grow throughout the cerebral hemispheres, usually in the frontal or parietal lobes in adults or in the thalamus of children. They present with a densely calcified, well-circumscribed subcortical mass. Patients with these neoplasms often have an extended history of seizures. Median survival length for these patients with treatment is approximately five years.

Ependymomas

Ependymal cells line the ventricles and central canal of the CNS. They are ciliated cells that function to move cerebral spinal fluid (CSF). Tumors arising from these cells are deeply situated and though not encapsulated, are well demarcated from the surrounding tissue. Ependymomas are more common in children then in adults and although they make up the majority of spinal cord and intermedullary neoplasms, they are most often found in the third and fourth ventricles. Common presenting symptoms are related to increased intracranial pressure (ICP) secondary to obstruction of cerebral spinal fluid. They can invade the ventricle floor and involve the cranial nerve nuclei. If this happens, total resection is impossible. Median survival length for these patients is approximately five years without a total resection.

Medulloblastomas

The medulloblastoma is thought to arise from mature neurons of the cerebellum. It is highly malignant, fast growing, not encapsulated, and can metastasize by way of CSF to the subarachnoid space. Secondary tumors are often found in the cervical or lumbar spinal areas. Their location and rapid proliferation cause them to occlude the fourth ventricle and infiltrate brain stem tissues. Medulloblastomas are most often found in children, with a higher incidence in males.

Meningiomas

The meninges are the three membranes lining the brain and spinal cord, the dura mater, the arachnoid, and the pia mater. Meningiomas arise from these membranes. They are the most common nonglioma cerebral tumor, accounting for 15% of all intracranial neoplasms. There is a higher incidence of meningiomas in women, and they tend to develop after the age of 50. Meningiomas primarily arise where arachnoid villi penetrate the dura mater. These tumors are slow growing, highly vascular, well circumscribed, often encapsulated, and considered benign. Total resection is usually possible unless the tumor is situated in an area where removal would jeopardize a vital blood vessel. Meningiomas can become malignant. Tumors of this type can invade adjacent bone and compress brain tissue. Without treatment, the median survival length is approximately one to two years.

Craniopharyngiomas

Craniopharyngiomas are located in the suprasellar regions of the brain and can extend to involve hypothalamic structures. They develop primarily in children and present as thin-walled cysts that produce a mucous fluid containing cholesterol that is very irritating to the CNS tissue. These tumors are considered histologically benign, but they can also be malignant.

Pituitary Tumors

Pituitary tumors account for 7% to 10% of all primary intracranial neoplasms. These growths are located in the intrasellar area but can extend beyond the sellar margins. They are usually slow growing, well encapsulated, and classified as either nonfunctional or hormonally active. Three types of pituitary cells give rise to these tumors: chromophobe, eosinophil, and basophil.[4]

Chromophobe adenomas tend to be nonfunctional growths. Of the three types of pituitary tumors, these growths are invasive and have a propensity to invade the temporal lobe of the brain. Presenting symptoms are usually associated with increased ICP and compression of the optic chasm. Although these tumors do not secrete hormones, they can suppress the pituitary gland and produce symptoms of hypopituitarism.

Eosinophilic adenomas usually produce growth hormone. These tumors have a tendency to remain small and noninvasive. The excess production of growth hormone results in symptoms of giantism or acromegaly.

Basophilic adenomas secret adrenocorticotropic hormone (ACTH) and stimulate excessive release of cortisol from the adrenal glands. The result of this imbalance is the clinical presentation of protein wasting, sodium and water retention, potassium reduction, and an impaired immune response to infections. This clinical condition is known as Cushing's syndrome.

Schwannomas

The schwannomas represent 10% of all intracranial tumors. The usual age of onset is between 30 and 60 years of age. These tumors arise from the Schwann's sheath surrounding the neurons and grow in association with several cranial nerves, most often the VIII cranial nerve (acoustic schwannomas). They are generally slow growing, well encapsulated, and benign, but peripheral nerve schwannomas can be malignant. The prognosis for patients with schwannomas is excellent for a cure by total resection; however, the larger the tumor the higher the risk of mortality.

Hemangiomas

Hemangiomas develop from embryonic vascular tissue and become benign neoplastic growths presenting with closely packed, abnormally dilated blood vessels. Hemangioblastoma is a type of hemangioma that presents with a peculiar mixture of capillaries and large lipid-laden stromal cells. Hemangiomas are found most often in the cerebrum or cerebellum, but they can be found anywhere in the central nervous system. They grow slowly, but even moderate growth or slight hemorrhage from these vessels can be dangerous in intracranial or spinal locations.

Primary Lymphomas

The recent increased incidence of primary lymphomas has been related to an increase in immunosuppression therapy (for transplant surgery) and to the spread of acquired immunodeficiency syndrome (AIDS). There has also been a correlation with the contraction of Epstein-Barr virus. These tumors contain intracellular or surface immunoglobulin. They are highly malignant and locally invasive, usually at cortical sites, and metastasize by subarachnoid seeding.

Metastatic Tumors

Tumors can metastasize to the central nervous system from any part of the body; however, the most common primary metastatic tumors are breast and lung carcinomas. Numerous CNS lesions often develop from these primary tumors. These metastatic lesions generally involve the cortical lobes, and most frequently the frontal lobes. The cerebellar region is less frequently involved, and the brain stem is the area least likely to be contaminated.

* * * * *

CASE STUDY

The following case study will provide a review of the diagnosis, pathology, and treatment of one type of brain tumor, glioblastoma multiforme.

A.D., a 54-year-old, well-developed, well-nourished white male, presented with a two-week history of increasing tingling, numbness, and weakness of his left upper extremity. He came to the hospital after suffering focal motor seizures of his left upper extremity and left facial muscles and a progressively worsening bilateral frontal headache over the previous four days. Past medical history was unremarkable. He was admitted to the neurology unit for a workup.

On neurologic exam, A.D. was alert and orientated times four. His pupils were equal and reactive to light on direct and consensual reflex stimulation. He displayed left facial weakness and left upper extremity weakness of 3/5 with decreased sensation. Speech was coherent and fluent; however, some dysarthria related to left-sided weakness was noted. His lower extremities moved strongly and purposefully, with the right lower extremity at 5/5 and the left at 4/5. His gait was slow and unsteady.

Cognitive testing revealed a deficit in calculation ability and emotional lability. See Tables 7-1 and 7-2 for additional details of examination.

In conversation with the patient's wife, it was learned that A.D. was experiencing significant personal stressors over the past month that included a move

Table 7-1 Case Study Neurologic Assessment

Category	Findings
General Appearance	Well groomed Anxious Left-sided weakness
Level of Consciousness	Orientated to person, place, time, and purpose
ICP	13 to 18
Short-term Memory	7/7 digits forward 6/7 digits backward
Calculations	273 + 135 = 308 (408) 741 − 420 = 520 (321) 11 × 33 = 483 (363)
Abstract Reasoning	A stitch in time saves nine = Waiting can be costly
Emotional Status	Affect—labile
Thought Content	Recognizes bell and finger snap Answers questions appropriately Recognizes body parts Recognizes right and left sides Identifies pen, scissors, cup Can read from a paper Can recite days of week Can write name and address
Sensory	Right side intact Left side presents with a loss of two-point discrimination Decreased ability to distinguish sharp from blunt touch at left upper extremity Complains of tingling and numbness at left upper and lower extremities Temperature discrimination intact bilaterally
Reflex Status	Right side intact Diminished left brachial and left patellar reflex Babinski reflex negative bilaterally
Cranial Nerves VII— XI—	All intact except for: Left-sided facial weakness Left shoulder shrug weakness
Motor	Left upper and lower extremity weakness
Gait	Unsteady with marked left-sided drooping

Table 7-2 General Assessment

Category	Findings
Cardiovascular	Pulses 3/4
	Capillary refill < 3 seconds
	Skin warm, dry, and pink
	Turgor good
	Heart tones regular rate/rhythm
	EKG monitor with NSR
	A—line intact
	IV—right forearm—NS, intact at 30 cc/h
	No edema noted
Respiratory	Respirations 16/min symmetrical and unlabored
	MA—1 ventilator at:
	TV 800, Fio$_2$ 40%, PEEP 5,
	rate 10/min IMV
	Breath sounds clear bilaterally
	Suctioned for moderate tan mucus
	Cough and gag present
	ABGs WNL
Gastrointestinal	Abdomen soft, non-tender
	Bowel sounds present
	NPO

across the country and starting a new job. According to family members, A.D. had been demonstrating changes in personality, especially a decrease in social inhibition. These changes had been attributed to the stress of the new environment and new job.

A computerized tomography (CT) scan was performed, which showed a bilateral frontal mass in the butterfly pattern that is typical of a glioblastoma multiforme. A second lesion was also detected in his right parietal lobe at the temporal lobe junction. A neurosurgical consult was called. A biopsy procedure was scheduled to be completed within the following two days.

Before the scheduled biopsy, the patient became lethargic and began to develop marked left-sided weakness. His attention span had decreased markedly. His biopsy was placed on an on-call urgent basis and was performed later that same day.

The surgical procedure, a craniotomy through the right superior parietal region, included both biopsy and debulking of the tumor mass. Total resection was impossible because of the size and location of the growth (involving bilateral hemispheres). This type of internal decompression or subtotal removal is performed in order to gain space for future tumor expansion.[3]

The patient was in the neurosurgical intensive care unit for two days after the craniotomy. Except for left facial droop and upper left extremity weakness, A.D.'s neurological deficits were relieved by the debulking.

He was then transferred to the neurosurgical floor for further observation and discharge planning. He was discharged to home later. Radiation therapy was scheduled to begin in two weeks.

* * * * *

PATHOLOGY

Benign tumors are usually slow growing, encapsulated or well demarcated from surrounding tissues, and, based on location, usually amenable to surgical resection. Malignant tumors of the central nervous system can grow by extending to and implanting beneath the leptomeninges (arachnoid and pia mater layers of the meninges) or the ependyma. This can occur by any of the following: formatting perineuronal and perivascular aggregates of tumor cells beyond the main tumor mass, seeding the cerebral spinal fluid and implanting areas not adjacent to the primary mass, contact with the circulatory system, and invasion of local adjacent tissues. CNS tumors can be very invasive of local adjacent tissue, but rarely metastasize outside of the CNS. There is no lymphatic system in the CNS.

Glial tumors grow by infiltrating the surrounding brain tissue as they extend. Glioblastoma multiforme is notable for its ability to migrate along myelinated structures of the brain to invade at sites distal to the primary mass. This migration allows the tumors to invade bilateral hemispheres of the brain and present with the butterfly-shaped mass.[2]

Tumors are surrounded by a stroma, a growth of new capillaries. The catalyst for this growth is an angiogenesis factor produced by the tumor that acts on surrounding capillary endothelium to induce new growth.[5]

Malignant gliomas also produce a vascular permeability factor that increases the vascular permeability of the peritumoral region.[5] This increased permeability results in the accumulation of edema around the tumor mass. Physiologically, it is thought that this seepage allows plasma to accumulate into extracellular spaces and into the areas between the layers of the myelin sheath. This results in changes in the potential of the cell membranes and can impair cellular function in the affected areas.

Highly anaplastic tumors, such as the glioblastoma multiforme, grow so rapidly that increased demands placed on the blood flow and oxygen supply of the regional tissues render them insufficient to sustain the growing tumor, and necrosis develops within the tumor.

Gliomas produce fibronectin, an adhesive cell-surface glycoprotein that mediates cellular adhesive interactions, forms part of the peritumoral matrix, and is interrelated with the blood-clotting mechanisms of the body. Other byproducts of these tumors include plasmin inhibitors and plasminogen activators. Together these factors are responsible for blood-clotting disturbances, such as hemorrhage or thrombophlebitis.[5]

Malignant glial tumors can also produce epidermal growth factor, glial growth factor, and fibroblast growth factor.[5]

In general, cerebral tumors affect the brain by compression, invasion, and infiltration. Common pathophysiological findings are cerebral edema, increased ICP, focal neurologic deficits, seizure activity, hydrocephalus related to obstruction of CSF flow, and changes in normal pituitary function.

The most common cause of death from brain tumors is a herniation syndrome resulting from the effects of increased mass in the rigid closed cerebral system.[3] Herniation usually results when the cerebellar tonsils or the temporal lobe uncus is forced against immovable bony structures. The outcome of herniation is often cerebral death. Space-occupying cerebral hemisphere lesions produce medial temporal lobe herniation as a result of the medial displacement of the uncus of the temporal lobe and compression of the brain stem. Posterior fossa lesions can compress the lower brain stem or herniate the cerebellar tonsils.

Cerebral lesions also demonstrate location-specific symptoms. Neural pathways throughout the brain are very specialized in their functions. Interference at any specific location will interrupt the function of the affected neural pathways (see Table 7-3).

The glioblastoma multiforme is thought to arise either spontaneously as a malignant tumor or resulting from changes in benign gliomas.[6] These tumors grow rapidly because of decreased adhesiveness, increased motility, and the lack of contact inhibition seen in normal cells.[5] Decreased adhesiveness is related to changes in the cancer cell membrane that inhibit the development of anchors that hold normal cells together. The membrane is also more negatively charged than normal cells, and this leads to a natural repulsion of adjacent cells.[5] The result of these changes is the natural shedding of cells into secretions, such as CSF, also known as seeding.

Motility is a natural ability of embryonic cells that is lost or inhibited in most mature cells. In cancer cells, this ability is no longer controlled.[5]

Contact inhibition is the natural tendency for cells to stop migrating when they touch other cells. In cancer cells, this inhibition is lost.[5]

In glioblastoma multiforme tumors, angiogenesis and necrosis are widespread. The cellular components very widely in these tumors, with only a small portion of cells being differentiated. They occur throughout the hemispheres, including the thalamus and basal ganglia, but are primarily found in the anterior portions of the cerebral cortex. They are especially noted for their ability to migrate along white matter pathways, such as the corpus callosum and the internal capsule. They grow very rapidly, invade surrounding tissue, and present with peritumoral edema.

Table 7-3 Symptoms according to Location

Location	Symptom
Frontal Lobe	Behavioral changes Inability to concentrate Emotional lability Decreased association ability Decreased intellectual ability Dysfunctional short-term memory
With dominant lobe	Decreased social inhibition Aphasia (expression) Slow movement Hemiparesis Hemiplegia
Temporal Lobe	Motor and/or sensory deficits of contralateral upper quadrant Receptive aphasia Psychomotor seizures Auras, auditory and/or visual Poor judgment Irritability Regressive behavior
Parietal Lobe	Paresthesia Decreased two-point discrimination Astereognosis Anosognosia Decreased right/left discrimination Agraphia Acalculia
Occipital Lobe	Focal or generalized seizures Visual hallucinations Contralateral homonymous hemianopsia
Fourth Ventricle	Headache Nausea/vomiting Nuchal rigidity Gag/swallow dysfunction Cardiorespiratory dysfunction (related to brain stem compression)
Pituitary	Hormonal dysfunctions Visual deficits Headache
Hypothalamus	Fluid and appetite imbalances Metabolism disturbances Changes in sleep patterns Temperature regulation problems

continues

Table 7-3 continued

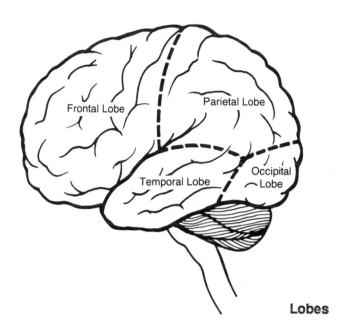

Lobes

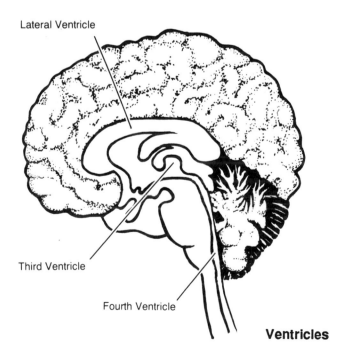

Ventricles

Table 7-3 continued

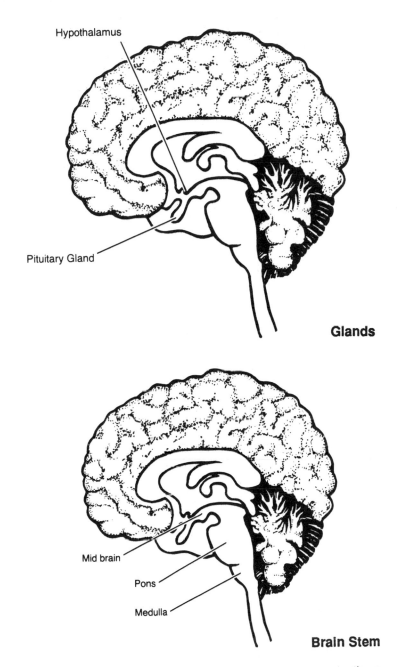

Hypothalamus

Pituitary Gland

Glands

Mid brain

Pons

Medulla

Brain Stem

continues

Table 7-3 continued

Cerebellum	Ataxia
	Decreased coordination
	Headache
	Nausea/vomiting
	Nuchal rigidity
Midbrain	Deafness
	Ptosis
	Decreased light reflex
Brain Stem	Unsteady gait/imbalance
	Dysphagia
	Vomiting
	Sensory disturbances

Source: Reprinted from *The Clinical Practice of Neurological and Neurosurgical Nursing,* ed 2 (pp 472–473) by J V Hickey with permission of J B Lippincott Company, © 1986.

Despite the rapid growth, the mitotic index of the glioblastoma is surprisingly low. Kinetic studies have shown that over 50% of the tumor cell population is in G0 phase at any one time.[3] This means that over half of the tumor is not in active division at the same time, which makes it difficult for radiation therapy and chemotherapy to disrupt the cell cycle and be effective against these tumors.

It is postulated that the lack of response of the glioblastomas to the body's immune system is related to a possible suppressor factor produced by the tumor, the reduction of lymphocytes and helper cells, and the production of the glycoprotein coat that protects the tumor mass.[3]

DIAGNOSTICS

Modern diagnostic techniques have made the discovery, location, and classification of cerebral neoplasms more of an exact science than in the past. Prior to modern imaging techniques, diagnosis of cerebral neoplasms was based on the patient's history and neurologic examination to detect the presence of a cerebral lesion, and then an exploratory craniotomy to identify the exact problem and possibly resect a growth once it was found. CT scans and magnetic resonance imaging (MRI) have made it possible for neurosurgeons to visualize these growths before risking a surgical procedure. Today, exploratory intracranial surgery no longer exists. The patient in the case study presented with a two-week history of progressive neurologic dysfunction in his left upper quadrant. Neurologic testing identified cognitive and emotional disturbances.

A thorough history and physical will identify the first indications of a possible tumor. The patient may present with a history of progressive neurological deficits. A complete neurologic examination will supply the physician with the information he or she needs to localize areas for further investigation. Prior to CT scan and MRI visualization abilities, the neurologic examination was the primary tool used by the neurologist and neurosurgeon in locating abnormal growths. Now the CT scan is the first diagnostic test ordered after the history and physical indicate the possible presence of a cerebral lesion. This was the procedure followed in our case study. The CT scan, used without contrast, detected the butterfly lesion indicative of a glioblastoma multiforme as well as the second lesion in the parietal lobe (see Figure 7-1).

Imaging Techniques

Imaging techniques confirm intracranial structure abnormalities, determine probable nature and degree of malignancy of detected growths, assess the extent and localization of growths related to critical structures, predict internal structure and probable consistency of detected growths, and evaluate response to treatment. Limitations of these techniques are related to the availability of the equipment and cost.

Computerized Tomography Scans

The CT scan detects density changes in the cerebral tissues. It can distinguish between CSF, blood, edema, tumors, and normal tissue. It is usually the first test ordered after the history and physical indicate a possible cerebral lesion. Limitations of the CT scan are that it does not visualize the actual tumor. Tumors with densities that are similar to that of surrounding tissues may not be detected. Tumors with diffuse infiltration are not easily identified.[2]

Magnetic Resonance Imaging

The MRI provides a high level of gray to white matter contrast and provides increased anatomical detail. There is also an absence of bone artifact to interfere with the visualization of lesions. Limitations of this pro-

A

B

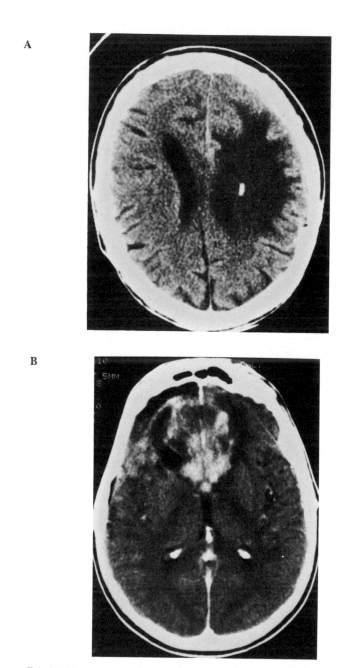

Figure 7-1 Glioblastoma. **A,** butterfly formation across the corpus collosum; **B,** unilateral advancement. *Source*: Courtesy of Kenneth Black, M.D., UCLA Medical Center, Los Angeles, CA.

cedure are the availability of equipment, cost of the procedure, and the fact that the patient must remain immobile for 5 to 20 minutes.

Positron Emission Tomography

The positron emission tomography (PET) scan depicts the metabolic activity of the cerebral tissue. Neoplastic tissues have a higher metabolic rate than normal tissue.

X-ray Films

Skull films are still used to detect calcification seen in some slow growth tumors. They can also detect bone invasion or growths around the sphenoid wing or supraorbital meningiomas, erosion of the sella, and abnormal osteoblastic activity. Chest x-rays and/or other films are also ordered to rule out primary lesions in other areas of the body.

Other Tests

Lumbar puncture. The lumbar puncture is used to detect CSF seeding. It is not performed as routinely as in the past. It is never performed when there is suspected increased ICP.

Electroencephalogram. This procedure records the electrical activity in the brain. It is used primarily when seizure activity is present.

Angiography. This procedure defines the circulatory system of the cerebral tissue and locates vascular landmarks. It is an important tool when tumor resection has a questionable risk due to its location in relation to major blood vessels.

MEDICAL TREATMENT

Preoperative Care

Preoperative medical therapeutics are concerned with controlling increased intracranial pressure (ICP). Steroids are the drugs of choice to reduce peritumoral edema. Gastrointestinal disturbances resulting from steroid treatment are controlled with medication such as an antacid. Acute increases in ICP are medically controlled with osmotic diuretics.

Some physicians prefer to start any patient with an intracranial tumor on anticonvulsants, such as phenytoin, as a prophylactic measure. The justification for this preventive measure is the risk of cerebral herniation associated with seizure activity.[3]

Surgery

In the past, mortality from surgical procedures was associated primarily with complications of infection or increased intracranial pressure. The advent of antibiotics has greatly reduced the risk of mortality related to infections. The identification and presurgical treatment of increased intracranial pressure have further reduced the risk of surgical mortality to less than 1%. Early administration of steroids to reduce peritumoral edema, especially of metastatic tumors such as the glioblastoma, has all but eliminated the risk of cerebral herniation associated with brain surgery in the past.[7] If cerebral spinal fluid obstruction is diagnosed, pressure is relieved by shunting done prior to resective surgery. Acute increased ICP is brought under control with the use of an osmotic diuretic.

In this case study, the glioblastoma multiforme was identified by CT scan imaging. A biopsy was scheduled to confirm the diagnosis histologically and debulking was performed to reduce the mass effect of the tumor and reduce the pressure-related neurological deficits. The highly metastatic nature of this high grade astrocytoma and the bihemispheral location of the primary lesion prevented this patient from being a candidate for total resection of his tumor. In cases of severely advanced growths of this type, a conservative neurosurgeon may consider this condition as inoperable. When cure is not an option, then the quality versus the quantity of life is the criterion that guides the physician's decision.

There are four basic types of surgical procedures performed for cerebral tumors. The first procedure is biopsy of the tumor tissue to confirm a histologic diagnosis. The other three types of surgery depend on the type, stage, and location of the tumor. Optimal conditions, such as an encapsulated, benign tumor that is not located adjacent to vital structures, would call for total tumor removal. Another type of surgery is called a lobectomy (or partial lobectomy), and as the name implies, all or a portion of a cerebral lobe is removed. The feasibility of this type of procedure depends on the location under consideration.

A unilateral frontal lobectomy will result in transient intellectual deficits. These temporary dysfunctions are often considered acceptable when balanced against death and dysfunction caused by an enlarging tumor. Bilateral frontal lobectomies, on the other hand, result in irreversible behavior and association losses.

A unilateral occipital lobectomy will result in hemianoptic loss, while a bilateral occipital lobectomy results in a state of total blindness.

A unilateral anterior temporal lobectomy can result in minimal deficits, while a bilateral will result in marked behavioral and memory problems, as well as expressive and receptive aphasia. Posterior temporal lobectomies are not surgically accessible areas because of their location in relation to vital cerebral structures, such as the hippocampal formation and dentate gyrus.

Lobectomy of the dominant parietal lobe (left side in right-handed patients) produces sensory and motor deficits, while in the nondominant parietal lobe (right side) deficits in spatial and abstract concepts will result.

The fourth and last type of surgical procedure discussed in this review is a partial resection, also known as decompression or debulking of the tumor. This is a palliative surgical procedure used to decrease the intracranial pressure and relieve the resulting neurological deficits from tumors that cannot be resected totally.[3] A complication of debulking is that metastatic tumor deposits appear to be stimulated to grow more rapidly once the primary tumor bulk is removed. Current theory suggests that either the primary tumor bulk has an inhibitory effect on the metastatic foci or that the surgery itself has a stimulating effect on these foci.[8]

There have been attempts at successive debulking of regrowth with a resulting increase in survival length and quality of life for these patients. The criteria for this type of palliative surgical approach concern the neurological deficits observed and not the extensive infiltration or destruction of brain tissue itself.[9]

Radiation Therapy

Radiation therapy is used in the treatment of 50% to 65% of all cancer patients. The primary goal is the eradication of the abnormal cancer cells. One advantage to the use of radiation is the ability to concentrate this therapy in localized areas. Delivery of radiation is not dependent on blood supply or diffusion through tissues. It is not restricted because of the tumor location in relation to vital structures, vessels, or bone. Sensitivity to radiation therapy increases over time; however, tolerance doses are volume dependent: the greater the dosage volume the lower the tolerance level.

The disadvantages of radiation therapy include the limited dose tolerated by normal tissues. Even with carefully controlled exposure, radiation necrosis of normal tissue can occur. Complications of radiation therapy may appear from several months to years after treatment. These include lesions with necrosis, volume loss, or glial cell reactions that may present similarly to a tumor. In addition, there is the potential for demyelination of cerebral white matter, vasculopathies, and neuronal changes that appear to increase over time.[10]

The survival length for patients treated with radiation therapy postoperatively has been increased, with the degree of success dependent on the type and grade of tumor being treated.

For high grade gliomas, such as the glioblastoma multiforme in this case study, radiation fields must encompass the whole brain. The doses must be significant, 4500 to 6000 rads, and given over an extended period of six to seven weeks.

Brachytherapy involves the implantation of up to four catheters, each containing one to five radionuclide sources, followed by a second debulking. The criteria for brachytherapy are that the tumor be well defined on CT imaging, not highly infiltrative, and peripherally located.[11]

Chemotherapy

Chemotherapy is another weapon in the arsenal to fight cancer. Generally, chemotherapeutic agents work by disrupting the cell during some stage of reproduction. The prolific nature of cancer cells makes them sensitive to these pharmaceutical agents. The major disadvantage is that the chemotherapeutic agents are not specific to tumor cells and disrupt normal cell reproduction and growth. Cells with high reproductive activity include bone marrow, hair follicles, and intestinal epithelium. The resulting side effects—alopecia, nausea and vomiting, anorexia, diarrhea, and a compromised immune system—require that a balance between quantity and quality of life be considered when evaluating the benefits and complications of chemotherapy.

The blood-brain barrier presents a problem for the administration of chemotherapeutic agents. This barrier prevents most of the common systemic drugs from being useful in the treatment of cerebral neoplasms. Even the increased permeability of the peritumoral capillaries does not permit a therapeutic dose to reach the tumor site.

As with the other treatment modalities, the benefits to be expected depend on the histology, grade, and location of the tumor being treated. Recent advances have made regional as opposed to systemic chemotherapy available for cerebral tumor patients. The advantage of this type of administration is the increased effectiveness at the tumor site and the decreased development of systemic side effects.

Intrathecal administration is carried out by the physician and is accomplished by injecting the drug into the CSF in the spinal canal by way of a lumbar puncture at L4 to L5. A proportionate volume of CSF is removed at the same time. This method eliminates the problem of crossing the blood-brain barrier. The fact that distribution to the cerebral tissue is not guaranteed and that there is a risk of infection are the major disadvantages of this method.

The intraventricular method of administration uses a reservoir, such as the Ommaya reservoir, surgically implanted into the lateral ventricle. This mushroom-shaped device is connected to the pericranium by a catheter that is sutured into place. Medications can be administered into the ventricle reservoir by infusion into the catheter. The advantages of this method are the ease of administration, better distribution to the cerebral tissue, and decreased drug dosages, resulting in a decrease of systemic side effects. It is also available for other types of medication, such as morphine for pain control. The two major disadvantages are the risk of infection and the potential for a technical malfunction or displacement of the reservoir.

The primary drugs used in the treatment of brain tumors are the alkylating agents (nitrosoureas), carmustine (BCNU), lomustine (CCNU), and procarbazine hydrochloride (Matulane).

BCNU and CCNU are effective because they are highly lipid soluble, nonionized, and molecularly small. They have the ability to cross the blood-brain barrier. Their major side effect is bone marrow depression, but they also can cause dose-related nausea and vomiting, hepatic toxicity, nephrotoxicity, pulmonary infiltration, and alopecia.

Matulane can also cause bone marrow depression, confusion, depression and hallucinations, nystagmus, photophobia, diarrhea, and alopecia.

In this case study, chemotherapy was not prescribed. As stated earlier, the glioblastoma multiforme has a relatively low mitotic index. Since more than half of the tumor is not reproducing at any one time, it is less sensitive to chemotherapeutic drugs. To date, chemotherapy has not increased the survival length of these patients or increased the time between debulking and recurrence of symptoms.

Research

Other methods of treatment are currently being studied. These include hyperthermia to the tumor mass, laboratory enhanced lymphocytes injected into the tumor, new chemotherapeutic agents, and hyperbaric enhanced radiation therapy. Research into the treatment of cerebral neoplasms, especially the lethal glioblastoma multiforme, is a dynamic area of study.

NURSING INTERVENTIONS

Nursing interventions begin with a thorough history, physical, and neurologic assessment. By establishing a baseline, one can observe, document, and report changes that may indicate increased or changing neurological deficits.

Preoperatively, observation and assessment should be focused on monitoring the tumor's effect on the patient. Changes in pupillary reaction, level of consciousness, and motor functioning can alert the nurse to increasing ICP. When increased ICP is evident, nursing interventions such as proper positioning, hyperventilation, and osmotic diuretics can avert serious consequences for the patient.

Monitoring side effects of medication, such as gastrointestinal bleeding or nausea and vomiting from steroid administration, can avoid unnecessary complications resulting from medical therapeutics. Precautionary measures to prevent injury from motor or sensory deficits and/or seizures should be implemented.

Postoperative monitoring for complications from surgery, such as increased ICP and infection, are primary nursing concerns. The surgical dressing should be assessed for CSF loss or excessive drainage.

While in intensive care, A.D. was on a Bear II ventilator for 24 hours. His breath sounds were clear bilaterally and he was successfully weaned by post-op day two. His ICP remained between 15 and 18 and the ICP fiberoptic catheter was removed on day two. Vital signs remained stable: his blood pressure was at approximately 130/85, respirations were at 16 and unlabored, and he remained afebrile. Fluid intake was restricted to 1,500 cc/day and urine output was adequate. A.D. had a good cough and was encouraged to breathe deeply and turn often. He complained of a headache and was medicated with Tylenol, 650 mg every four hours.

A.D. focused mainly on increasing the function of his left upper extremity. He was encouraged by his nurses to exercise to his optimal ability. His family was very concerned about his dismal prognosis and required emotional support from the nurses.

Throughout the patient's hospitalization, psychosocial support for the patient and his or her significant others is of utmost importance. As mentioned earlier, the diagnosis of a brain tumor is devastating to the patient and the family. As in this case study, the prognosis often is poor. Entering a therapeutic helping relationship with the patient and those he or she loves can help to preserve the quality of the patient's life.

NURSING CARE PLAN

Increased Intracranial Pressure

As an intracranial tumor expands, the limits of the rigid cranial vault will eventually be unable to accommodate the increased volume. When this period of decompensation is reached, symptoms will emerge. Without treatment, the pressure inside the cranial vault will continue until herniation occurs. The vital centers of the brain then become depressed and death may ensue.[2]

1. Nursing Diagnosis: Potential Alteration in Cerebral Tissue Perfusion Related to Increased Intracranial Pressure Secondary to Mass Effect of a Glioblastoma Multiforme Tumor

Expected Patient Outcome

The patient will maintain an adequate cerebral perfusion pressure as evidenced by:

1. no further deterioration of neurological status
2. maintenance of ICP pressure readings between 0 and 15 mm Hg
3. maintenance of CPP pressure between 70 and 100 mm Hg

Nursing Interventions

1. Monitor and document neurologic status every one to two hours.
2. Monitor and record ICP/CPP every one to two hours.
3. Keep head of bed elevated at 30 degrees at all times.
4. Maintain Pco_2 between 25 and 35 mm Hg.
5. Maintain O_2 saturation $>95\%$.
6. Hyperventilate for ICP >20 mm Hg.
7. Position patient to prevent neck flexion, rotation, extension, or hip flexion.
8. Administer steroids as ordered.
9. Prevent Valsalva maneuvers.
10. Maintain a quiet restful environment.
11. Organize nursing care to allow for undisturbed periods of rest.

Infection

Any compromise of integumentary integrity, such as that experienced with surgical procedures, increases the patient's risk of developing an infection. For the patient undergoing a craniotomy for a cerebral neoplasm, the risk of developing an infection is further increased because of the administration of steroids. These pharmacological agents decrease the body's ability to overcome invasive pathogens. In addition, access to cerebral spinal fluid, which contains a high (60%) concentration of glucose and is an excellent medium for bacterial growth, becomes a potential via the surgical site and ICP monitor.

2. Nursing Diagnosis: Potential for Infection Related to Surgical Procedure and Invasive Therapies Secondary to Cerebral Tumor

Expected Patient Outcome

The patient will not develop an infection as noted by chart records indicating:

1. afebrile state
2. surgical site clean and free of purulant drainage
3. all invasive catheter sites normal
4. negative wound and/or blood cultures, if performed

Nursing Interventions

1. Monitor and record vital signs every two hours.
2. Use sterile technique when changing dressing.
3. Assess surgical site for inflammation or drainage every day or when dressing change is performed.
4. Assess IV sites for signs of inflammation or infiltration.
5. Change IV fluids every 24 hours.
6. Change IV tubing every 48 hours.
7. Change IV site every 72 hours.
8. Administer antibiotics as ordered.

Potential for Injury

About 30% of adults with brain tumors develop seizure activity.[12] The hyperactivity of these neuronal cells is related to cerebral edema and alterations in the normal electrical potential of the cell. This hyperactivity produces paroxysmal electrical discharges (seizures) that may be either localized or general. Muscle weakness as well as decreased sensory discrimination can result in an unsteady gait and/or a lack of balance.

3. Nursing Diagnosis: Potential for Injury Related to Potential for Seizure Development Secondary to Craniotomy and Unsteady Gait Secondary to Left-Sided Weakness

Expected Patient Outcome

Patient will not sustain injury.

Nursing Interventions

1. Administer anticonvulsants as ordered.
2. Institute seizure precautions (i.e., padded siderails, bed in lowest position, oral airway at bedside, etc.).

Pain

The manifestation of headache following a craniotomy can be related to the pressure of the tumor mass on the cerebral structures or from meningeal irritation related to the surgical procedure. Inflammation of the meningeal layers can result from residual blood in the subarachnoid space or contamination of the wound following surgery.[2]

4. Nursing Diagnosis: Alteration in Comfort Related to Pain Secondary to Craniotomy Procedure and Intracerebral Mass

Expected Patient Outcome

The patient will maintain an adequate level of pain relief as noted by verbal report by the patient.

Nursing Interventions

1. Assess quality of pain every eight hours using a scale from 0 to 10.
2. Administer pain medication as ordered.
3. Assess effectiveness of pain medication dosage and frequency.
4. Teach patient and family alternative methods of pain control, ie, relaxation, meditation.
5. Provide comfort measures, ie, back rub, foot massage, bed bath.
6. Maintain a quiet restful environment and/or diversional activities according to patient's preference.

Nutrition

Many patients with intracranial lesions have difficulty maintaining an adequate intake of food prior to hospitalization due to malaise, fatigue, nausea, difficulty swallowing, or a loss of appetite in general. Usually such symptoms are not severe and result in only moderate weight loss. However, in addition to the surgical insult of the craniotomy, there may be food and fluid restrictions, osmotic diuretics, and steroid therapy, all of which combine to produce a catabolic state with a negative nitrogen balance in the patient.[6]

5. Nursing Diagnosis: Potential Alteration in Nutrition Related to Surgical Stress and Anorexia Secondary to Cerebral Neoplasm and Chemotherapy

Expected Patient Outcome

The patient will maintain body weight within 10% of baseline.

Nursing Interventions

1. Monitor intake and output every two hours.
2. Consult with nutritionist.
3. Monitor serum albumin.
4. Assess ability to swallow.
5. Start diet appropriate to patient's gastrointestinal status and ability to tolerate liquids and solids.

Ineffective Coping

Cerebral tumors can arise in otherwise healthy adults. This outward appearance of vitality can give conflicting messages to both the patients and their families. Brain surgery and cancer are two frightening situations to confront. In situations such as the case study we have been reviewing, in which the prognosis is bleak, coming to terms with the reality of the situation can be overwhelming. Feelings of hopelessness, helplessness, and the need to grieve are powerful emotions that can be made more bearable with the help of therapeutic communication and a helping relationship between the patient, the family, and the health care team.

6. Nursing Diagnosis: Potential for Ineffective Coping Related to Hopelessness and Helplessness Secondary to Terminal Prognosis

Expected Patient Outcome

The patient will develop coping strategies to deal with the situation as evidenced by:

1. verbalization of feelings
2. proactive participation in plans and goals for hospitalization and discharge planning

Nursing Interventions

1. Encourage verbalization of feelings.
2. Provide social support via brain tumor support groups or religious counsel.
3. Provide honest information as requested.
4. Provide a therapeutic relationship.

PROGNOSIS

The biologic malignancy of a cerebral tumor depends on its rate of growth and its location. Prognosis is based largely on a grading and staging system of evaluation that considers factors such as the type of tumor, histologic grade, anatomic site, size, ability to invade surrounding tissue, and ability to metastasize.

Other factors that must be considered when determining the prognosis of a cerebral neoplasm are characteristics such as whether or not it is encapsulated, cystic, or solid; the vascularity of the tumor and the peritumoral area; and any limitations to resection related to location, radiosensitivity, potential obstruction of CSF flow, and seeding of the subarachnoid space.

Grading

Grading of a tumor is based on its histology and is a determination of its degree of malignancy. The less differentiated or the more anaplastic a tumor's cells are, the more malignant it is. Tumors are graded using Roman numerals I to IV. The higher the number, the more malignant the tumor. In our case study, the glioblastoma multiforme has very little differentiation in its cell population; therefore, it is a highly anaplastic and malignant tumor. Generally, the higher the grade, the poorer the prognosis.[5]

Staging

Staging is usually done according to the TNM system. It is based on the extent (T) or size of the tumor; lymph node involvement (N); and the presence or absence of distant metastases (M).[5]

A localized tumor that has not invaded surrounding tissue is designated as T0. T1 through T4 indicate the increasing size of the tumor.

If no lymph nodes are involved, the tumor is designated as N0. N1 through N3 indicate increasing lymph node involvement.

If the primary tumor has not metastasized to other areas of the body, it is designated as M0. If it has metastasized, it is designated as M1.

Physicians use the TNM evaluation to determine their method of treatment. In this case study, the classification was an astrocytoma grade IV. The TNM evaluation is T4N0M0.

PET scanning can supplement pathologic grading by identifying the metabolic rate of the tumor mass. With high grade gliomas, such as in this case study, patients have a 78% one-year survival rate if the tumor is hypometabolic, or a 27% one-year survival rate if the tumor is hypermetabolic.[13] Since the PET scan was not ordered, we cannot make that distinction for A.D.

Unfortunately, the prognosis for a patient with a glioblastoma multiforme is very poor. Survival rate for a grade III astrocytoma is usually one to two years. With a grade IV, the survival rate is 15 to 30 weeks after surgery. Age appears to be a significant factor determining survival length. The younger the patient, the longer the survival length.[12]

A.D. survived for seven months. Radiation therapy had little effect on the spread of the tumor. Surgical debulking provided him with several months of increased neurologic functioning and gave both the patient and his family time to come to terms with his prognosis and to attend to final arrangements.

During the course of his disease, A.D. and his family received support from the nursing staff, not only in the physical and comfort-related realm, but also in the very important psychosocial and spiritual domains.

Cerebral tumors are devastating, regardless of the prognosis. They confront patients and their loved ones with human mortality. The intensive care nurse interacts with these patients when they are most vulnerable. To care for them competently and holistically requires implementation of a wide range of skills, from the highly technical to the uniquely human art of therapeutic communication.

NOTES

1. *Nurse's Reference Library: Diseases.* Springhouse, Pa: Springhouse Corp; 1984:178–183.

2. Hickey JV. *The Clinical Practice of Neurological and Neurosurgical Nursing.* 2nd ed. Philadelphia: JB Lippincott Co; 1986:461.

3. Batzdorf U, Weisenburger TH. Neoplasms of the nervous system. In: Seydel HG, ed. *Tumors of the Nervous System.* New York: John Wiley & Sons; 1975:728.

4. Bullock BL, Rosenthal PK. *Pathophysiology: Adaptations and Alterations in Function.* Boston: Little, Brown & Co; 1984:717.

5. Muir BL. *Pathophysiology: An Introduction to the Mechanisms of Disease.* 2nd ed. New York: John Wiley & Sons; 1988:257.

6. Rudy EB. *Advanced Neurological and Neurosurgical Nursing.* St. Louis: CV Mosby Co; 1984:162.

7. Haskell CM, ed. *Cancer Treatment.* Philadelphia: WB Saunders Co; 1980:51–52.

8. Cheng EY. Growth factor and carcinogenesis. *Cope.* April 1988:56.

9. Bleehen NM, ed. *Tumours of the Brain.* New York: Springer-Verlag; 1986:3.

10. Ross AP. Non-traumatic neurologic problems. In: *Nurse Review.* Springhouse, Pa: Springhouse Corp; 1987:87.

11. Moser RP. Surgery for glioma relapse: factors that influence favorable outcomes. *Cancer.* July 15,1988;62:381–390.

12. Newhall J, Ransohoff J, Kaplan B. Glioblastoma in the older patient: how long a course of radiotherapy is necessary? *J Neuro-Oncol.* 1988;6:325.

13. Alavi JB, Alavi A, Chawluk J, et al. Positron emission tomography in patients with gliomas: a predictor of prognosis. *Cancer.* 1988; 62:1074–1078.

SUGGESTED READINGS

Burger C, Green SB. Patient age, histologic features, and length of survival in patients with glioblastoma multiforme. *Cancer.* 1987; 59:1617–1625.

Harper J. Use of steroids in cerebral edema: therapeutic implications. *Heart Lung.* 1988;17(1):70–73.

Kornblity PL, Walker MD, Cassady JR. *Neurologic Oncology.* Philadelphia: JB Lippincott Co; 1987.

Seydel HG, ed. *Tumors of The Nervous System.* New York: John Wiley & Sons; 1975.

Welsh DM, Zumwalt CB. Volumetric interstitial hyperthermia: nursing implications for brain tumor treatment. *J Neurosci Nurs.* 1988;20(4):229–235.

Wen HL, Dahele JS, Mehal ZD, Chan WHS, Wen D YK. Application of invasive microwave hyperthermia for the treatment of gliomas. *J Neuro-Oncol.* 1988;6:93–101.

Chapter 8

Brain Resuscitation

Elizabeth A. Henneman

INTRODUCTION

The goal of brain resuscitation is the amelioration of neurologic injury that occurs secondary to cardiac arrest. Brain resuscitation therapy is still in its infancy. The majority of proposed interventions have only been studied in animals and are still considered experimental. The nurse plays a pivotal role in brain-oriented therapy. The complexity of brain injury coupled with the critical condition of the patient after arrest demands expert clinical judgment and skill. Constant monitoring and assessment of the patient allow the nurse to detect subtle changes in the patient's condition, evaluate the effectiveness of therapy, and facilitate prompt, potentially life-saving intervention.

* * * * *

CASE STUDY

Mr. G. was a 75-kg Caucasian male admitted to the intensive care unit (ICU) from the emergency department following resuscitation from a cardiac arrest of unknown etiology. A brief history obtained from the patient's wife revealed the patient had passed out at home while reading the newspaper. The patient's son had immediately initiated cardiopulmonary resuscitation (CPR) and the paramedics arrived approximately ten minutes later. The paramedics' report stated that upon their arrival, Mr. G. was pulseless, in ventricular fibrillation, with adequate CPR being performed. Advanced cardiac life support (ACLS) was immediately initiated. The patient was successfully converted to a sinus tachycardia after three attempts (200-200-300 joules) at defibrillation and one milligram(mg) of epinephrine (intravenous [IV] bolus). Following this conversion, the patient was orally intubated and manually ventilated with 100% oxygen. The patient began to develop occasional premature ventricular contractions (PVCs). A bolus of 75 mg of lidocaine was administered IV, followed by a continuous infusion of lidocaine at 2 mg/min. The patient's blood pressure was palpated at 70 mm Hg (systolic). Dopamine was started at 10 mcg/kg/min (400 mg/250 mL D5W).

Mr. G.'s past medical history was significant for a 30 pack per year history of smoking and a family history of cardiac disease (father died of myocardial infarction at age 50). On admission to the ICU, vital signs were: heart rate—130 beats/minute with 4–6 unifocal PVCs/minute; respiratory rate 12 (on ventilator); blood pressure—80/50 mm Hg (MAP = 60 mm Hg); temperature 37°C. A complete systematic assessment was immediately performed with attention initially paid to cardiopulmonary function.

The patient was orally intubated and mechanically ventilated on a volume ventilator with the following settings: Fio_2—100%, tidal volume (TV)—800 mL, assist-control (AC) mode, rate—12 breaths/minute. A test of the patient's ventilatory function revealed no attempt at spontaneous breathing (ie, apnea). Breath sounds were equal and clear bilaterally. Arterial blood gases drawn after 30 minutes in the ICU were: pH—7.47, $Paco_2$—45 mm Hg, bicarbonate—22 mEq, Pao_2—480 mm Hg, O_2 saturation—100%.

Continuous electrocardiographic (EKG) monitoring revealed a sinus tachycardia, rate 120 to 130 beats/minute with 4 to 6 PVCs/minute. The patient was cool and clammy, with weak peripheral pulses. Blood pressure was 100/60 (MAP = 73 mm Hg) on 10 mcg/kg/minute of dopamine. Heart sounds were normal without appreciable murmurs, gallops, or rubs.

The patient did not open his eyes and was unresponsive to verbal command, but responded with purposeful (withdrawal) movements to painful stimuli. A Glascow coma scale score of 1/ 4/ intubated was recorded. Pupils were 8 mm in diameter and reactive (sluggishly) to light. Corneal and oculocephalic reflexes were normal. An electroencephalogram (EEG) showed slow, low-voltage activity. A computerized tomographic (CT) scan was unremarkable.

All blood tests performed on Mr. G. were within normal limits of the biochemical parameters: glucose—140 mg%, sodium—140 mEq, potassium—4.0 mEq, hematocrit—38%.

The status of the patient's gastrointestinal and genitourinary systems was unremarkable. A nasogastric tube and Foley catheter were in place.

$$* \quad * \quad * \quad * \quad *$$

PATHOPHYSIOLOGY

The brain injury resulting from cardiac arrest is due not only to the arrest itself, but to processes that occur after circulation has been reestablished. To complicate matters, some of the detrimental processes initiated during the arrest are carried over into the postresuscitation period.

Processes Occurring during Cardiac Arrest

Cardiac arrest results in the complete cessation of blood flow and oxygen to the brain (ischemia-anoxia) (Figure 8-1). The brain has a very high meta-

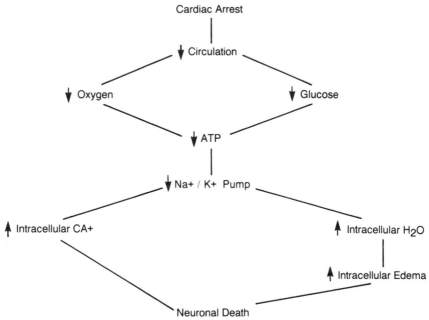

Figure 8-1 Processes occurring during the cardiac arrest resulting in brain injury. *Source*: Adapted with permission from *Heart and Lung* (1986;15(1):3–11), Copyright © 1986, CV Mosby Company, St. Louis.

bolic rate, requiring a significant amount of energy to function. As a result, it is extremely vulnerable to this ischemic injury. Ten seconds after a complete ischemic-anoxic event, oxygen and glucose stores are depleted. Approximately 15 seconds after a cardiac arrest, consciousness is lost, and by 1 minute, brain stem function has ceased. Five minutes after an arrest, all processes requiring adenosine triphosphate (ATP) come to a halt.[1]

Without ATP, all transmembrane pumping mechanisms (eg, sodium[Na$^+$]/potassium[K$^+$] pump) fail. The result is an increase in extracellular potassium and intracellular sodium. High levels of intracellular sodium are responsible for the cytotoxic edema and consequent destruction of neurons, which occur during the cardiac arrest. Excessive extracellular K$^+$ triggers the influx of calcium ions. This intracellular accumulation of calcium is now believed to play a major role in postresuscitation brain injury. If ischemia is prolonged, the blood-brain barrier (BBB) is damaged and vasogenic edema occurs, complicating the injury.[2]

Despite this rapid, devastating sequence of events, researchers believe that successful intervention is possible even after prolonged periods of injury.

Animal studies have demonstrated complete neurological recovery after 60 minutes of complete ischemia.[3]

Postreperfusion Injury

Despite the successful reestablishment of circulation after a cardiac arrest, continued injury occurs in the brain. This postreperfusion insult, with its potentially devastating consequences, is believed to result from events triggered by the brain's renewed blood supply (Figure 8-2). The following theoretical mechanisms are being investigated for their role in postreperfusion brain injury: hypoperfusion, free radicals, arachidonic acids, intraneuronal calcium, and hypermetabolism.

Hypoperfusion, or the "no-reflow" phenomenon, has been documented by Ames et al and others who noted diminished brain perfusion during the postischemic insult period.[4-8] Their findings indicate that 15 to 90 minutes after reperfusion, cerebral vascular resistance increases and perfusion is reduced to less than 40% of normal. Mechanisms believed to play a role in this low flow state include: cerebral vasoconstriction,[9,10] decreased red blood cell deformability,[9,11] platelet aggregation,[12-14] pericapillary cellular edema,[15] and abnormal calcium ion influx.[16]

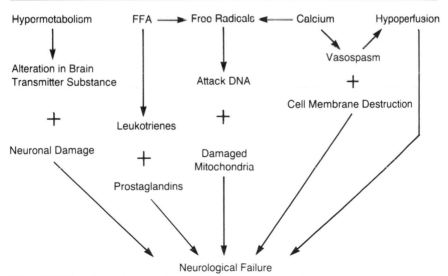

Figure 8-2 Hypothesized mechanisms of injury in the postreperfusion period.

Free radicals are extremely reactive substances with an unpaired electron in their orbital ring. These free radicals are produced during reperfusion and are believed to contribute to neuronal death, possibly by attacking dioxyribonucleic acid (DNA) and damaging mitochondria.[17] The re-oxygenation of neurons postresuscitation results in the liberation of free fatty acids (FFA), such as arachidonic acid. These FFAs serve as substrates for prostaglandin synthesis and are metabolized to form free radicals and leukotrienes. Prostaglandin and leukotrienes have been implicated in the postreperfusion vasospasm and membrane damage that contributes to neuronal death.

Much emphasis is being placed on the role of calcium in postreperfusion injury. Some experts speculate that calcium shifts may be responsible for most of the injury occurring during the postreperfusion period.[1,18] Maintenance of normal intracellular calcium ion concentrations requires intact transmembrane pumping systems and ATP. Loss of this mechanism during cardiac arrest allows the buildup of intracellular calcium. The reestablished blood supply in the postresuscitation period together with high levels of intracellular calcium precipitates a series of destructive events, including vasospasm, cell membrane destruction, and the release of cytotoxic substances, such as free radicals, prostaglandins, and leukotrienes.[16,19]

A renewed supply of blood and oxygen postresuscitation allows the brain to step up its activities but in a disorganized and chaotic fashion. This hypermetabolic state is believed to result from the release of endogenous catecholamines (eg, dopamine, norepinephrine) in the early reperfusion period. This hypermetabolic activity is detrimental to the vulnerable brain because it results in increased glycolysis, lipolysis, proteolysis, and the cerebral metabolic rate of oxygen (CMRO). These processes contribute to neurological failure either by directly damaging neuronal cells or by altering levels of brain transmitter substances.[20]

CLINICAL ASSESSMENT

A comprehensive assessment of the patient with an ischemic-anoxic injury is vital both to making an accurate diagnosis and in predicting prognosis. Initial evaluation of the brain-injured patient requires obtaining a health history, performing a physical assessment, and securing appropriate diagnostic studies. The emergent nature of brain resuscitation frequently necessitates that assessment and intervention be performed simultaneously. In fact, it would not be uncommon for interventions to be started prior to a final diagnosis being made. Intensive, continuous monitoring of neurological status and vital signs allows the clinician to appreciate subtle changes in the patient's condition and intervene promptly.

History

Obtaining an accurate history is frequently difficult in the early postarrest period, particularly if the arrest occurred outside the hospital. Family, friends, and medical personnel can offer useful information regarding the circumstances surrounding the arrest. Details, such as the length of time prior to the onset of cardiopulmonary resuscitation (CPR) and the duration of the resuscitation, should be elicited as they are useful in predicting neurologic recovery. An account of the resuscitation, including medications administered, should also be noted. Many of the pharmacologic agents used routinely in advanced cardiac life support (ACLS) can mask or mimic neurological emergencies. Atropine, for example, an anticholinergic drug, causes pupillary dilatation and altered light responses, findings that might be misinterpreted as abnormal.

Information regarding the patient's metabolic status and temperature prior to the arrest is also important as they may impact neurologic outcome. High glucose levels prearrest may adversely affect cerebral viability while hypothermia provides a protective effect on the brain.[21,22]

Pertinent details of the patient's past medical history should also be explored, including past surgeries or trauma, pre-existing neurological or cardiovascular disorders, and medication and alcohol history.

PHYSICAL ASSESSMENT

Priority in brain resuscitation (cardiopulmonary cerebral resuscitation [CPCR]) (Table 8-1) is given to an evaluation of cardiopulmonary function. Once ventilation and circulation is reestablished, the neurologic system becomes the focus of the evaluation.

Respiratory Status

The patient postarrest is usually intubated and mechanically ventilated to ensure an open airway and provide adequate minute ventilation. Care should be taken to evaluate proper placement of the endotracheal tube immediately after intubation (eg, by auscultation and chest x-ray). The adequacy of ventilation is best assessed initially by blood gas analysis. Thereafter, continuous evaluation of oxygenation and ventilation is possible via pulse oximetry and capnography.

It is not uncommon for a patient postarrest to have absent or abnormal respirations. Because global ischemic-anoxic injury is associated with dif-

Table 8-1 Phases of Cardiopulmonary Cerebral Resuscitation (CPCR)

Phase I: Basic life support
  A. Airway control
  B. Breathing control and oxygenation
  C. Circulation control

Phase II: Advanced life support
  D. Drugs and fluids
  E. Electrocardiography
  F. Defibrillation

Phase III: Prolonged life support
  G. Gauging the soundness of resuscitative efforts
  H. Humanizing resuscitation with neuron saving measures
  I. Intensive care

Source: Adapted with permission from *Heart and Lung* (1986;15[1]:3–11), Copyright © 1986, CV Mosby Company, St. Louis.

fuse brain stem depression, alterations in respirations are generally nonspecific. Apnea in particular is an important finding in evaluating patient prognosis as well as in the determination of brain death.

Cardiovascular Status

An evaluation of cardiovascular function should begin during the resuscitation itself by assessing the effectiveness of both basic and advanced life support. Particular attention should be paid to the adequacy of CPR, as research has indicated that even when flawlessly performed, cardiac compressions provide less than ten percent of normal brain perfusion.[23,24]

Heart rate, rhythm, and blood pressure must be continuously monitored in the postresuscitation period. Additional compromise in cardiac function resulting in further ischemia may have more serious consequences than the cardiac arrest itself.[25,26] Both hypotension and hypertension may adversely affect neurologic recovery. Hypotension postarrest worsens the no-reflow phenomenon and contributes to the production of lactic acidosis. Hypertension may exacerbate cerebral edema and increase intracranial pressure.

Neurologic Status

Once respiratory and cardiovascular function has stabilized, the priority of the clinical assessment becomes the neurologic system. The actual exam performed postarrest will vary depending on the extent of neurologic damage and the patient's level of wakefulness. Ischemic-anoxic injury generally affects both cerebral hemispheres and the brain stem, leaving the patient in a comatose state. As a result, the assessment guidelines for brain resuscitation are essentially those used in the evaluation of any comatose patient.

A comprehensive neurologic assessment of the comatose patient postarrest should include an evaluation of level of consciousness, the neuro-ophthalmic exam, and an assessment of motor function. The Glasgow Coma Scale (GCS)[27] is a commonly utilized tool designed to eliminate the subjectivity that accompanies an evaluation of level of consciousness. The following indices are tested when using the standardized scoring system: eye opening, verbal response, and motor response. Possible scores range from 3 to 15, with a score of 3 indicating severe neurologic impairment. If the patient is intubated, it is impossible to evaluate verbal responses, and the score should reflect this fact (ie, 2/ 3/ intubated).

Testing of motor function in a comatose patient frequently requires the application of a noxious stimulus, such as nailbed or supraorbital pressure (although gentler methods should always be tried first). The response to this stimulus may be normal (eg, localizes or withdraws), abnormal (eg, decorticate or decerebrate posturing), or absent. Decerebrate posturing is a particularly ominous sign in the postarrest period because it implies brain stem involvement. The complete absence of any motor response is indicative of severe brain stem damage and frequently accompanies the terminal stages of coma.[28]

The neuro-ophthalmic examination, including testing of the pupillary, oculovestibular, and oculocephalic reflexes, is a useful aid in determining neurologic status. Pupils are frequently wide and fixed postischemia-anoxia, but then quickly become smaller and reactive. Pupil dilation lasting longer than several minutes is suggestive of severe brain damage.[29] As previously mentioned, many of the drugs used in ACLS may alter pupillary size and the light reflex (eg, atropine, dopamine).

The oculovestibular (doll's eyes) and oculocephalic (ice-water calorics) reflexes are used in testing the integrity of the third, sixth, and eighth cranial nerves in comatose patients (Figure 8-3). The oculovestibular reflex is tested by instilling approximately 50 milliliters of iced water into the ear canal with the head at a 30 degree elevation. A normal response in a comatose patient is tonic deviation of the eyes towards the irrigated ear. The oculovestibular reflex is elicited by briskly rotating the head laterally. A normal response in a comatose patient is conjugate deviation of the eyes to the side opposite of the direction in which the head was turned. Absence of these reflexes suggests a deterioration in brain stem function. Several brain-oriented therapies, such as barbiturates and neuromuscular blocking agents, will inhibit these reflexes.

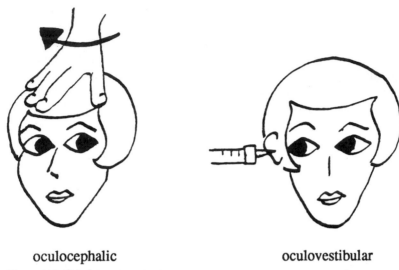

oculocephalic   oculovestibular

Figure 8-3 Normal oculocephalic and oculovestibular reflexes in the comatose patient. Suggest intact brain stem function.

The corneal reflex is also used in testing brain stem integrity. A normal response to passing a wisp of cotton over the cornea is bilateral eyelid closure and upward deviation of the eye.[29]

Metabolic Function

A variety of metabolic conditions have the potential to affect neurologic outcome and therefore require careful evaluation in the postresuscitation period. Particular attention should be paid to serum glucose, sodium, potassium, and calcium levels in the patient postarrest.

Abnormal blood glucose levels prearrest have been associated with poor neurologic outcome.[21] Hyperglycemia during anoxic-ischemia allows for continuing anaerobic glycolysis and the production of lactic acidosis. This additional acidosis may have serious consequences for the patient with a low pH from other metabolic or respiratory causes related to the arrest. Hyperglycemia is also detrimental in that glucose may enter brain cells, pulling water with it, worsening cerebral edema. Hypoglycemia not only impedes the brain's energy-requiring processes (eg, sodium-potassium pump), but also leads to a breakdown of phospholipids and the accumulation of FFAs.

Serum sodium, potassium, and calcium may also affect neurologic viability. Both hypo- and hypernatremia may result in an altered level of consciousness (LOC) and/or seizures. Imbalances in serum potassium do not affect the brain directly, but have the potential to induce further injury via their potential to alter cerebral blood flow by affecting cardiac function. Dysrhythmias and/or recurring cardiac arrests will have devastating consequences for the brain that has suffered a prior ischemic insult. Normal calcium levels are important not only in maintaining neurologic function (eg, maintaining muscle strength) but potentially in ameliorating the devastating events of the postreperfusion period.

NEURODIAGNOSTIC TESTS

A variety of neurodiagnostic tools are available to assist the clinician in determining the extent and location of injury, guide therapy, and predict prognosis after cardiac arrest. These tests are of limited value unless used in conjunction with findings from laboratory tests and the clinical assessment.

Intracranial Pressure (ICP) Monitoring

Monitoring of ICP is not routinely warranted in the postarrest setting, because increases in ICP are generally not seen in these patients. However, prolonged arrests may result in cerebral edema and a sustained increase in ICP.[30] In these instances, ICP monitoring may be of value in ongoing evaluation of cerebral perfusion pressure (CPP) and evaluation of the effectiveness of various therapies (eg, drugs, hyperventilation) and nursing interventions (eg, suctioning) on ICP.

Electroencephalographic (EEG) Monitoring

Electroencephalographic monitoring is used to evaluate the functional state of the brain. It is of particular value in the comatose patient postarrest who is unable to cooperate with a neurological exam and in paralyzed or sedated patients. Abnormal EEG patterns, with slower than normal frequencies and low voltage background activity, are frequently seen postarrest. Intermittent bursts of high voltage waves against an otherwise low voltage EEG, termed suppression bursts, which occur postresuscitation, are associated with a grave prognosis.[31]

EEG studies are also frequently included in the evaluation of brain death. An isoelectric EEG in the absence of drugs or hypothermia is generally accepted as indicative of absent brain stem and cerebral function.

Computerized Tomographic (CT) Scanning

Computerized tomographic scanning may be used after an ischemic-anoxic event to determine the extent of cerebral edema but is of limited value in this setting. Edema develops slowly with ischemic-anoxic injury; therefore, early scans (0–3 days) are generally not helpful.

Evoked-Potential (EP) Monitoring

Evoked-potential monitoring uses a stimulus to evoke an electrical response in the brain. The resultant waveforms are analyzed and the findings used in determining the location and degree of brain dysfunction. A variety of EP can be used in evoking a response including: brain stem auditory (BAER), somatosensory (SER), and visual (VER).

Both brain stem and cerebral functioning can be evaluated using EPs. In addition, EPs are able to detect neurologic function in comatose, sedated, or paralyzed patients. This is particularly valuable in patients requiring brain resuscitation. The use of EPs has been found to be more reliable than the clinical exam in predicting neurologic outcome, suggesting that they may be useful in determining prognosis while the patient is still in coma.[32]

Cerebral Blood Flow (CBF) Studies

Much of our understanding of the pathophysiology of the postresuscitation period has come from animal studies that measured CBF during CPR and after the reestablishment of circulation. Despite the knowledge gained from this research, the clinical usefulness of CBF studies in patient management postarrest remains unclear.

MEDICAL INTERVENTIONS

The goals of brain resuscitation are (1) to optimize cerebral perfusion pressure either through a reduction in ICP or by optimizing mean arterial pressure (MAP) (CCP = MAP − ICP), and (2) to minimize the deleterious events that contribute to continued brain injury in the postresuscitation period (Table 8-2). The medical approach to the brain-injured patient must be multi-faceted because of the many processes involved in neuronal pathology. General postresuscitation therapies, as well as more specific brain-focused interventions, are aimed at halting, avoiding, or reversing those processes believed to occur after an ischemic-anoxic event, namely, hypoxemia, edema, acidosis, hypoperfusion, and membrane damage. Many brain-oriented therapies are still in the experimental phases; none have proven

Table 8-2 General Brain-Oriented Interventions

Goal	Therapy
1. Optimize CPP	
ICP—0 to 15 mm Hg	Hyperventilation
	$Paco_2$ 25 to 35 mm Hg
	Diuretics (eg, furosemide)
	Osmotics (eg, mannitol)
	Steroids (eg, dexamethasone)
	Serum osm 280 to 330 mOsm/L
MAP—90 to 100 mm Hg	Fluids
	Vasoactive
	medications (eg, dopamine)
2. Enhance cell recovery	
$Pao_2 >$ 100 mm Hg	Optimize oxygenation
pH 7.3 to 7.6	Hyperventilation
decrease CMR	Manage seizures
	(eg, phenytoin, diazepam)
	Light anesthetic
	(eg, barbiturate)
	Sedatives (eg, diazepam)
	Normothermia/hypothermia
normalization of biochemical parameters	
HCT	Blood transfusions
K^+—3.5 to 4.5 mEq	Electrolyte replacement or removal
Na^+—135 to 145 mEq	
Glucose—100 to 300 mg%	Glucose replacement/insulin
reduction of extracranial complications (eg, sepsis)	Aseptic technique Routine cultures

Source: Adapted with permission from *Critical Care Medicine* (1978;6[4]:215–227), Copyright © 1978, Williams and Wilkins Company, Baltimore.

worthy of routine use in postresuscitation management. The current recommendation for brain-oriented therapy is to normalize all parameters via maximal intensive care.

General Brain-Oriented Therapies

The emphasis in brain resuscitation (ie, cardiopulmonary cerebral resuscitation [CPCR]) continues to be placed on basic and advanced life support (Table 8-1). This necessitates stabilizing respiratory and cardiac function prior to initiating specific brain-oriented measures. The following interventions are considered appropriate therapies for the patient postarrest: oxygenation, hyperventilation, blood pressure control, diuretics and osmotic therapy, steroids, normalization of biochemical parameters (eg, pH, electrolytes, blood glucose, and hematocrit), temperature control, treatment of seizures, immobilization and sedation, and reduction of extracranial complications such as sepsis (Table 8-2).

Oxygenation

Optimizing oxygenation in the postresuscitation period allows for normal cell function and reparative processes to begin.[1] The partial pressure of arterial oxygen (Pao_2) should be maintained above 100 torr or oxygen saturation greater than 90%. This may require the use of high fractions of inspired oxygen (Fio_2) and/or the use of positive end-expiratory pressure (PEEP). When PEEP is required, its effect on cardiac output (CO) and ICP must be monitored as it may adversely influence both.[33,34]

Hyperventilation

Hyperventilation is employed in postresuscitation management to maintain acid-base balance as well and lower ICP. Maintaining the partial pressure of carbon dioxide ($Paco_2$) between 25 and 35 torr decreases CBF by 40 percent while optimizing pH.[30] Although acute changes in $Paco_2$ effectively decrease CBF and therefore ICP, this effect lasts only about four hours and therefore is of limited usefulness.[1]

The major role for hyperventilation in the postresuscitation period appears to be protection of the brain via the correction of acidosis. However, it has also been hypothesized that hyperventilation may play a role in neuronal recovery via a phenomenon known as the "reverse steal" effect, meaning that blood is shifted from normal to injured vascular beds. This is believed to occur because normal vessels retain their vasoconstrictive properties while injured vessels do not.[35] The result is a shifting of blood to the more vulnerable areas of the brain. Recently, this theory has been disputed, by suggestions that CO_2 responsiveness is retained in injured vessels, so that hyperventilation actually decreases blood flow to injured areas rather than shunting blood to them.[36]

Blood Pressure Control

It is of critical importance that every effort be made to stabilize BP immediately following the restoration of circulation. As previously mentioned, both hypertensive and hypotensive periods may be deleterious to the already traumatized brain. Experts now suggest maintaining a brief (one to five minute) period of moderate hypertension (MAP of 110 to 130 mm Hg) followed by sustained normotension or slight hypertension (MAP of 90 to 100 mm Hg). This transient period of moderate hypertension has been reported to improve neurologic recovery in animal studies.[37] Maintenance of MAP within this narrow range may require the use of pharmacologic agents (e.g., vasopressors or vasodilators) and/or fluid therapy.

Diuretics, Osmotics, and Steroids

Diuretic and osmotic agents are utilized in cerebral injury to decrease ICP and optimize cerebral perfusion. Because increases in ICP are rare following ischemic-anoxic injury, these agents are of limited value.

Hyperosmolar agents, such as mannitol, draw water from the intracellular as well as interstitial compartments of the brain into the vasculature. The result is decreased ICP as well as plasma expansion, resulting in improved cerebral perfusion. Unfortunately, mannitol draws only water and not sodium from brain cells, and only from normal, not edematous tissue. If the blood-brain barrier is disrupted in the postarrest period, mannitol may leak out into brain tissue, drawing water with it, resulting in further edema.

Mannitol administration must be accompanied by careful monitoring of the patient's cardiovascular, renal, fluid, and electrolyte status. Most of the toxic effects accompanying the administration of mannitol result from the increased solute load and diuresis that occurs with its use. When possible, osmotherapy should be titrated according to ICP values and serum osmolality rather than blindly by protocol.[30]

Furosemide, a potent loop diuretic, is the favored diuretic agent for reducing cerebral edema.[38] It acts by diminishing systemic blood volume, thus creating a pressure gradient that allows edematous fluid to diffuse into the vasculature. Furosemide is often given simultaneously with osmotic agents because it has the advantage of selectively dehydrating traumatized versus normal brain tissue. It also does not increase systemic blood volume or intracranial blood flow.[39] Because furosemide induces a significant diuresis, close monitoring of cardiovascular, renal, fluid, and electrolyte status is mandatory.

Steroids have long been used in the management of many types of brain injury, despite the fact that their effectiveness has only been documented in patients with intracranial tumors, and may in fact be deleterious in the co-matose patient.[40] The theoretical advantages of steroids include their ability to decrease cerebral edema, stabilize cell membranes, increase the seizure threshold, scavenge free radicals, and decrease CSF production.[30]

Normalization of Biochemical Parameters

Every attempt should be made to maintain blood variables (eg, hematocrit, glucose, electrolytes, and pH) within normal limits in order to prevent or minimize further injury and maximize cerebral recovery. The importance of each of these variables in influencing neuronal recovery is unclear at this time. Some research suggests that the manipulation of these factors out of the normal range may be warranted in the early postresuscitation period (eg, hemodilution). Currently, however, the recommendation is to normalize these values as much as possible. The one exception is the maintenance of pH in the mildly alkalotic range that results from hyperventilation therapy.

A hematocrit of 30 to 40 percent will optimize the oxygen-carrying capac-ity of the blood. Although normalizing hematocrit is recommended at this time, researchers are in investigating the effectiveness of a more dilute blood in improving reflow postresuscitation.

Serum glucose levels must also be maintained within normal limits (100–300 mg%) because both hyperglycemia and hypoglycemia have adverse effects on the injured brain. Treatment of hyperglycemia may require insulin administration; hypoglycemia should be treated with dextrose.

Electrolytes, especially sodium and potassium, may directly impact brain recovery and therefore should be monitored closely. Hypernatremia does not require treatment unless significant (>150 mEq). If therapy is indicated, fluid replacement must be given slowly to prevent cerebral edema. Hypo-natremia (<135 mEq) may require sodium replacement and/or fluid restriction.

Low serum potassium (<3.5 mEq) is treated with intravenous or na-sogastric administration of potassium chloride (KCl). Hyperkalemia, if se-vere (>6.5 mEq), requires prompt intervention. A variety of methods are used in the treatment of hyperkalemia, including intravenous glucose and bicarbonate administration, Kayexalate, or dialysis.

Efforts directed at preventing acidosis in the postresuscitation period have been found to be beneficial to the injured brain.[41] The primary cause of pH imbalance in the patient postarrest is lactic acidosis, which accumulated both during and after the ischemic-anoxic event. Both hyperventilation and bicarbonate administration are currently recommended for the treatment of lactic acidosis. Hyperventilation offers only short-term effects. Bicarbonate is also of limited value in that it crosses the BBB and may actually exacerbate cell damage.[41,42]

Temperature Control

The cerebral metabolic rate increases eight percent with each degree rise in body temperature.[1] Thus, hyperthermia contributes significantly to the demand placed on the injured brain. Conversely, hypothermia decreases the CMR and has been shown to protect the brain when it occurs prior to an ischemic insult.[22] However, studies documenting the effectiveness of hypothermia induced following an ischemic event are inconclusive.

Therapeutic hypothermia is still in the experimental phases. Current recommendations are to maintain normothermia using available methods. Patients on cooling blankets require vigilant monitoring. Complication of iatrogenic hypothermia include myocardial depression, arrhythmias, hypotension, increased blood viscosity, and depressed defense mechanisms. Any of the complications could prove disastrous to the already injured brain.

Treatment of Seizures

Seizure activity increases the CMR 300 to 400 percent, resulting in serious neurologic compromise.[1] Postischemic seizures require rapid intervention with pharmacologic agents, such as barbiturates, phenytoin, and diazepam.

Phenytoin, the most widely used anticonvulsant, is believed to improve neurologic recovery via its anticonvulsant effects as well as other mechanisms, including membrane stabilization, cerebral vasodilation, diminishing cerebral O_2 consumption, and increasing the brain's stores of glucose, glycogen, and phosphocreatine.[1,43]

Immobilization and Sedation

Immobilization may be useful in brain-injured patients by decreasing the CMR and in improving ventilation. Neuromuscular blocking agents, such as pancuronium, are often used in conjunction with sedatives or anesthetic agents to blunt the patient's response to external stimuli, thus decreasing oxygen demand. Immobilization can also maximize the efficacy of mechanical ventilation in the patient who is agitated and breathing out of synchronization with the ventilator. Some clinicians prefer the administration of a light anesthetic (eg, barbiturate) in addition to a muscle relaxant to suppress hypermetabolic brain activity.[30]

It is imperative that patients who are paralyzed also be sedated because the use of neuromuscular blocking agents alone may cause severe anxiety. A comprehensive neurologic exam should also be performed prior to the initiation of immobilization and sedative therapy.

Treatment of Extracranial Factors

As soon as the patient has stabilized, efforts to identify and treat the underlying problem that led to the arrest should be initiated. In addition, steps must be taken to ensure that preventable complications, such as sepsis, be prevented.

EXPERIMENTAL BRAIN-ORIENTED THERAPIES

There are many specific brain-oriented therapies currently under investigation. They include high dose barbiturates, calcium channel blockers, prostaglandin and free radical inhibitors, and cardiopulmonary bypass. The goal of these therapies is the amelioration of neurological deficits resulting from processes that occur in the postreperfusion period.

Barbiturate therapy was once considered a promising brain-oriented intervention. Researchers were attracted to the use of barbiturates in brain resuscitation because these agents had been shown to reduce cerebral metabolism, cerebral edema, intracranial pressure, and seizure activity. Early studies in animals suggested that the administration of barbiturates after complete global ischemia resulted in improved neurologic outcome. Clinical pilot studies continued to support this benefit, particularly when barbiturates were administered in high doses.[44,45] Recently, however, the results of a large clinical trial suggested that large dose barbiturate therapy (thiopental) did not affect neurologic outcome and therefore should not be routinely used in brain resuscitation. The authors of this study did suggest that barbiturate therapy could still be used safely for specific purposes, such as sedation, anticonvulsant therapy, or to reduce ICP.[46]

Barbiturates, particularly in high doses, must be administered with caution, as they have the potential for serious side effects. The use of barbiturate coma is especially challenging because it results in the loss of many of the reflexes normally used in the evaluation of neurologic status (eg, pupillary, oculocephalic, and corneal). The administration of large doses of barbiturates mandates total ventilatory support and vigilant cardiac monitoring. Because these drugs suppress brain electrical activity (EEG), as well as other neurologic indices, they should be withdrawn and serum drug levels monitored prior to any decision-making regarding diagnoses (eg, determination of brain death) or the withdrawal of life support.

Calcium Channel Blockers

The proposed role of calcium in the pathophysiology of brain ischemia has led investigators to study the effects of calcium antagonists on brain recovery. Potential benefits of calcium channel blockers include: decreasing cerebral vasospasm, improving cerebral blood flow, and protecting cellular integrity.[1] Animal studies suggest that calcium antagonists, administered after a global ischemic anoxic event, improve neurologic recovery.[47,48] A clinical trial is presently under investigation to examine the efficacy of lidoflazine in improving neurologic recovery in comatose patients after cardiac arrest.

Miscellaneous Experimental Brain Resuscitation Therapies

Several promising brain-oriented therapies are now in the preliminary stages of investigation. They include prostaglandin inhibitors, free radical scavengers, and cardiopulmonary bypass.

Prostaglandin inhibitors prevent the destruction of cell membranes during the postreperfusion period. Their use has been associated with an improvement in CBF and neurologic recovery in animal studies.[49]

Free radical scavengers, such as superoxide dismutase, ascorbic acid, and dimethyl sulphoxide (DMSO), are also being investigated for their effectiveness in inhibiting cell membrane destruction. DMSO has been demonstrated to reduce neurological deficits following a focal ischemic event (ie, stroke); its benefit after a global event has not been established.[50]

Cardiopulmonary bypass has also shown promise as a brain resuscitation measure when employed following a prolonged ischemic insult. It has been postulated that its use in the postresuscitation period may allow for the restoration of circulation in patients refractory to standard life support measures, improve cerebral perfusion, and result in the amelioration of post-ischemic brain damage.[1,51]

PROGNOSIS POSTRESUSCITATION

Neurologic recovery following out-of-hospital cardiac arrest is very poor. As a result, physicians are frequently interested in knowing the patient's prognosis in order to determine if continued aggressive therapy is appropriate. Several factors have been shown to be predictors of neurologic outcome postarrest, including the initiation and duration of CPR, findings of the neurologic exam, and length of coma.[52-58] Studies suggest that the shorter the length of time prior to the initiation of CPR and the less time required to restore spontaneous circulation with CPR, the better the outcome.[52-54] Neu-rologic recovery has also been shown to correlate with the results of simple neurologic tests. Intact brain stem reflexes (eg, corneal, pupillary, ocu-locephalic) and normal motor responses are suggestive of a favorable neuro-logical outcome.[55-57]

The duration of coma postarrest has also been found to be a useful and reliable prognostic tool. Essentially, patients who awaken postarrest do so early (within 48 hours). Patients in coma for greater than 48 hours face almost certain death or vegetative survival.[58]

OUTCOME NARRATIVE

Following a complete assessment of Mr. G., general brain-oriented ther-apy was initiated. Immediate attention was given to the patient's cardiac status, particularly his low blood pressure. The dopamine infusion was in-creased to 15 mcg/kg/min with an increase in BP to 130/90 mm Hg. A pulmonary artery catheter was placed to assist in the management of Mr. G.'s therapy. Initial readings were: pulmonary artery pressure—18/5, pulmonary capillary wedge pressure (PCWP)—5, right atrial pressure (RA)—5, cardiac output (CO)—4.0. Based on those readings, the decision was made to in-crease the patient's fluid intake. Several hours later, his BP had improved (130/80 mm Hg, MAP = 97 mm Hg).

The results of Mr. G.'s pulmonary assessment suggested that his oxygena-tion was normal but the $Paco_2$ was too high, necessitating an increase in the number of breaths per minute being delivered to the patient. The ventilator rate setting was increased to 16 breaths/minute with a resultant decrease in $Paco_2$ to 30 mm Hg. Measurement of end-tidal CO_2 levels were then used in evaluating CO_2 and guiding further therapy, limiting the need for ABGs. Because oxygenation was normal, the Fio_2 was gradually decreased to 30%.

Once Mr. G.'s cardiopulmonary status had stabilized, attention was turned to his neurologic status. His neurologic assessment remained unchanged from baseline until four hours after admission when he began to exhibit generalized seizure activity. Dilantin one gram was administered intra-venously over 30 minutes and a daily dose ordered. No further seizure activity occurred during the remainder of Mr. G.'s ICU stay.

Twelve hours after his admission to the ICU, Mr. G. began to show signs of neurologic improvement. He opened his eyes spontaneously and was able to localize painful stimuli. A GCS score of 4/ 5/ intubated was recorded. As he awoke, he became increasingly restless and began to breathe out of synchronization with the ventilator, resulting in a drop in O_2 saturation to 80%. In an attempt to improve the patient's ventilatory status, barbiturate therapy (phenobarbital) was initiated. A neuromuscular blocking agent was considered but deemed unnecessary after the sedative action of the barbiturates took effect.

Identifying the cause of Mr. G.'s arrest was a primary focus of the medical staff. Serial EKGs, evaluation of cardiac enzymes, and echocardiographic testing were undertaken while the patient was still in the ICU.

Forty-eight hours after his admission to the ICU Mr. G.'s barbiturates were discontinued and he began to awaken. He opened his eyes spontaneously and began to follow simple commands. Spontaneous ventilatory mechanics demonstrated an adequate tidal volume, vital capacity, and inspiratory force, allowing Mr. G. to be weaned successfully from the ventilator and be extubated. Mr. G.'s cardiac status improved and ectopy ceased, allowing the dopamine and lidocaine to be discontinued.

Three days after his admission to the ICU, Mr. G. was transferred awake and oriented (GCS = 15) to an observation unit for further cardiac workup and monitoring. Mr. G. was discharged home five days later with no evidence of neurological deficit.

NURSING CARE PLAN

Effective nursing care of the patient undergoing brain resuscitation therapy requires ongoing assessment, diagnosis, intervention, and evaluation. Continuous monitoring allows for accurate assessment and identification of appropriate nursing diagnoses. The nursing care plan organizes diagnoses and associated interventions and allows for consistency in the delivery of patient care. A nursing care plan for the patient undergoing brain resuscitation should reflect standards of care as well as an individualized plan designed to meet the specific needs of both the patient and the family. Ongoing evaluation of the current plan is critical to effective treatment and patient outcome.

Caring for the brain-injured, critically ill patient requires extensive knowledge of the pathophysiology of ischemic-anoxic injury as well as an understanding of the therapies used in brain resuscitation. Nurses caring for these complex patients must keep abreast of current research in order to provide optimal care.

Meeting the needs of families of the brain-injured, postarrest patient requires excellent communication skills and empathetic caring. The stress of having a critically ill loved one in the ICU can be overwhelming and may disrupt normal coping mechanisms. As a coordinator of patient management, the nurse can be instrumental in facilitating the exchange of information between families and the various disciplines involved in the patient's care.

1. Nursing Diagnosis: Airway Clearance Ineffective Related to Central Nervous System Depression, Pharmacologic Therapy (eg, Paralyzing Agents, Sedatives), and Thick Copious Secretions

Expected Patient Outcome

Patient will have a patent airway as evidenced by:

1. bilateral breath sounds
2. absence of adventitious breath sounds (eg, crackles, rhonchi, wheezes)
3. vital signs within normal limits (WNL) for the patient
4. mental status WNL for the patient
5. ABGs WNL for the patient
6. absent or small amounts of thin, clear secretions

Nursing Interventions

1. Assess airway patency. Auscultate lungs every two hours.
2. Assess for signs or symptoms of ineffective airway clearance:
   - tachypnea
   - tachycardia
   - use of accessory muscles
   - dyspnea
   - Pao_2 < 80 mm Hg
   - O_2 saturation < 90%
   - $Paco_2$ > 45 mm Hg
3. Maintain airway patency:
   - assist with intubation of patient postarrest
   - provide humidification of artificial airway
     - (a) bronchial hygiene
       - turn patient every two hours
       - chest physical therapy every two to four hours as tolerated (evaluate effect on ICP)
     - (b) suction patient
       - assess need for suctioning—crackles, rhonchi, ventilator pressure limit alarm sounding
       - utilize aseptic technique
       - suction for no more than 10 seconds, only while withdrawing catheter
       - monitor heart rate, rhythm, and O_2 saturation during suctioning

4. Explain procedures and treatments to patient and family as appropriate.
5. Document interventions and outcomes in nursing notes.

2. Nursing Diagnosis: Ineffective Breathing Pattern Related to Brain Injury, Pharmacologic Therapy (eg, Neuromuscular Blocking Agents, Sedatives), and Agitation

Expected Patient Outcome

Patient will have an effective breathing pattern as evidenced by:

1. respiratory rate, depth, and pattern WNL for the patient
2. vital signs WNL for the patient
3. ABGs WNL for the patient
4. patient receiving full tidal volume from ventilator

Nursing Interventions

1. Assess patient's respiratory status:
   - evaluate respiratory rate, depth, rhythm every one to two hours
   - monitor ABGs as ordered
   - monitor O_2 saturation continuously
   - monitor VS every one to two hours
2. Assess patient for signs or symptoms of ineffective breathing pattern:
   - altered respiratory rate, depth, or pattern
     - (a) apnea
     - (b) bradypnea
     - (c) tachypnea
     - (d) hyperventilation
     - (e) hypoventilation
     - (f) Cheyne-Stokes respirations
   - Pao_2 < 80 mm Hg
   - O_2 saturation < 90%
   - $Paco_2$ > 45 mm Hg
   - pH < 7.35 or > 7.45
3. Evaluate need for artificial ventilatory support:
   - apnea
   - tidal volume < 5 to 10 mL/kg
   - vital capacity < 10 to 15 mL/kg
   - negative inspiratory force < 20 mm Hg

4. Assist with maintenance of artificial ventilatory support:
   - adjust respiratory therapies in determination of appropriate ventilatory settings to maintain $Paco_2$ in proper range (25 to 35 mm Hg during first 24 hours)
   - evaluate physiologic response to changes in ventilator settings on:
     (a) ABGs
     (b) cardiovascular status (particularly with use of high levels of PEEP)
     (c) ICP (if applicable)
5. Administer and evaluate effectiveness of pharmacologic therapy on ventilation.
6. Assist in obtaining spontaneous ventilatory mechanics in patients who are awakening.
7. Explain procedures and treatments to patient and family as appropriate.
8. Document intervention and outcome in nursing notes.

3. Nursing Diagnosis: Impaired Gas Exchange (Potential/Actual) Related to Ventilation/Perfusion Mismatching Secondary to Aspiration Pneumonia, Congestive Heart Failure, Pulmonary Embolism, and Adult Respiratory Distress Syndrome

Expected Patient Outcome

Patient will have adequate gas exchange as evidenced by:

1. vital signs WNL for the patient
2. mental status WNL for the patient
3. ABGs WNL for the patient
4. O_2 saturation WNL for the patient
5. $ETCO_2$ levels WNL for the patient

Nursing Interventions

1. Monitor gas exchange:
   - auscultate breath sounds every one to two hours
   - monitor ABGs as ordered
   - monitor O_2 saturation continuously
2. Monitor patient for signs or symptoms of impaired gas exchange including:
   - altered mental status
   - tachycardia/bradycardia

- arrhythmias
- use of accessory muscles
- Pao_2 < 80 mm Hg
- O_2 saturation < 90%
- $Paco_2$ > 45 mm Hg

3. Maintain patent airway (see Airway Clearance Ineffective).
4. Institute measures to improve oxygenation:
   - head of bed at 30 to 90 degrees
   - increase PEEP as necessary—evaluate effect on cardiac output and ICP
5. Optimize O_2 delivery:
   - maintain cardiac output between 5 and 7 liters/minute
   - maintain hematocrit between 35% and 45%.
6. Explain procedures and treatments to patient and family as appropriate.
7. Document interventions and outcomes in nursing notes.

4. Nursing Diagnosis: Cardiac Output Decreased Related to Inadequate CPR, Arrhythmias, Heart Failure, and Hypovolemia

Expected Patient Outcome

Patient will exhibit signs of adequate cardiac output:

1. mental status WNL for the patient
2. vital signs WNL for the patient
3. cardiac output > 5 L/minute
4. normal sinus rhythm without ectopy
5. urine output > 30 mL/hour
6. skin warm and dry
7. peripheral pulse strong

Nursing Interventions

1. Evaluate cardiovascular status:
   - monitor heart rate and rhythm continuously
   - monitor PAPs, PCWP, RA, and cardiac output every two to four hours
   - monitor urine output every one to two hours
   - monitor skin temperature and peripheral pulses every two to four hours
   - evaluate effect of interventions (eg, drugs, PEEP) on cardiac output

2. Assess patient for signs or symptoms of decreased cardiac output:
   - altered mental status
   - tachycardia
   - ectopy
   - hypotension
   - decreased urine output ($<$ 30 mL/hour)
   - cool, clammy skin
   - weak peripheral pulses
3. Maintain cardiac output WNL with fluid and/or drug therapy, including:
   - vasopressors
   - vasodilators
   - antiarrhythmics
   - cardiotonics
4. Explain treatments and procedures to patient and family as appropriate.
5. Document interventions and outcomes in nursing notes.

5. Nursing Diagnosis: Potential for Injury Related to Hypothermia/Hyperthermia

Expected Patient Outcome

Patient will be free from signs or symptoms of injury as evidenced by:

1. hypothermia (arrhythmias, infection, skin breakdown)
2. hyperthermia (altered mental status, increased ICP, shivering, seizures)

Nursing Interventions

1. Monitor temperature every one or two hours.
2. Treat hyperthermia:
   - reduce fever
     (a) administer antipyretics
     (b) cooling blankets
     (c) tepid baths
     (d) promote air circulation
3. Treat hypothermia (therapeutic—still considered experimental):
   - maintain temperature within a narrow prescribed range (approximately 35° C)
   - prevent shivering

- monitor for arrhythmias
- monitor for signs or symptoms of infection
- obtain routine cultures (blood, urine, sputum)
- monitor serial hematocrits
- utilize strict aseptic technique
4. Explain procedures and treatments to patient and family as appropriate.
5. Document interventions and outcomes in nursing notes.

6. Nursing Diagnosis: Alteration in Tissue Perfusion (Cerebral) Related to Global Ischemic-Anoxic Injury

Expected Patient Outcome

Patient will exhibit signs of adequate cerebral tissue perfusion as evidenced by:

1. mental status WNL for the patient
2. VS WNL for the patient
3. cerebral perfusion pressure 80 to 100 mm Hg (if ICP monitor is in place)

Nursing Interventions

1. Assess neurologic status every hour:
   - level of consciousness (use Glasgow Coma Scale)
   - pupil size and reactivity
   - respiratory rate, depth, and pattern
   - ICP
2. Assist in obtaining EEG, EP, and CT studies.
3. Maintain adequate CPP (MAP − ICP):
   - maintain MAP between 90 and 100 mm Hg (utilize fluids and vasoactive medications as necessary)
   - maintain ICP within normal range (0 to 15 mm Hg):
     (a) maintain $Paco_2$ between 25 and 35 mm Hg
     (b) facilitate venous outflow by
       - elevating head of bed
       - avoid head rotation, neck flexion, hip flexion
     (c) control agitation with sedatives
     (d) administer medication to decrease ICP
       - diuretics (eg, furosemide)
       - osmotics (eg, mannitol)

    (e) restrict fluids as necessary
    (f) control seizures (eg, phenytoin, diazepam)
    (g) decrease patient anxiety
- provide caring supportive environment
- orient patient frequently
- explain all treatments and procedures to patient
- reduce cerebral metabolic rate (CMR):
    (a) normothermia/therapeutic hypothermia (select cases)
    (b) immobilization (eg, pancuronium bromide)
    (c) sedation (eg, barbiturates, diazepam)

4. Explain treatments and procedures to patient and family as appropriate.
5. Document interventions and outcomes in nursing care plan.

7. Nursing Diagnosis: Alteration in Skin Integrity Related to Depressed Neurologic Function, Pharmacologic Therapy (eg, Sedation, Neuromuscular Blocking Agents), Cooling Blanket, and Immobility

Expected Patient Outcome

Patient will be free from any alteration in skin integrity as evidenced by absence of redness, edema, or broken areas on skin.

Nursing Interventions

1. Monitor patient for signs or symptoms of skin breakdown:
- redness
- edema
- broken areas on skin
2. Institute preventive measures to decrease incidence of alterations in skin integrity:
- special mattress
- turn patient every two hours
- promote circulation with massage and range of motion exercises
    (a) support bony prominences
    (b) heel and elbow pads (lamb's wool)
- maintain proper body alignment
- ensure adequate nutrition
3. Explain treatments and procedures to patient and family as appropriate.
4. Document interventions and outcomes in nursing notes.

8. Nursing Diagnosis: Knowledge Deficit (Family) Related to Brain Resuscitation and ICU Environment

Expected Patient Outcome

Family will demonstrate knowledge of brain-oriented therapies as evidenced by:

1. ability to verbalize purpose and goal of therapies
2. ability to accurately describe patient condition
3. ability to describe purpose of ICU (eg, policies, equipment)

Nursing Interventions

1. Assess family's level of understanding regarding ICU, patient's condition, and therapeutic regime.
2. Orient family to ICU environment, including roles of various personnel, visiting hour policy, procedures, equipment.
3. Keep family informed of patient's condition and current therapies; ensure that information is appropriate for family's level of understanding.
4. Assist family in maintaining a positive but realistic outlook.
5. Encourage questions and verbalization of concerns.
6. Document interventions and outcomes in nursing notes.

NOTES

1. Abraham NS. Brain resuscitation. In: Rosen P, ed. *Emergency Medicine*. St. Louis: CV Mosby Co; 1988: 143–157.

2. Jordan R. Pathophysiology of brain injury. *CCQ*. 1983;5:1–11.

3. Hossman KA, Zimmerman V. Resuscitation of the monkey brain after one hour complete ischemia. Part 1. *Brain Res*. 1974;81:59.

4. Ames A, Wright RL, Kowada M, et al. Cerebral ischemia, II: the no reflow phenomenon. *Am J Pathol*. 1968;52:437–453.

5. Snyder JV, Nemoto EM, Carrol RG, et al. Global ischemia in dogs: intracranial pressure, brain blood flow and metabolism. *Stroke*. 1975;6.21–27.

6. Gadinski DS, White BC, Hoehner PJ, et al. Alterations in canine cerebral blood flow and vascular resistance post cardiac arrest. *Ann Emerg Med*. 1982;11:58–63.

7. Dewes LR, Gilboe DD, Betz AL. Metabolic alterations in brain during anoxic-anoxia and subsequent recovery. *Arch Neurol*. 1973;29:385–390.

8. Rehncrona S, Abdul-Rahman A, Siesjo BK. Local cerebral blood flow in the post ischemia period. *Acta Neurol Scand*. 1979;60(suppl):294–295.

9. Van Neuten JM, Van Houtte PM. Improvement of tissue perfusion with inhibitors of calcium ion influx. *Biochem Pharmacol*. 1980;29:479.

10. White BC, Gadinski DS, Hoehner PJ, et al. Effect of flunarizine on hypothesis extension: a tale of two ions? *Ann Emerg Med*. 1984;13:862.

11. De Cree J, De Crok W, Genkins H, et al. The rheologic effects of cinnarizine and flunarizine in normal and pathologic conditions. *Angiology*. 1979;30:505.

12. Kleihues P, Hossman KA, Pegg AE, et al. Resuscitation of the monkey brain after one hour complete ischemia. Part 3. *Brain Res*. 1975;95:61.

13. Obrenovitch TP, Hallenbeck JM. Platelet accumulation in regions of low blood flow during the postischemic period. *Stroke*. 1983;16:224.

14. Hossman KA, Hossman V, and Takagi N. Effect of intravascular platelet aggregation on blood recirculation following prolonged ischemia of the cat brain. *J Neurol*. 1980;222:159.

15. Klatzo I. Brain edema following brain ischaemia and the influence of therapy. *Br J Anaesth*. 1985;27:18.

16. Siesjo BK. Cell damage in the brain: a speculative synthesis. *J Cereb Blood Flow Metab*. 1981;1:155.

17. Del Maestro RF, Thaw HH, Bjork J, et al. Free radicals as mediators of tissue injury. *Acta Physiol Scand*. 1980;492:43–58.

18. White BC, Wiegenstein JG, Winegar CD. Brain ischemic anoxia. *JAMA*. 1984; 251:1586–1590.

19. Siesjo BK. Cerebral circulation and metabolism. *J Neurosurg*. 1984;60:883.

20. Nemoto EM. Pathogenesis of cerebral ischemia-anoxia. *CCM*. 1978;6:203–214.

21. Pulsinelli WA, Waldman S, Rawlinson D, et al. Moderate hyperglycemia augments ischemic brain damage: a neuropathologic study in the rat. *Neurology*. 1982; 32:1239.

22. Jagger JA, Bobovsky J. Nonpharmacologic therapeutic modalities of brain resuscitation. *CCQ*. 1978;5:31–41.

23. Niemann JT. Differences in cerebral myocardial perfusion during closed chest resuscitation. *Ann Emerg Med*. 1984;13:849–853.

24. Niemann JT. Artificial perfusion techniques during cardiac arrest: quest of experimental focus vs clinical need. *Ann Emerg Med*. 1985;14:761–768.

25. Canter RC, Ames A, DiGicianto G, et al. Hypotension: a major factor limiting recovery from cerebral ischemia. *J Surg Res*. 1969;9:525.

26. Becker DP, Verity MA, Povlishock J, et al. Brain cellular injury and recovery. Horizons for improving medical therapies in stroke and trauma. *West J Med*. 1988;148:670–684.

27. Teasdale G, Jennet B. Assessment of coma and impaired consciousness. A practical scale. *Lancet*. 1974;2:81–84.

28. Corronna JF. Clinical evaluation of acute brain failure. In: Grenvik A, Safar P, eds. *Brain Failure and Resuscitation*. New York: Churchill-Livingstone; 1981:55–65.

29. Plum F, Posner JB. *The Diagnosis of Stupor and Coma*. 3rd ed. Philadelphia: F.A. Davis Co; 1980.

30. Safar P, Bleyaert A, Menoto EM, et al. Resuscitation after global brain ischemia anoxia. *CCM*. 1978;6:215–227.

31. Ramsey RE. Electrophysiologic recovery in the ICU. In: Green BA, Marshall LF, and Gallagher TJ, eds. *Intensive Care for Neurological Trauma and Disease*. New York: Academic Press Inc; 1982:177–199.

32. Greenburg RP, Becker DP, Miller JD, et al. Evaluation of brain function in severe head trauma with multimodality evoked potentials, part 2: localization of brain dysfunction and correlation with post traumatic neurological condition. *J Neurosurg*. 1977; 47:163–177.

33. Quist J, Pontoppidan H, Wilson RS, et al. Hemodynamic responses to mechanical ventilation with PEEP. The effect of hypovolemia. *Anesthesiology.* 1975;42:45–55.

34. Aidinis SJ, Lafferty J, Shapiro HM. Intracranial responses to PEEP. *Anesthesia.* 1976; 45:275–286.

35. Safar P. Cerebral resuscitation: current state of the art. *Ann Emerg Med.* 1982;11:162–165.

36. Olsen TS, Larsen B, Hernig M, et al. Blood flow and vascular reactivity in collaterally perfused brain tissue: evidence of an ischemic penumbra in patients with acute stroke. *Stroke* 1983;14:332.

37. Nemoto EM, Endmann W, Strong E, et al. Regional brain Po_2 after global ischemia in monkeys: evidence for regional differences in critical perfusion pressure. *Stroke.* 1979;10:44.

38. Eilers M. Pharmacologic therapeutic modalities: osmotic and diuretic agents (in brain resuscitation). *CCQ.* 1983;5:44.

39. Cottrell JE, Robustelli A, Pask K, et al. Furosemide and mannitol induced changes in intracranial pressure and serum osmolality and electrolytes. *Anesthesiology.* 1977;47:27–30.

40. Warrell DA, Looareesuwan S, Warrell MJ, et al. Dexamethasone proves deleterious in cerebral malaria. *N Engl J Med.* 1982;306:313–318.

41. Rehncrona S. Brain acidosis. *Ann Emerg Med.* 1985;14:770.

42. Weil MH, Ruiz C, Michaels S, et al. Acid base determinants of survival after cardio-pulmonary resuscitation. *Crit Care Med.* 1985;13:888.

43. Martin ML. Pharmacologic therapeutic modalities: phenytoin, dimethyl sulfoxide, and calcium channel blockers (in brain resuscitation). *CCQ.* 1983;5:72–81.

44. Goldstein A, Wells BA, Keats AS. Increased tolerance to cerebral anoxia by pentobarbital. *Arch Int Pharmacol Ther.* 1966;161:138.

45. Bleyaert AL, Nemoto EM, Safar P, et al. Thiopental amelioration of brain damage after global brain ischemia in monkeys. *Anesthesiology.* 1978;45:390.

46. Abramson NS, Safar P, Detre KM, et al. Randomized clinical study of thiopental loading in comatose cardiac arrest survivors. *N Engl J Med.* 1986;314:397.

47. Vangenes P, Cantador R, Safar P, et al. Amelioration of brain damage by lidoflazine after 10 minutes ventricular fibrillation in dogs. *Crit Care Med.* 1984;12:846.

48. Winegar CP, Henderson O, White BC, et al. Early amelioration of neurological deficits by lidoflazine after 15 minutes of cardiopulmonary arrest in dogs. *Ann Emerg Med.* 1983;12:471.

49. Hallenbeck JM, Leitel DR, Dutka AJ, et al. Prostaglandin 12, indomethacin, and heparin promote post ischemia neurological recovery in dogs. *Ann Neurol.* 1982;12:145.

50. de la Torre JC, Surgeon JW. Dexamethasone and DMSO in experimental transorbital cerebral infarction. *Stroke.* 1976;7:577.

51. Tishman S, Chabel C, Safar P, et al. Resuscitation of dogs from cold water submersion using cardiopulmonary bypass. *Ann Emerg Med.* 1985;14:389.

52. Liberthson RR, Nagel EL, Hirshman JC, et al. Prehospital ventricular fibrillation: prognosis and follow-up course. *N Engl J Med.* 1974;291:317.

53. Pionkowski RS, Thompson BM, Gruchow HW, et al. Resuscitation time in ventricular fibrillation, a prognostic indicator. *Ann Emerg Med.* 1983;12:733.

54. Szcygiel M, Wright R, Wagner E, et al. Prognostic indicators of ultimate long term survival following advanced life support. *Ann Emerg Med.* 1981;10:566.

55. Bates D, Corrobna JJ, Cartlidge NF, et al. A prospective study of nontraumatic coma: methods and results in 310 patients. *Ann Neurol.* 1977;2:211–220.

56. Earnest MP, Breckenridge JC, Yarnell PR, et al. Quality of survival after out of hospital cardiac arrest: Predictive value of early neurological evaluation. *Neurology.* 1979;29:56–60.

57. Levy DE, Bates D, Corrona JJ, et al. Prognosis in nontraumatic coma. *Ann Intern Med.* 1981;94:293–301.

58. Yarnell PR. Neurological outcome of prolonged coma survivors of out of hospital cardiac arrest. *Stroke.* 1976;7:279–282.

Index